Obama's Washington: political leadership in a partisan era

Edited by

Clodagh Harrington

INSTITUTE OF
LATIN AMERICAN
STUDIES

SCHOOL OF ADVANCED STUDY
UNIVERSITY OF LONDON

British Library Cataloguing-in-Publication Data
A catalogue record for this book is available from the British Library

ISBN: 978-1-908857-10-1

INSTITUTE OF
LATIN AMERICAN
STUDIES

SCHOOL OF ADVANCED STUDY
UNIVERSITY OF LONDON

INSTITUTE FOR THE STUDY OF THE
A M E R I C A S

ECCLES CENTRE FOR
AMERICAN STUDIES

Institute of Latin American Studies
School of Advanced Study
University of London
Senate House
London WC1E 7HU

Telephone: 020 7862 8844
Fax: 020 7862 8886

Email: ilas@sas.ac.uk
Web: http://ilas.sas.ac.uk

Contents

Contributors   v
Acknowledgements   viii
Abbreviations   ix
List of Tables and Figures   xi

Introduction: Obama's Washington   13
Clodagh Harrington

1. Voting in Obama's America: highs and lows   21
   Philip Davies

2. Obama's burden: governing in polarized times   41
   George C. Edwards III

3. The Obama administration, Congress and the battle of
   the budget   71
   Tim Hames

4. Beast of burden: the weight of inequality and the second
   Obama administration   89
   Steven Pressman

5. The Affordable Care Act: cure or train wreck?   113
   Daniel Béland and Alex Waddan

6. The politics of food: sense and sustainability   135
   Clodagh Harrington

7. Obama and the environment   157
   John Berg

8. 'Heart and hand'? US–UK relations under President Obama   175
   Ashlee Godwin

9. Obama's foreign policy: process, personnel and policy
   direction   199
   John Dumbrell

Index   225

Contributors

Daniel Béland is Professor and Canada Research Chair in Public Policy (Tier 1) at the Johnson-Shoyama Graduate School of Public Policy (University of Saskatchewan campus). A student of comparative social and fiscal policy, he has published more than ten books and 85 articles in peer-reviewed journals. Recent books include *The Politics Policy Change* (Georgetown University Press, 2012; with Alex Waddan); *Ideas and Politics in Social Science Research* (Oxford University Press, 2011; co-edited with Robert Henry Cox) and *What is Social Policy?* (Polity, 2010).

John C. Berg is Professor of Government and Director of the Environmental Studies Program at Suffolk University. He is the author of *Unequal Struggle: Class, Gender, Race, and Power in the US Congress* and editor of *Teamsters and Turtles? Progressive US Political Movements in the 21st Century*. His current research focuses on the potential for minor parties and protest movements, including the environmental movement, to effect change in the American party system. He lives in Dorchester, Massachusetts, and can be found on Twitter@jcberg.

Philip Davies has authored and edited some 30 books and special journal issues and many articles and chapters, often in partnership with respected colleagues, on many aspects of US elections, and on such subjects as US politics and film, politics and science fiction, the American city, the US constitution, political marketing, the US presidency. He is president of the European Association for American Studies, and director of the Eccles Centre for American Studies at the British Library in London. The Centre is home to one of the UK's leading conference, lecture and fellowship programmes in American studies, based on the Library's holdings relating to Canada and the USA (see www.bl.uk/eccles).

John Dumbrell is Professor of Government at Durham University. He has written books on Presidents Jimmy Carter, Lyndon B. Johnson and Bill Clinton and most recently was the author of: *Rethinking the Vietnam War* (Palgrave Macmillan, 2012). Professor Dumbrell is editor of a volume entitled *Issues in American Politics: Polarized Politics in the Age of Obama* (Routledge, 2013), a selection of essays designed to showcase the work of the American Politics Group of the Political Studies Association. He is also co-editor of the Routledge book series, 'Studies in US Foreign Policy'.

George C. Edwards III is Distinguished Professor of Political Science and Jordan Chair in Presidential Studies at Texas A&M University and Distinguished Fellow at the Rothermere Institute, Oxford. He is also editor of *Presidential Studies Quarterly*. Among his 25 books, *On Deaf Ears* examines the effectiveness of presidential leadership of public opinion; *The Strategic President* offers a new formulation for understanding presidential leadership; and *Overreach* analyzes leadership in the Obama presidency. Professor Edwards has served as president of the Presidency Research Section of the American Political Science Association, which has named its annual Dissertation Prize in his honor and awarded him its Career Service Award.

Ashlee Godwin is a Fulbright Scholar in US national security policymaking with a particular research interest in US–UK relations. She is currently deputy editor of the *RUSI Journal*, the flagship publication of the Royal United Services Institute for Defence and Security Studies, a London-based defence think-tank. Ashlee is also a blogger for the *Huffington Post* and volunteers for Centenary News, a website dedicated to events commemorating the Great War.

Tim Hames is director general of the British Venture Capital Association. He was a lecturer in politics at Oxford University between 1989–96, specialising in American and British government. Since then he has continued publishing and has more than 25 pieces on US and UK public policy to his name. He worked at *The Times* from 1996 to 2008, where he became assistant editor, chief leader writer and a regular columnist and often edited the newspaper as a whole. Tim also served as special adviser to the Speaker of the House of Commons from 2009–10 and continues to have a formal link to that office.

Clodagh Harrington is a senior lecturer in American politics at De Montfort University in Leicester. She received her MA and PhD in US politics from London Metropolitan University. Her main area of research is the politics of scandal in the US. She also works on presidential character and issues relating to public integrity. Clodagh recently contributed an essay on the rise of the Tea Party to John Dumbrell's *Issues in American Politics: Polarized Politics in the Age of Obama*. Clodagh is vice-chair of the UK American Politics Group. Twitter@ DMUClodagh.

Steven Pressman is Professor of Economics and Finance at Monmouth University in West Long Branch, New Jersey. He also serves as co-editor of the *Review of Political Economy*, associate editor and book review editor of the *Eastern Economic Journal*, and treasurer of the Eastern Economic Association. Steven has published more than 160 articles in refereed journals and as book chapters, and has authored or edited 16 books including *A New Guide to Post Keynesian Economics* (Routledge, 2001) and *50 Major Economists*, 3rd edn. (Routledge, 2013), which has been translated into five different languages.

Alex Waddan is a senior lecturer in American politics and American foreign policy at the University of Leicester. A specialist of fiscal and social policy, he has published numerous journals and articles, and several books dealing primarily with US politics and welfare state reform. His books include *The Politics Policy Change* (Georgetown University Press, 2012; co-authored with Daniel Béland) and *Clinton's Legacy? A New Democrat in Governance* (Palgrave Macmillan, 2002).

Acknowledgements

Thanks are due to a number of institutions and many individuals for bringing this project to fruition. My most sincere gratitude goes to all the speakers and participants who were so generous with their time and expertise. Special thanks go to Steve Pressman who was kind enough to travel from Monmouth University, New Jersey and act as keynote speaker at the 'State of the Union' conference held at the British Library's Eccles Centre in 2013. I am enormously grateful to the Institute for the Study of the Americas (ISA) at the School of Advanced Study (SAS), University of London, who provided conference funds, a contribution generously matched by my own institution, De Montfort University.

Philip Davies and his staff at the Eccles Centre were crucial to the proceedings throughout, kindly hosting the event and offering support from start to finish. Olga Jimenez at ISA (now the Institute of Latin American Studies) was continuously charming and helpful in ensuring the smooth administration of the event.

My sincere thanks go to all the book contributors, whose collective knowledge and wisdom resulted in an insightful and intellectually rigorous consideration of the trials and tribulations of the Obama presidency to date. All involved were admirably punctual and professional throughout the publication process, which helped to ensure a speedy turnaround. Editorial staff, including Emma Bohan in SAS Publications, were invariably a pleasure to deal with, and I would like to express particular gratitude to the copy editor Valerie Hall for her patience, professionalism and warmth in all our dealings.

Overseeing the project has been a great pleasure from start to finish, specifically due to the good will and cooperation of all involved.

Abbreviations

ACA	Affordable Care Act
AND	Academy of Nutrition and Dietetics
ARRA	American Recovery and Reinvestment Act
BCA	Budget Control Act
CAP	Climate Action Plan
CBO	Congressional Budget Office
CCES	Cooperative Congressional Election Study
CCF	Center for Consumer Freedom
CDC	Centers for Disease Control
CIA	Central Intelligence Agency
COP	Conference of the Parties
CPI	Consumer Price Index
FAC	Foreign Affairs Committee
FY	fiscal year
GCHQ	Government Communications Headquarters
GDP	Gross Domestic Product
GMA	Grocery Manufacturers Association
GOP	Grand Old Party (Republicans)
HSA	Health Security Act
ISAF	International Security Assistance Force
LIS	Luxembourg Income Study
MENA-TIP	Middle East and North Africa Trade and Investment Partnership Initiative

MoD	Ministry of Defence
NARAL Pro-Choice America	National Association for the Repeal of Abortion Laws
NATO	North Atlantic Treaty Organization
NCSL	National Conference of State Legislatures
NDC	National Dairy Council
NSA	National Security Agency/National Security Advisor
NYCAH	New York Coalition Against Hunger
OIRA	Office of Information and Regulatory Affairs
OMB	Office of Management and Budget
PAC	Political Action Committee
PIRG	Public Interest Research Group
PPP	purchasing power parity
RUSI	Royal United Services Institute for Defence and Security Studies
SDSR	Strategic Defence and Security Review
SNAP	Supplemental Nutritional Assistance Program
SNAP-Ed	SNAP educational programmes
SSCI	Senate Select Committee on Intelligence
TARP	Troubled Asset Relief Program
TPP	Trans-Pacific Partnership
TTIP	Trans-Atlantic Trade and Investment Partnership
UNFCCC	United Nations Framework Convention on Climate Change
USDA	US Department of Agriculture
USEPA	US Environmental Protection Agency

List of Tables and Figures

Chapter 2

Figure 1:   Polarized states in 2012 presidential election

Table 1:   Self-reported ideology of the public

Table 2:   Ideological self-identification of party groups

Table 3:   Public support for larger government

Table 4:   The policy divide in public opinion, 2012

Table 5:   Party differences in presidential public approval

Table 6:   Presidential support in Congress, 1953–2012

Chapter 3

Table 1:   US federal budget deficit 2007–15
              (2014–15 projected)

Chapter 4

Figure 1:   Shares of income received by the top decile

Figure 2:   US annual productivity growth in manufacturing

Figure 3:   Federal minimum wage's real value, 1968–2012
              (in 2012 dollars)

Table 1:   Public social expenditures as % GDP, 2011

Table 2A: The impact of child allowances on child poverty

Table 2B: The impact of child allowances on middle-class
              children

Table 3:   Paid parental leave and baby bonuses, 2003–06

Table 4A: The impact of paid parental leave on child poverty

Table 4B: The impact of paid parental leave on middle-class
              children

Introduction: Obama's Wash

Clodagh Harrington

'I hope he fails.'[1] The sentiment that radio host Rush Limbaugh shared with his 14 million listeners at the prospect of a progressive Obama administration encapsulated the mood of angry American conservatives in early 2009. The speed with which the Democratic roar of Hope and Change became a faint echo was little short of astonishing.

It was not unreasonable to think, in the wake of the electoral outcomes of 2006 and 2008, that incremental policy shift in favour of the Democrats would become the logical progression. Liberals high-fived each other at the prospect of the Republican agenda being banished to the political wilderness for a generation. Books were written on Obama's campaign magic, and elements within the media embraced the 'skinny kid with the funny name' as the new Messiah, or at least as the new Franklin Delano Roosevelt.[2] Comparisons with deified predecessors abounded, and the man himself was not slow to invoke the spirit of Abraham Lincoln in his public addresses. Expectations in those early months of Obamamania were stratospheric. Could a 21st-century US administration really be post-imperial, post-racial and post-partisan? Clearly, when the soaring rhetoric subsided, the answer turned out to be a resounding No. Once the 2008 election was won, the only direction for presidential public support was down. Barack Obama was merely human after all but his supporters and opponents respectively viewed him as a saviour or scourge.

The circumstances in which the new president took office could hardly have been more challenging. The economic collapse of late 2008 was a domestic catastrophe of epic proportions, and such a moment provided a once-in-a-lifetime opportunity for fundamental change. *Time* magazine ran a cover in November 2009 superimposing Obama's face on a classic Roosevelt image with the caption 'The New New Deal.'[3] There was no question mark after the sentence. Fleetingly, anything seemed possible. Reality rapidly kicked in and

---

1   The Rush Limbaugh Show, 16 Jan. 2009, www.rushlimbaugh.com/daily/2009/01/16/limbaugh_i_hope_obama_fails (accessed 29 Jan. 2014).

2   Pew Research Journalism Project, Winning the Media Campaign, 22 Oct. 2008, www.journalism.org/2008/10/22/winning-media-campaign/ (accessed 29 Jan. 2014).

3   *Time* magazine, 24 Nov. 2008, http://content.time.com/time/covers/0,16641,20081124,00.html (accessed 29 Jan. 2014).

political atmosphere toxified with lightning speed. Less than a month after Obama's 2009 inauguration speech, the first Tea Party protest took place. The anger-fuelled momentum gathered pace on a weekly basis and to the dismay of Democrats, the 2010 mid-terms saw the Tea Party-fuelled Grand Old Party (GOP)[4] make a triumphant return. Instead of quietly disappearing to lick their wounds, opponents of the new president and his liberal agenda regrouped, recharged and recalibrated their position. Political opponents conducted themselves in a less-than-becoming manner, arguing, berating and insulting each other with increasing vigour. That no love should be lost between those on opposite sides of the ideological fence was hardly breaking news. However, the increasingly personal nature of the attacks and capacity to put partisan politics above the national interest was astounding. It is the impact of this gridlocked political environment, and the government's perceived inability to put its house in order that provides the framework for the contents of this book.

The project began with a conference at the British Library in May 2013, organised by Clodagh Harrington and made possible by the support of Professor Philip Davies and the hospitality of the Eccles Centre. This was in addition to the generosity of the Institute for the Study of the Americas (ISA) in the School of Advanced Study, University of London, and De Montfort University, Leicester. Sincere gratitude goes to Jean Petrovic and Kate Bateman at the Eccles Centre, and ISA's Olga Jimenez who were enormously helpful in ensuring the smooth running of the day.

Space does not allow for this volume to offer a full overview of the administration's achievements and failures to date, but instead some salient issues are considered in the context of the times. The book begins with a focus on getting to office and how Obama managed once he arrived there, along with a section on the economy, focusing on the budget and the ever-growing scourge that is income inequality. The opening chapter provides reflections on the rollercoaster journey from the giddy 2008 Obama campaign to the far more sombre 2012 victory, via the 'shellacking' of Democrats in the 2010 mid-terms. Philip Davies discusses a range of issues that directly affect election outcomes. We are reminded of the significance and consequences of the political exercise that is constitutional boundary design. As the parties have the opportunity to manipulate these political borders once every ten years, in 2010 it was the Republicans' turn to ensure electoral spoils. Such adjustments can be of great importance in a nation whose voting demographics are shifting significantly. In addition, the importance of the relationship between the Supreme Court and elections is examined, both in terms of appointments to the bench, and rulings that are made. George Edwards then sets the scene for the challenges the president faced when attempting to implement the policy changes that

4   The Republican party is often referred to as the GOP.

he campaigned on. Even a second electoral victory was insuffic
such luxury. Simply put, Edwards' thesis proposes that presid
believe that they can create, rather than exploit, circumstan
Obama made this assumption, and was naive in thinking that he could we.
constructively with Republican opponents on weighty policy issues on which
they did not agree. In addition, the American public is not especially liberal,
and so gathering public support for what many perceived as liberal policies,
was always going to be a challenge. The successful branding of Obama by his
opponents as an unknown entity, even as a 'radical socialist' ensured that the
ideological chasm between left and right, or perceptions of it, increased daily.
Edwards' conclusion is downbeat and pragmatic in equal measure. Obama's
opportunities for implementing meaningful change were significantly limited
from the first moment. Politically, the system and environment were not
conducive to his liberal plans. These findings provide an insightful platform for
the book's remaining chapters.

The figures displayed with regard to the nation's debt and deficit are as
dramatic as they are unnerving, and Tim Hames offers a stark reminder of the
profound economic challenge that faced the president-elect in late 2008. The
pace at which the situation deteriorated was staggering and the situation that
the new president faced in early 2009 was a radical departure from even a few
months earlier. The Tea Party mindset, momentum and then movement washed
over the country faster than the Democrats could say 'Economic Recovery and
Reinvestment Act' and the reality of this development was encapsulated in
the Republican House victories of 2010. Whilst the presidential incumbent
won a comfortable majority in the 2012 election, the political atmosphere
deteriorated by the hour. Playing politics with the debt ceiling became the
order of the day. Falling off the fiscal cliff was narrowly avoided in January
2013, as the president stood his ground. Again, with the government shutdown in autumn 2013 linked to the funding of the Affordable Care Act,
the president won the battle, but all the while the wider war continued, and
crucially, the nation's international standing was reduced.

As America lost ground as an economic hegemon, domestic income
inequality was on the rise. This trajectory dated back to the 1980s but the gap
between rich and poor had reached new levels by 2012. Even factoring in the
2008 economic collapse that adversely affected virtually all Americans, those
at the higher end of the income bracket recovered far more rapidly than their
less well-off counterparts. Steve Pressman proposes that the relentless focus by
politicians and the media on the national debt and deficit distracts attention
from the more consequential issues of unemployment and income inequality.
Pressman considers the causes, costs and consequences of increased income
inequality, and suggests that the Obama administration efforts at dealing

with the issue have been economically viable, but far less so politically. The short-term solution of increasing the minimum wage and longer-term plan to improve pre-school education were sensible and constructive. In 2013, the president proposed partial cuts in Social Security in conjunction with a tax increase on the wealthy. The latter was not a winning strategy for Republicans. Pressman proposes an alternative solution involving tax and benefit reform. The former would go some way to reducing the high entitlement that wealthy Americans currently hold, and the benefit reform would focus on adjustments to childcare and maternity pay.

No book on the Obama presidency would be complete without a chapter on the poisonous politics of healthcare. A daring campaign promise was made in 2008 – to boldly go where no president had gone before. Federal efforts to deal with healthcare issues date back to the mid-19th century, and in the modern era there has been a catalogue of piecemeal presidential successes and categorical failures. Candidate Obama declared that patient protection and affordable healthcare would be top of his first-term agenda. Alex Waddan and Daniel Béland consider how, despite ferocious opposition, the administration struggled to ensure that 'Obamacare' became the president's landmark piece of legislation. However, the reasons for this were not only about what it was, but about the epic political battle that accompanied it. The making of the law itself was traumatic, and the sustaining of it equally so, with challenges coming from every angle, culminating in a landmark Supreme Court ruling in 2012. Then, in a dramatic turn of events, the implementation of Obamacare caused a whole new series of headaches for the beleaguered administration. As one former Congressman put it, the president tried to force the policy equivalent of a 50-ounce steak on the public in one sitting, instead of offering filleted portions of a digestible size.[5] A key lesson from the Obamacare saga is that implementation matters.

Continuing with the theme of income and health is a section on the prevalence of food stamps and obesity in a country ranked among the world's top ten wealthiest (based on per capita Gross Domestic Product – GDP). This chapter considers the plight of those on the lower end of the socio-economic scale who not only struggle to make ends meet, but to afford nutritious food. The term 'food insecurity' conjures up images of developing nations compromised by war or drought, but in 21st-century America, food insecurity is an increasing problem. In 2013, one in six Americans was a recipient of the government's Supplemental Nutritional Assistance Programme. As the chapter on income inequality outlines, poorer Americans have been disproportionately affected by the post-2008 economic decline, and a part of this is demonstrated by the

---

5   Former Member of Congress John Tanner speaking at Congress to Campus, De Montfort University, Leicester, 13 Nov. 2013.

impact of government subsidies and heavy marketing of highly-processed, low nutrition foods to people on minimal incomes who have to prioritise calories-per-dollar over nutritional-content per dollar. Clodagh Harrington examines how government spending on the food stamps programme more than doubled during President Obama's first term in office, and the ways in which his political opponents used this development to goad him. In addition, while obesity-reduction efforts such as those implemented by first lady Michelle Obama have had partial success, being overweight and undernourished has become the norm for a significant portion of the US population.

The food crisis comprises one small part of the nation's wider environmental challenge, which remains an area of enormous governmental neglect. In a landmark speech on climate change in 2013, President Obama admitted, with some understatement, that 'we haven't done as much as we need to.'[6] The campaign pledges of 2008 included cutting carbon dioxide emissions by 80 per cent before 2050, and investing hundreds of billions of dollars in green technology. John Berg tracks the progress that has been made, including the $90 billion spent on energy-saving technologies during Obama's first term. Nonetheless, the president's environmental agenda has met with consistent roadblocks from Congress. Public attitudes have changed since 2008, when a majority of Americans believed that global warming, if it did exist, was not manmade. By 2012, this figure had shifted to 54 per cent believing that it was caused by human actions, and 57 per cent said that they considered it to be a threat to themselves, their families and communities, rather than just the concern of others.[7] Environmentalists have criticised the administration for not rising sufficiently to this most serious challenge, and congressional opponents point to a lack of public will to prioritise the issue above the economy and jobs. The administration did attempt to marry these priorities by promoting a green jobs initiative, and while not without its problems, there were some solid outcomes in relation to electric cars and clean energy sourcing. However, in the scheme of what is to be done, Berg concludes that the administration has yet to step up. Environmental progress made in spite of the adverse political climate is little to be proud of. This needs to become the number one policy agenda item as a matter of national and international urgency.

Staying with the theme of America's global priorities, Ashlee Godwin examines how relations with the UK took a back seat relative to more consequential players during Obama's first term, hence the Asia pivot, and its perceived impact on that Churchillian nugget the 'special relationship'. No-one could deny that broad geopolitical changes were afoot and observers pondered the

6   President Obama's Climate Change speech, Georgetown University, 25 June 2013.
7   Yale University Study, 'America's global warming beliefs and attitudes in September 2012', http://environment.yale.edu/climate-communication/article/Climate-Beliefs-September-2012/ (accessed 29 Jan. 2014).

t Powers in an era of Asian ascent. Although the previously
l' relationship was recalibrated to a more open 'essential'
s did share a common experience in the early years of the
Iraq and Afghanistan, responding to the associated global
managing the post-2008 economic meltdown, brought
..., .. both nations, albeit on differing scales. In the wake of the
deeply controversial Bush-Blair relationship, creating some emotional distance
between the executives was to be applauded. If the relationship between
Prime Minister Cameron and President Obama appeared civil and cordial, for
many this was an improvement on the submissive-dominant roles that their
respective predecessors embraced. Nonetheless, as details unfolded in 2013 of
the scale of National Security Agency (NSA) intelligence gathering, observers
were reminded of the power dynamic within the relationship, as Europeans
subject to surveillance techniques demonstrated their displeasure. Momentary
embarrassments notwithstanding, joint diplomatic endeavours remain the
order of the day, and clearly mutual trust is present. This is a real, sustainable
and for the most part uncontroversial liaison in a complex and ever-changing
multi-polar arena.

In wider foreign policy terms, John Dumbrell reminds us of how the world
noted the changing of the guard with interest. An exit strategy from Iraq and
drawdown from Afghanistan were key priorities for the new administration,
along with a noticeable adjustment of rhetoric in relation to the 'War on
Terror'. It was in the realm of foreign policy that the hope of change inspired
by the campaign promise of 'Hope and Change' was most urgently sought.
A decade of war, with no meaningful end in sight, had reduced the nation
on many levels – internationally, economically, militarily and spiritually. As
tradition dictates, the power of an executive is most keenly displayed via
international affairs, and the Obama presidency is no exception. Congress
may have hobbled him at every turn in the domestic arena, but on the world
stage he spoke for his country. Rational, measured, pragmatic and cautious, the
president's own position clearly mirrored the decline in political will among
voters for future international intervention. Withdrawal, leading from behind,
and not intervening at all became the new normal in a country that was war-
weary and broke. The Bush-era chatter of 'imperial overstretch' faded in the
light of this new reality. Reactions were mixed. Liberals at home and abroad
increasingly voiced concern at drone strikes on civilian populations and the
force-feeding of prisoners in Guantanamo. In the end, when the rhetorical
2008 campaign flourishes had subsided, the nation was left with what Indyk

et al. term a 'progressive pragmatist.'[8] It remains to be seen if this p
live up to his liberal credentials by retaining an appropriate ratic
progressive and the pragmatic.

The election of President Obama brought with it an array of joy, controversy
and indignation. Disappointing many liberal supporters and igniting political
enemies across the entire spectrum of right-wing ideology, he sometimes
united the most unlikely groups in their loathing of him. Few presidents
inspire apathy. In recent decades, the culture wars have provided full-volume
background noise to any presidential activities, from Democrat healthcare
plans to Republican foreign wars. This book does not attempt to second guess
what the Obama legacy may be. A definitive judgement is still some time away.
There is still potential for a catalogue of 'unknown unknowns' and in any case,
those judging through the lens of history often reach a conclusion far removed
from that of the opinion polls and pundits of the day. At the very least, his
obituary will state in addition to being the first African American to shatter the
highest glass ceiling, he won two terms, as had only 16 men before him.

In addition, he inspired a political awakening, however momentary,
among those whom his predecessors had failed to reach. Fred Greenstein
complimented the president on having that rare combination of a first-class
intellect and a first-class temperament. There is little doubt that Obama was
always the smartest guy in the room, and one who conducted his presidency
with personal dignity. However, all presidents want to be remembered for what
they did, rather than simply for what they were. Machiavelli wrote that 'there is
nothing more difficult to plan, more doubtful of success, nor more dangerous
to manage, than the creation of a new order of things.'[9] This conclusion
applies even more when trying to implement progressive change in a political
context as complex as that which Obama faced. A genuinely transformative
presidency is all but impossible in a polarised political environment where
unprecedented blockage of the executive agenda is the norm. In the end, it
is jobs and economic growth that voters care about most, and patience with
partisan squabbling quickly wears thin. As the economy shows signs of delicate
recovery in the second Obama term, he may yet be remembered not only as
the first black president, but the one who drew two controversial wars to a close
and got a healthier America back to work. Only time will tell.

---

8   Martin S. Indyk, Kenneth Lieberthal and Michael O'Hanlon, 'Obama's foreign policy',
     Brookings Institute, 9 March 2012, www.brookings.edu/research/opinions/2012/03/09-
     obama-foreign-policy (accessed 29 Jan. 2014).
9   Niccolo Machiavelli, *The Prince* (Longman, 2003), p. 71.

1. Voting in Obama's America: highs and lows

Philip Davies

On Sunday 20 January 2013 there was a particularly happy and relaxed air about the centre of Washington, DC. With President Barack Obama's second inauguration due to take place the following day, hundreds of thousands of people were arriving from all over the country. Many wanted to scout the lie of the land before rising early to be in place for Monday's ceremony. Eastern Market had more than its usual visitation of tourists for breakfast and stall browsing, while around the Capitol visitors took advantage of photo opportunities, traded souvenirs and shared campaign stories.

It was a crowd of enormous diversity, but with a common purpose, signalled by the designs on many hats, shirts, buttons, balloons: to launch the second term in office of the first African-American president of the USA. For some this re-election may have been cause for particular celebration – after all, the reasoning would go, what would be the effect on unorthodox candidate choices in the foreseeable future if the first president who was not a white male fell after one term?

Political parties can be pragmatic, and an increasingly diverse electorate might be expected to clear the way for a similarly diverse range of candidates. But tried and tested routes to political victory are not abandoned in any cavalier manner and candidate characteristics that fall outside the expected norm are likely to provoke anxiety among campaign managers until they have been demonstrated not to damage the potential for victory, and a failed Obama re-election effort would have provided no such demonstration.

There was evidence that the pragmatic response among some party leadership groups, especially within the Republican party, was a willingness to erect barriers to diversity in the electorate rather than to accommodate diversity. In a wide variety of states Republican politicians have led attempts to tighten voter identification requirements, purge electoral rolls, reduce early voting opportunities, limit the opportunity for organisations to mount voter registration drives and in other ways to make the route to casting a vote more difficult. These attempts often attracted robust counter reactions from organisations representing those affected, but where successful they were likely to suppress voting especially by Democratic voters. Arguments that such actions were prompted by an objective, reasonable and non-partisan fear of electoral fraud are not strongly supported by the history of voter fraud cases in these states. They were further undermined by post-elections statements by some leading Republicans in Florida that their party had intended their adjustments to voter regulation, in that important battleground state, to depress Democratic voting turnout.[1] The major parties' responses to the growing diversity in the US electorate and the related issues of voting regulation are likely to remain important to the future landscape of electoral politics in the USA.

President Obama's first inaugural was a cause for massive national celebration and self-congratulation. After a collapse of public confidence in the George W. Bush administration there was a widespread sense of relief that new leadership, with a new political agenda, was being installed. There was also a perhaps exaggerated sense that at a time of considerable political, international and financial stress, a new president would bring a new dawn. And, of course, an historic first inaugural for an African American achieving the office of president was a momentous event. Even many of the Republicans who had campaigned for their party's candidates in the 2008 elections were proud that their nation had matured to the point that an African American could be elected to occupy the White House.

It did not take long for Washington politics to return to their recent norm of deeply entrenched inter-party combat and not two years later the 2010 mid-term elections were greatly encouraging for the Republicans. The GOP gained 64 more House seats than in 2008, becoming the majority party in that chamber. Republican gains were also made in the Senate, but left them short of a majority, with 47 seats. This reflected a genuine swing in public opinion. The economic situation showed few signs of improving, American military interventions overseas seemed to be bogged down and without obvious benefits, the Obama healthcare plan had sharpened party political divisions and its outcomes were still subject to much speculation. Conservative voters were unlikely to warm to Obama, but interpreting his as an overspending, overbearing, overreaching administration, anticipated that it would eventually threaten to increase taxes and undermine gun rights. The most extreme of these critics suspected further that Obama was subject to un-American influences – that he may be Muslim, foreign-born and a socialist. Some erstwhile Obama supporters were also disappointed, perceiving the administration as having failed to implement its healthcare promises in full, of not having grasped the opportunities provided by its 2008 election success, and of having failed to provide strong presidential leadership.

---

1   Keyssar, 'Voter suppression returns: voting rights and partisan practices'; ACLU, 'Voter suppression in America'; Dianis, 'Top 10 voter suppression moments of 2012'; Kam and Lantigua, 'Former Florida GOP leaders say voter suppression was reason they pushed new election law'; Ungar, 'How GOP voter suppression efforts contributed to Obama win'.

Mid-term and presidential elections attract different proportions of the electorate, with the mid-terms achieving a turnout only about two-thirds that of a presidential year. This fall in turnout will be affected by public engagement with the issues of the day, but also reflects the different voting habits of groups within the electorate. Turnout fell from around 62 per cent of eligible voters in 2008 to around 42 per cent in 2010. Among the smaller voting population in 2010 the proportion of white voters increased from 74 to 77 per cent as the African Americans and Hispanics who had turned out in record numbers for Obama failed to return for generic Democrat congressional candidates. Voters aged up to 29 fell from 18 per cent of the electorate in 2008 to 12 per cent in 2010. White Protestants made up 44 per cent of the 2010 electorate, an increase of 2 per cent, and those who reported weekly church attendance, traditionally a very conservative-leaning group, made up 48 per cent of the 2010 electorate, an increase of 8 per cent on the 2008 figure. A different electorate defeated the Democrats in 2010 from the one that elected Obama in 2008.[2]

The mid-term setbacks were interpreted by many as an indication that Obama was in danger of failing in his bid for re-election, and certainly the Republicans made more than usually clear their determination to make this so. In a 2010 interview Republican Senate Minority Leader Mitch McConnell stated that 'The single most important thing we want to achieve is for President Obama to be a one-term president.'[3] While said in the context of a broader-ranging interview, McConnell's comment captured the spirit of the period. Party political positions in Washington over the next two years appeared entrenched and uncompromising, setting battle lines for the election campaign. As the 2012 election approached, the Republican campaign for Mitt Romney anticipated victory. The effects of the economic crisis were still being felt across the nation, unemployment had only just fallen below 8 per cent, the president had achieved few notable legislative victories since the mid-terms, anxiety over the Obama healthcare reforms remained high, a poor showing by Obama in the first presidential debate had not been erased by later improvement, Independent voters[4] were polling much more strongly for the Republican ticket than four years earlier, and victory in the battlefield states seemed plausible – even likely.

The depth of the Republicans' misreading of the runes became evident during the Fox News election-night coverage. When Fox declared a victory for

2   *New York Times* National Exit Polls Table, 5 Nov. 2008, elections.nytimes.com/2008/results/ president/national-exit-polls.html (accessed 29 Jan. 2014); CNN, ElectionCenter2008: Results, edition.cnn.com/ELECTION/2008/results/polls/ (accessed 29 Jan. 2014); CNN, ElectionCenter2010. The Results, http://edition.cnn.com/ELECTION/2010/results/polls/ (accessed 29 Jan. 2014).

3   Garrett, 'After the wave'.

4   Reference to Independents throughout the book relates to the unaffiliated, not the American Independent Party.

Obama in the key state of Ohio, based on exit polls and early results, Karl Rove, Republican activist and former senior adviser to President George W. Bush, found the evidence so difficult to accept that he spent 20 minutes on air volubly, but uselessly, denouncing it, embarrassing even his fellow conservatives. Rove's key role in investing Republican money in the campaign may have increased his resistance to the reality of election night. Donald Trump, another high profile Obama critic, is reported to have tweeted, 'Congrats to @KarlRove on blowing $400 million this cycle'.[5]

The 2012 presidential result may have come as a surprise to many Republicans, but the Democrats' success in the US Senate was at least as remarkable. With 23 of their Senate seats at risk (including two held by Independents who caucused with the Democrats), the Democrats presented a much larger target than the Republicans, who held ten of the seats being contested. In a year when the vote might be expected to swing against the incumbent presidential party, the Democrats faced a tough challenge and the prospect of losing their party majority in the chamber. In the event the Democrats made a net gain of two seats.

In this year, as in 2008, Republican chances of gaining more Senate seats were undermined by a few individual candidacies that weakened the party. In 2008 ideological divisions within the party had resulted in Tea Party candidates gaining the Republican nominations in some states where they were unable to turn their popularity among those committed to the party into a general election majority, undermining otherwise likely GOP victories in Delaware and Nevada. In 2012 strange pronouncements on pregnancy and on rape severely undermined the credibility of the Republican nominees in Missouri and Indiana, both of whom lost. The unintended help given to the Democrats by these Republican candidates should not disguise the success of the Democrats' state-level campaigns in preserving their Senate position in these years.

The Republicans' greatest electoral success in the federal elections of 2012 came in the House of Representatives. The Democrats recouped some of their mid-term losses in this chamber, winning 201 seats, eight more than in 2010, but the Republicans retained a majority of seats in the House, in spite of the fact that the aggregate vote in all House seats gave the Democratic party candidates about 1.4 million more votes than their Republican opponents.[6] In the words of commentator and voting expert Rhodes Cook the Republicans have become in recent years 'the Congressional Party', a significant change from most of the second half of the 20th century, when the Democrats dominated that chamber.[7]

5   Alter, *The Centre Holds: Obama and his Enemies*.

6   Haas, *Statistics of the Presidential and Congressional Election of November 6, 2012*.

7   Cook, 'The Rhodes Cook Letter: The Congressional Party', p.1.

Recalling the late Speaker Tip O'Neill's dictum that 'all politics is local', a plausible case can be made that the GOP has in recent years managed to appeal better to the electorate on local matters than have the Democrats. The 2012 elections brought the total number of state governorships in Republican hands to 30 out of the 50 available. As 2013 opened the GOP controlled both chambers of state government in 26 states, as opposed to the Democrats' 19, and in 23 states the Republicans held the governorship and both chambers. Additionally, while Nebraska's unicameral legislature is nominally nonpartisan, the GOP occupied the governorship and dominated the state's other partisan offices. The Democrats made gains in 2012, but finished the year with 199 fewer seats than the Republicans in the nation's state level house chambers, and 133 fewer in state Senate chambers.[8] As the most locally based part of the federal government, the Republican party's success in the US House of Representatives could be seen as part of its contemporary achievement at this level of politics.

The Democratic popular vote lead of 1.2 per cent in the 2012 House elections was under a third of the 3.9 per cent lead Barack Obama held over Mitt Romney, and about 7.7 million fewer voters cast ballots in congressional elections than in the contest for the presidency, resulting in different electorates for these parts of government, even in the same election year. Nevertheless an aggregate Democratic vote lead was turned into a Republican victory in terms of number of seats.

The key to this Republican victory lies in the gerrymandering of congressional constituencies. In most states the design of constituency boundaries is a political exercise, seen by the leaderships of both major parties as a legitimate spoil of victory. The exercise is usually performed by some combination of the state governor and legislature. This is where party success in state elections can be parlayed into increased representation in the federal government. Rhodes Cook points for example to the important states of Ohio, Michigan, Pennsylvania and Wisconsin. In 2012 Obama carried all four states against Romney, and Democratic congressional candidates on aggregate out-polled their Republican opponents, but only 17 Democrats were sent to the US House from these states, as opposed to 39 Republicans.

In most states Republican administrations had controlled the post-2010 census process of redrawing congressional boundaries, and took the opportunity to concentrate Democratic voters in districts with large Democratic majorities, while capturing Republican voters more parsimoniously to create smaller, but potentially safe, Republican majorities in more constituencies. Nationally, it has been calculated that '1.7 million votes ... were effectively packed into

8   National Conference of State Legislatures (NCSL), '2013 state and legislative
     partisan composition (as of January 31, 2013)', www.ncsl.org/documents/statevote/
     legiscontrol_2013.pdf (accessed 9 July 2014).

Democratic districts and wasted'.[9] Constituency boundaries are subject to review after every decennial national census, giving the parties an opportunity at ten-yearly intervals to manipulate constituencies to their benefit, and making the state elections, held immediately before the reapportionment process goes into effect, particularly important. Only a handful of states use non-partisan commissions or some similar mechanism to redesign constituency boundaries. One of these, the California Citizens Redistricting Commission, was established in 2010 after California voters used that state's ballot initiative process to replace an established process of self-serving negotiation between the state's political parties. In other states, without citizen direct access to the legislative process, there seems little appetite for change.

The 2012 elections resulted in the continued divided control of US central government between the major parties as has been the norm in recent decades. While single party control of the presidency and both chambers of Congress typified US government until 1968, since that year three-quarters of elections have resulted in divided government control. For one congressional term after the election of 2008 President Obama had the benefit of Democratic control of the executive, the US Senate and the US House. But while his 2012 victory did not propel his party back into that position, and while it would be false to interpret his success as a strong endorsement of Obama's political agenda, the re-election was no mean feat.

It had been more than half a century since a presidential candidate had won more than 51 per cent of the vote in consecutive elections. President Eisenhower achieved it in 1956, while the last Democrat to do so was President Franklin Roosevelt in 1944.[10] Roosevelt in particular helped create an electoral coalition that influenced American politics to the benefit of the Democratic party for decades beyond the end of his presidency. If the general sense of celebration felt at the 2009 inauguration did not apply in 2013, the Obama campaign had still won a famous re-election victory after a bitter inter-party campaign, and some analysts detected indications that Obama's two elections may signal similarly long-lasting changes.

The consideration of national elections inevitably concentrates the 'horse race' between the most visible candidates. This focus can become all-consuming to the point of obscuring central themes and significant alternative policy consequences that might follow an election. In an effort to concentrate the minds of the campaign team, and to keep them from being diverted from the central message of President Clinton's 1992 campaign, key strategist James Carville hung a sign in the campaign headquarters saying 'the economy, stupid'. While this phrase is the one most remembered, it actually sat below 'Change

---

9   Wang, 'The great gerrymander of 2012'.
10   Giroux, 'Final tally shows Obama first since '56 to win 51% twice'.

vs more of the same' and above 'Don't forget health care', thereby linking one campaign theme used as a regular standard by non-incumbents, and one issue that has tortured Democrats in elections for decades, and may yet do so again. It is perhaps not surprising that the novel middle phrase is the one that caught the public imagination.

While not so ubiquitous in the political lexicon as the suffix '-gate' (since the 1972 Republican break-in to Democratic offices in the Watergate complex started a sequence of events leading to President Richard Nixon's resignation, no political scandal has been complete without a '-gate' added to its name), Carville's phrase has neither been forgotten, nor lain dormant. One such recycling occurred in 2000. In August of that election year *Womensenews.org* reported from Los Angeles that 'A catchy, off-camera election slogan is catching on fast with the women here: "It's the Supreme Court, stupid!"' Later that month, New York's *Village Voice* advised Democrat Al Gore that this phrase might best encapsulate a key difference between him and his opponent George W. Bush.[11]

The US reproductive rights campaigning organisation NARAL Pro-Choice America produced an 'It's the Supreme Court, stupid' campaign button for the 2000 presidential election, since when the slogan has continued to appear on campaign items and is unlikely to disappear soon.[12] It is easy to understand the importance of the Supreme Court to women's political organisations. There have been repeated attempts to erode the reproductive rights gained by women after the Supreme Court decision in *Roe v. Wade* (1973), and the Court has shown itself almost evenly divided when presented with subsequent cases related to this topic. In such a case any alteration in the Court's membership may have dramatic policy consequences.

The significance of the Supreme Court in election campaigns is not restricted to the debate over women's rights. Political and policy matters have ended up being argued before the US Supreme Court repeatedly in the nation's history. The US judiciary has made decisions affecting states' rights, the rights of different racial, ethnic and religious groups in American society, the balance of power between the branches of American government, the boundaries of constituencies for federal office and many other issues. These issues start their journey to the higher reaches of America's judicial system in many ways, but the results can have substantial impact on the government, politics, policies and people of the United States.

Traditionally pictured as a relatively objective arbiter of the issues that come before it, there is evidence that the political role of the Court has become more

11 Johnson, 'The new slogan: it's the Supreme Court, stupid!'; Otis, 'It's the Supreme Court, stupid'.

12 Rudin, 'Contraception, abortion: a reminder that it's not just the economy, stupid'.

sharply defined. Justices are appointed to the Court only when an incumbent leaves office through death or retirement. In that case the president makes a nomination and the US Senate has the power of confirmation or rejection. It is evident that this process has become more contentious since the late 1960s, and that the confrontations over judicial appointments in the past half century have been firmly along party lines.[13] In such a situation it is unsurprising that even if the economy continues to be the core motivation of voters' decisions in successive elections, the potential impact of any election on the membership of the Supreme Court, and hence on its decisions relating to key policy issues, may also be a significant issue for some groups of voters.

In 2000 those campaigners emphasising the significance of the Supreme Court in making an electoral choice between Al Gore and George W. Bush were anticipating an opportunity for the next president to alter the composition of the Supreme Court. In the event, the election of 2000 itself became a case study on the political impact of the Court, when the exceptionally close and contested result in Florida, the key to who would enter the White House, could not be decided by the generally accepted technique of counting all the votes, but was instead confirmed by the Supreme Court's Justices.[14] The resulting eight-year administration led by President George W. Bush confirmed the point that had been in the minds of the NARAL Pro-Choice campaigners and their allies, when two opportunities to nominate to the Supreme Court fell to Bush, one for the very important position of Chief Justice.

Most Supreme Court Justices can be seen in hindsight to have followed a relatively consistent path of judicial decision-making during their careers. Predicting this pattern is more difficult than post-hoc analysis. There are classic examples of Justices who have diverged from the parameters hoped for by the president who nominated them, but generally the political expectations for the behaviour of Justices are broadly fulfilled. Presidents are tempted to extend the influence of their own political beliefs beyond their own term by appointing Justices whom they believe to be close to their own political beliefs; senators take into account the presumed political leanings of the nominees. The recent era of strong party confrontation in Washington, DC has served to sharpen the attention given to judicial appointments by politically engaged groups.

During the Bush administration the conservative Chief Justice Rehnquist died, and Justice Sandra Day O'Connor, also perceived as a conservative on most issues, retired from the Court. A Gore presidency would have presented the opportunity to present nominees of a radically different judicial inclination, but Bush was able to maintain and extend the life of the conservative tilt on the

---

13 McKeever and Davies, *Politics USA*, pp. 284–91.

14 See, for example, Ackerman, *Bush v. Gore: The Question of Legitimacy*; Rakove, *The Unfinished Election of 2000*.

Supreme Court, finding in the appointments of Chief Justice John Roberts and Associate Justice Samuel Alito the opportunity to consolidate and strengthen the conservative tendency of the Supreme Court. The Democrats, having missed the opportunities presented in the first presidency of the 21st century to remould the Supreme Court, have found some solace in the administration of President Barack Obama.

In 2009 and 2010 President Obama was successful in nominating Associate Justices Sonia Sotomayor and Elena Kagan. Each of these women replaced Republican-nominated Justices – David Souter (nominated by President George H.W. Bush) and John Paul Stevens (nominated by President Ford) – both of whom had shown a more liberal voting pattern on the Court than it is likely the presidents nominating them had expected. So President Obama, like President George W. Bush, managed to consolidate the group on the Court that he preferred, in this case the liberals, and possibly even to strengthen its ideological core, but did not fundamentally alter the balance of the Court. And the Republicans, having failed at the 2008 elections, had for the moment lost their opportunity to shift the Court firmly and sharply to the right.

Both political parties, and especially the groups within those parties who felt theirs were issues likely to be impacted by judicial decisions, can be said to have missed critical opportunities to remodel the Supreme Court through their failures in the closely fought elections that took place in the early 21st century. The significance of the Supreme Court's relationship to elections and to important policy issues is sharpened by such an experience, and the importance to both parties of the Court's political impact is not lost on their leaders, nor on at least some of their followers.

A number of Supreme Court decisions handed down in June 2013 brought ample evidence of the political reach of the judicial branch. Two of these cases addressed the issue of gay marriage. While public opinion nationally has shifted towards greater toleration of same-sex unions, this has been a deeply contested issue in recent politics, and while an increasing number of jurisdictions allow same sex marriage, over half the states had legislative or constitutional provisions that specifically prohibited same-sex marriage at the time the Supreme Court made its ruling.[15] In decisions handed down on the same day, *United States v. Windsor* and *Hollingsworth v. Perry*, the Court declared part of the federal Defense of Marriage Act unconstitutional (the denial of federal benefits to same-sex couples who were legally wed), and cleared the way for California to resume same-sex marriages after they had been stopped by an earlier Proposition referendum.[16] This was a landmark day in the history of

15 Teixeira, 'The coming end of the culture wars'.

16 NCSL, 'Defining marriage: state defense of marriage laws and same-sex marriage', 14 Feb. 2014, www.ncsl.org/research/human-services/same-sex-marriage-overview.aspx (accessed 18 Feb. 2014).

gay rights in the USA, extending federal benefits to legally married gay couples even in states that themselves ban gay marriage, and establishing the potential for further erosion of restrictions on gay marriage using the precedent set by these cases. Both of these decisions came from a divided Court, with a bare majority of five Justices supporting each decision.[17]

The Court's partial reshaping of the landscape of gender politics might itself be seen as a vindication of the earlier 'It's the Supreme Court, stupid' women's movement button, and it had been preceded one day earlier by another notable decision, *Shelby County v. Holder*. Again by a 5–4 vote, in this case widely interpreted as reflecting the political and judicial ideologies of its members, the Supreme Court ably demonstrated its relevance to the electoral process when it declared unconstitutional a central element of the Voting Rights Act of 1965, a piece of legislation whose defenders saw as protecting the core rights of the electorate.

The passage of the Voting Rights Act during President Lyndon B. Johnson's administration was considered to be a major achievement of the civil rights movement. The law, contested in the 2013 Supreme Court hearing, had required nine states plus a number of counties and municipalities to gain advance federal approval before making any changes in their electoral laws. The impact of the requirement for pre-clearance was felt mainly in the south. Of the states subject to this federal oversight, seven were in the south – Alabama, Georgia, Louisiana, Mississippi, South Carolina, Texas and Virginia – to which were added the southwest state of Arizona, and Alaska, from the Pacific Rim. And while the law reached out to places in New York, California and elsewhere, most of the other local government jurisdictions covered were in southern states, for example Florida and North Carolina.[18]

Writing for the majority, the Chief Justice opined that while voting discrimination continues to exist in the United States the country has changed so much over time that any rationale for stringent oversight of particular states could not be justified on the basis of '40-year-old facts having no logical relationship to the present day'. Congress had on occasion renewed the original 1965 legislation, but continued to refer to data from 1975 in deciding which states and other communities were affected. Chief Justice Roberts acknowledged that the Voting Rights Act had been fundamental to the nation making great strides; indeed, so successful had this process been that it would be necessary for Congress to make new evidence based identifications of jurisdictions where federal oversight could currently be justified for that section of the law to be considered constitutional.

17 Liptak, 'Two 5–4 decisions', pp. A1, A18.
18 Liptak, 'Justices void oversight of states, issue at heart of Voting Rights Act', pp. A1, A16.

American government is a system of separated institutions, shared powers and checks and balances. The legislature may respond to judicial decisions with new laws written to tackle an issue in the light of previous court cases. At times, however, the elected branches of government have found it difficult to agree a path on some policies. In these areas the ability of the Supreme Court to interpret law and its willingness to hear critical cases has on occasion provided the polity with a valuable arena in which to move on matters that contemporary circumstances may cause to stall if left to the other branches.

The degree to which the Court is seen as being politicised by these cases may depend on any particular observer's sympathy with the resulting decision, but it should be no surprise that the Court's actions sometimes indicate that the other branches should take up responsibility for the issue. Without bipartisan support it is likely to be difficult to progress a contentious issue, so an extended period of divided party control does not provide an easy context for a positive legislative response. There is some congressional support for a renewed Voting Rights Act, with a leading role being taken by Congressman John Lewis, former civil rights activist and a speaker at the Lincoln Memorial in August 1963 on the occasion of Dr King's 'I have a dream' speech,[19] and President Obama declared his deep disappointment at the Court's decision, calling on Congress to respond. Others sense that the Court has made an important decision in favour of states' rights that should be vigorously defended, especially among Republicans who see the foundation of their party's strength as being in the states. Any cross-party compromise that came out of a divided Congress to renew the Act would be likely to result in a rather different piece of legislation, and even if this was forthcoming there is no guarantee that a future case would not be used by the Court to strike down other sections of the Act not considered closely in the June 2013 decision.

James Carville undoubtedly had a point in declaring that the state of economy needs to be at the core of all US election campaigns. Voters are strongly influenced by whatever impacts on their life directly, and the economy has to be a perennial for virtually all sectors of society. When women first entered the US electorate in all parts of the nation in 1920, *Needlecraft* magazine published an election design for its now enfranchised readership on 'the high cost of living', an issue 'we are all vitally interested in'.[20] Other issues wax and wane in significance, and the filtering action of the Supreme Court and other political institutions is distant from the direct impact of policy – it is unlikely to emerge as public opinion priority often but this does not diminish the connection between election results and subsequent Supreme Court activity.

19   Stolberg, 'Still marching on Washington, 50 years later'.

20   *Needlecraft*, 'Attractive campaign pillows' repr. in *The Keynoter* from Nov. 1920.

The Court is generally known by its Chief Justice, with the Roberts Court dating from the appointment of Chief Justice John Roberts in 2005. Appointments in the early years of the 21st century may have consolidated the political divisions on the Court, but it has continued a recent trend of close decisions, often by five votes to four, along relatively predictable political lines. The Justice most often providing the swing vote in those 5–4 decisions is Associate Justice Kennedy. In the judicial term that ended in June 2013 Kennedy had been on the winning side in close decisions more than any other Justice – a position he had occupied for some years. Some commentators consider this situation to indicate that a Kennedy Court exists rather than a Roberts Court. It is important to recognise that while Justice Kennedy was in the dissenting group only seven times in the 2012/13 session, the Chief Justice was also almost always in the majority, dissenting only 11 times.[21]

Legislators as well as the executive are well aware of the political significance of America's judiciary. Federal judicial nominations include all trials and appeals court judges, and the major parties look for political gains and party benefits here, as in other parts of the political process.[22] Supreme Court Justices come to that office with some maturity and generally show little inclination to leave before serving a substantial term. The median age of those Justices who have left the Court since 1970 is 80/81 years. The 2013 Court had just one member aged 80 (Justice Ginsburg). Only slightly younger are Justices Kennedy (77), Scalia (77) and Breyer (75). The eldest of the other four is Justice Thomas (65) and the youngest Justice Kagan (53). Ginsburg, who wrote the dissenting opinion for *Shelby County v. Holder*, calling the majority decision an egregious error on the part of the Court, is on the liberal side of the Court, as is Breyer. Scalia is reliably conservative. Mortality and retirement cannot be well predicted, but the continued significance of election results to the political make-up of the Court, and the demeanour of its decisions, is particularly clear. With such a key swing voter as Kennedy, and other more predictable conservative and liberal Supreme Court Justices entering their eighth decade a two-term president taking office in 2017 might have a strong and long-term impact on the complexion of the Court and the array of questions that subsequently come before it.

The re-election of Barack Obama was followed by much speculation about demographic change in the USA, and the implied inevitable decline of the Republican party in a country where, for example, projections suggest that over a quarter of the population will be defined as Hispanic/Latino by 2050.[23]

21 Greenhouse, 'The real John Roberts emerges', pp. SR1, SR6; Cohen, 'This is Kennedy's court – the rest of the justices just sit on it'; Wolf, 'From gay marriage to voting law, Kennedy is the key'.
22 Leonhardt, 'The endless battle over judicial nominees', p. SR4.
23 Passel and Cohn, 'US population projections: 2005–2050'.

Obama's re-election success owed a great deal to his appeal to this voting group. Seventy-one per cent of Latino voters – one tenth of the 2012 electorate – voted for Obama. In recent elections this group of voters has increased steadily as a proportion of the electorate, and has increasingly swung to back the Democratic presidential candidates. In 2004 the Latino vote for Democrat John Kerry was equivalent to 4.2 per cent of the electorate. In 2008 Obama's Latino vote made up 6 per cent of the electorate, which rose to 7.1 per cent in 2012.[24] The increase in Democratic party support in this group alone resulted in a benefit to the Democrats of almost 3 per cent of the electorate – a vital boost in a period when national elections have been decided by relatively modest margins.

Furthermore, the impact of this voting group is projected to accelerate as a larger proportion of the Latino population engages with the US political process. The turnout rate for Hispanic/Latino voters increased in 2012, but remains up to 15 per cent lower than that for white and black American voters. This ethnic community is destined to become an increasingly important sector of the voting population. Naturalisation rates among legal Hispanic immigrants to the USA lag behind that of other groups. Millions of unauthorised immigrants would be affected by any move by Congress to create a pathway to citizenship. Hispanics have the youngest age profile of any ethnic group in the USA, and 93 per cent of Hispanics under the age of 18 years are US-born citizens who will automatically enter the electorate as they come of age.[25]

The experience of previous groups suggests that turnout and naturalisation rates of the Hispanic/Latino community will converge to match approximately those of the general population. Congressional action and future immigration rates are hard to predict, but it is hard to conceive of anything but further growth, and the ageing process will inevitably expand the number of potential voters. If this group remains loyal to the Democratic ticket, the argument goes, as the Hispanic/Latino vote grows, then by mid-century the Democrats could have a potential vote approaching 25 per cent of the electorate from this group alone.

Simultaneously with the maturation of the Latino/Hispanic population, ageing in another population group potentially works to the disadvantage of the Republican party. In 1980 Ronald Reagan began his influential period as president with a clear victory over incumbent Jimmy Carter. At the core of this overwhelming result was the support of 56 per cent of the white vote.

24 CNN, Election Results, 2004, us.cnn.com/ELECTION/2004/pages/results/president/ (accessed 29 Jan. 2014); CNN, ElectionCenter2008: Results, edition.cnn.com/ ELECTION/2008/results/polls/ (accessed 29 Jan. 2014); CNN, America's Choice 2012: ElectionCenter: Races & Results, http://edition.cnn.com/election/2012/results/main (accessed 29 Jan. 2014).

25 Taylor et al., 'An awakened giant: the Hispanic electorate is likely to double by 2030'.

In 2012 Mitt Romney had the support of 59 per cent of the white vote, and still lost. Almost nine out of ten American voters in 1988 were white, but by 2012 this had fallen to about seven out of ten. Mature voters have a high turnout rate, but America's white population is ageing and declining as a sector in the electorate. At about the time of the Obama re-election, birth records in America showed that white babies no longer formed a majority of births, definitive evidence that the country was headed for a future where America's white, Asian, black and Hispanic/Latino populations would all be minorities. In June 2013 updated US Census estimates recorded for the first time that deaths exceeded births in the nation's white population. The total of those aged under five was recorded as about half non-white, with those people aged under the age of 18 years projected to be more than half non-white by 2018, and the national population projected to be majority-minority around 2043.[26]

If the major parties retain the respective advantages in different ethnic groups in the US electorate that they held at the start of the 21st century, then the Democratic party should steadily gain a political advantage.[27] Furthermore, the Obama campaign attracted large majorities among young voters, gaining 66 per cent of voters under the age of 30 years in 2008 and 60 per cent of that group in 2012. Political choices made at the time of entering the voting population tend to predict the electoral decisions made by the members of those population groups throughout their lifetime. Voting behaviour will shift according to contemporary issues and contexts, but the trends indicated by those initial voting decisions remain evident. Young voters have tended to be more supportive of Democratic candidates than the national population average throughout the 21st century, and the Obama victories have emphasised the potential for this to be part of the foundation for long-term political advantage.[28]

If the demographics suggest a real opportunity for the Democrats to forge a long-term winning electoral coalition built on the work of the Obama campaign, there remain plausible arguments that the Republicans can create an alternative political future. Much has been made of the Democrats' more skilled use of social media, for fund-raising as well as messaging, of that party's extraordinarily skilful data management operation, and a superb 'ground game' that amalgamated the latest data analysis with dogged door-to-door canvassing.[29] All of these were true in 2008, and the Republican party did not

26 Yen, 'Census: white majority in US gone by 2043'.

27 Some researchers were documenting this trend well before it entered the broader popular consciousness. See, for example, White, *The Values Divide: American Politics and Culture in Transition*; Teixeira, *Red, Blue and Purple America: The Future of Election Demographics*.

28 Pew Research Center, 'Angry silents, disengaged millennials'.

29 Issenberg, *The Victory Lab: The Secret Science of Winning Campaigns*; Rutenberg, 'Data you can believe in', pp. 22–9, 36.

seem to have closed the gap by 2012, but they are techniques and skills that can be learned and transferred. Campaigns are always seeking to break new ground, and such advantages should not remain with one party in the long term.

Candidate Obama broke the mould of presidential campaign funding when, in 2008, he became the first major party nominee to refuse the federal campaign funding introduced in the 1970s. The Supreme Court also altered the campaign funding landscape with decisions liberating independent and anonymous spending in campaigns. The Obama fundraising machine has led a surge in Democratic campaign spending at the same time as some major Republican funders have seen some of their own highly expensive campaigns fail. There was no doubt some Democratic *schadenfreude* that the hundreds of millions invested in the campaign by Republican supporter Sheldon Adelson, by Karl Rove on behalf of teams of Republican supporters, and by other wealthy backers of Romney and Republican candidates had failed to achieve its aims. It is plausible to argue that these investors would be more cautious in their political spending should the demographic imperative be against them. But the potential for political investment remains strong if the appetite for it remains. Adelson's losses in 2012 amount to tens of millions, but his estimated worth by September 2013 was $28.5 billion.[30] Few people in the world are fortunate enough to be so wealthy, and even fewer of them are openly engaged in politics, but the willingness of people to contribute in support of policies, platforms and candidates they believe to be important shows no sign of diminishing and Republican candidates will continue to accumulate considerable war chests. The fundraising advantage does not necessarily lie with the Democrats and the Republicans have opportunities to invest.

The federal nature of US politics gives the Republican party's strength at state and local level real value. Most domestic policy spending is done at these levels. Political groups at state level can use ballot initiatives and referenda to influence the political agenda, and conservative groups have already shown the potential of operating at this level in certain policy areas. These include abortion, where state-level actions have imposed extra burdens on those seeking and trying to provide abortion options, and on gay rights, where legislative and constitutional changes have prevented the introduction of gay marriage. While the federal judiciary is appointed by the President with the advice and consent of the US Senate, some states hold elections for their judicial offices. These contests have traditionally not been strongly politicised, but the substantial rise in spending on state judicial elections, observed in 2012, may be an indication of increasing awareness of the potential of state-level political arenas.[31]

30 *Forbes*, 'Sheldon Adelson', www.forbes.com/profile/sheldon-adelson/ (accessed 29 Jan. 2014).

31 Hoy and Moore, 'Judicial election TV spending sets new record, yet voters reject campaigns to politicize the judiciary'.

The GOP has not been slow to recognise the national potential of politics fought at the state level. Operation Redmap has been aimed at maximising the party's strength within the states, including in its targets, for example, the presidential battleground of North Carolina, which after the 2012 elections had both a Republican governor and the two chambers of the state legislature under Republican control for the first time in more than a century. The state has seen a sharp change of direction in policies on such matters as abortion, gun control, the death penalty and Medicaid.[32] It was also one of the states that moved quickly to take advantage of the regulatory space created by the Supreme Court's 2013 decision affecting the Voting Rights Act. Within two hours of the decision, Texas implemented strict voter-identification law which had previously been blocked. Alabama and Mississippi announced plans to move forward with similar regulations that had been passed in the state, but not submitted for the federal approval formerly required. North Carolina's legislation introduced photo-ID requirements and limits on early voting opportunities.[33]

Politically pragmatic voter suppression and careful attention to constituency boundaries may do something to protect a political party's fortunes in the face of demographic shifts, but there are serious dangers in relying too heavily on these approaches. In themselves they may provide a locus around which an aggrieved opposition can organise, but they also tend to decrease the potential for compromise and adaptation that are likely to lie at the centre of a long-term strategy for party political growth. Constituencies carefully manipulated for party political benefit increase the opportunity for the politically committed groups unrepresentative of public opinion to dominate candidate selection. Processes that daunt voters from taking part are likely to act more strongly on some groups than others, potentially adding a more unrepresentative quality to the polity. While the states have long been seen as 'laboratories of democracy', and have jealously protected their right to take different policy decisions, a problem develops when diversity and political compromise within individual states is sacrificed to the skilful and (some might think) cynical protection of policies and office holders that do not command broad-based support.

The US House of Representatives is currently districted such that the Democrats would need a national aggregate popular vote lead of around 5 per cent to win the majority of seats. The success of the Obama electoral coalition provided a base for the second mid-term election campaigns in 2014, but the presidential party usually does not do well in mid-term elections, especially in second mid-terms. The Democrats' gain of four seats in 1998 is the only example of a presidential party gaining House seats in a second mid-term in well over a century. In the US Senate most of the seats up for election in 2014 are

32 Mayer, 'State for sale'; Robertson, 'North Carolinians fear the end of a middle way'.

33 Cooper, 'After ruling, states rush to enact voting laws'.

held by Democrats, and about one-third of those in states that voted for Romney in 2012. The Democrats therefore presented a large and potentially vulnerable target. Turnout declines at mid-terms, and elements of the Obama electoral coalition that performed so well for the party in 2012, may be less enthusiastic without Obama on the ballot. The Republican party hoped that 2014 would demonstrate how extremely difficult it might be to convert the Obama electorate coalition into a broader and long-lasting Democratic party electoral coalition.

James Carville's exhortation has become a cliché for good reason: there are elections when above and beyond all 'It's the economy, stupid', and this could be particularly evident in 2016. His other campaign reminder 'Change vs more of the same' also taps firmly into the habits of the American electorate, which has shown an inclination to change its presidency regularly. Only once since 1952 has a party held on to the presidency for more than two terms. President Obama will not be on the 2016 ticket, and while the Obama generation of new voters may incline to the Democrats, it will be up to a new candidate to demonstrate an appeal that can hold on to the new Democratic coalition and persuade it to turn out.

An alternative, unintended legacy of Barack Obama's remarkable presidential victories could be a period of considerable Republican electoral achievement. There is real potential for this, and certainly a likelihood of at least partial success. That said, the degree to which any such success is based on political legerdemain, rather than the creation of a broadly based electoral coalition with mutually compatible policy aims, is likely also to be an indication of the eventual fragility or strength of the GOP's long-term prospects.

The Democrats cannot rely on the unfailing loyalty of the voting groups that helped project President Obama to the White House, and the Republicans cannot rely on the groups that have been their traditional bastions to continue to put them in control of national government. The electorate is changing quite quickly, and the battle to gain and maintain political leadership in this shifting landscape will energise US elections for some time to come. It is safe to predict that the streets of Washington, DC will be crowded with happy people at future inaugurations. The political complexion of those crowds is much less easily predictable.

References

ACLU (2013) 'Voter suppression in America', www.aclu.org/voter-suppression-america (accessed 29 Jan. 2014).

B. Ackerman (2002) Bush v. Gore: The Question of Legitimacy (New Haven, CT: Yale University Press).

J. Alter (2013) The Centre Holds: Obama and his Enemies (New York, NY: Simon & Schuster).

A. Cohen (2013) 'This is Kennedy's court – the rest of the Justices just sit on it', *The Atlantic*, 29 May, www.theatlantic.com/national/archive/2013/05/this-is-kennedys-court-the-rest-of-the-justices-just-sit-on-it/276309/ (accessed 29 Jan. 2014).

R. Cook (2013), 'The Rhodes Cook Letter: The Congressional Party', Feb., see http://cookpolitical.com/.

M. Cooper (2013) 'After ruling, states rush to enact voting laws', *New York Times*, 5 July, www.nytimes.com/2013/07/06/us/politics/after-Supreme-Court-ruling-states-rush-to-enact-voting-laws.html?pagewanted=all&_r=0 (accessed 29 Jan. 2014).

J.B. Dianis (2012) 'Top 10 voter suppression moments of 2012', *HuffPost Politics* blog, 26 Dec., www.huffingtonpost.com/judith-browne-dianis/top-10-voter-suppression_b_2348574.html (accessed 29 Jan. 2014).

S. Issenberg (2012) *The Victory Lab: The Secret Science of Winning Campaigns* (New York, NY: Random House).

M. Garrett (2010) 'After the wave', *National Journal*, vol. 42, no. 43, pp. 60–1.

G. Giroux (2013) 'Final tally shows Obama first since '56 to win 51% twice', *Bloomberg*, 4 Jan., www.bloomberg.com/news/2013-01-03/final-tally-shows-obama-first-since-56-to-win-51-twice.html (accessed 29 Jan. 2014)

L. Greenhouse (2013) 'The real John Roberts emerges', *New York Times*, 30 June, http://opinionator.blogs.nytimes.com/2013/06/29/the-real-john-roberts-emerges/?_php=true&_type=blogs&_r=0 (accessed 29 Jan. 2014).

K. Haas (2013) *Statistics of the Presidential and Congressional Election of November 6, 2012*, http://clerk.house.gov/member_info/electionInfo/2012election.pdf, (accessed 29 Jan. 2014).

S. Hoy and E. Moore (2012) 'Judicial election TV spending sets new record, yet voters reject campaigns to politicize the judiciary', 7 Nov., www.brennancenter.org/press-release/judicial-election-tv-spending-sets-new-record-yet-voters-reject-campaigns-politicize, (accessed 29 Jan. 2014).

C. Johnson (2000) 'The new slogan: it's the Supreme Court, stupid!', *WEnews*, 16 Aug., womensenews.org/story/campaign-trail/000816/the-new-slogan-its-the-supreme-court-stupid (accessed 29 Jan. 2014).

D. Kam and J. Lantigua (2012) 'Former Florida GOP leaders say voter suppression was reason they pushed new election law', *The Palm Beach Post*, 25 Nov., www.palmbeachpost.com/news/news/state-regional-govt-politics/early-voting-curbs-called-power-play/nTFDy/ (accessed 29 Jan. 2014).

A. Keyssar (2012) 'Voter suppression returns: voting rights and partisan practices', *Harvard Magazine*, July–Aug., harvardmagazine.com/2012/07/voter-suppression-returns (accessed 29 Jan. 2014).

D.Leonhardt (2013) 'The endless battle over judicial nominees', *New York Times*, 23 June, www.nytimes.com/2013/06/23/opinion/sunday/the-endless-battle-over-judicial-nominees.html?_r=0 (accessed 29 Jan. 2014).

A. Liptak (2013) 'Justices void oversight of states, issue at heart of Voting Rights Act', *New York Times*, 25 June, Appears under headline 'Supreme Court invalidates key part of Voting Rights Act' at www.nytimes.com/2013/06/26/us/supreme-court-ruling.html?pagewanted=all (accessed 29 Jan. 2014).

— (2013) 'Two 5–4 decisions', *New York Times*, 26 June. Appears under headline 'Supreme Court bolsters gay marriage with two major rulings' at www.nytimes.com/2013/06/27/us/politics/supreme-court-gay-marriage.html (accessed 29 Jan. 2014).

R. McKeever and P. Davies (2012) *Politics USA*, 3rd edn, (London: Longman).

J. Mayer (2011) 'State for sale', *The New Yorker*, 10 Oct., www.newyorker.com/reporting/2011/10/10/111010fa_fact_mayer (accessed 29 Jan. 2014).

Needlecraft (1986) 'Attractive campaign pillows', repr. from Nov. 1920 in *The Keynoter*, vol. 86, no. 2, pp.16–18.

G.A.Otis (2000) 'It's the Supreme Court, stupid', *New York Village Voice*, 29 Aug., www.villagevoice.com/2000-08-29/news/it-s-the-supreme-court-stupid/ (accessed 29 Jan. 2014).

J.S. Passel and D'Vera Cohn (2008) 'US population projections: 2005–2050' (Washington, DC: Pew Research Hispanic Trends Project), www.pewhispanic.org/2008/02/11/us-population-projections-2005-2050/ (accessed 29 Jan. 2014).

Pew Research Center (2011) *'Angry silents, disengaged millennials: the generation gap and the 2012 election'* (Washington, DC), www.people-press.org/files/legacy-pdf/11-3-11%20Generations%20Release.pdf (accessed 29 Jan. 2014).

J.N. Rakove (2001) *The Unfinished Election of 2000* (New York, NY: Basic Books).

C. Robertson (2013) 'North Carolinians fear the end of a middle way', *New York Times*, 13 Aug., www.nytimes.com/2013/08/14/us/north-carolinians-fear-the-end-of-a-middle-way.html?nl=todaysheadlines&emc=edit_th_20130814&_r=0 (accessed 29 Jan. 2014).

K. Rudin (2012) 'Contraception, abortion: a reminder that it's not just the economy, stupid', *Political Junkie*, 13 Feb., www.npr.org/blogs/

politicaljunkie/2012/02/13/146672116/contraception-abortion-a-reminder-that-its-not-just-the-economy-stupid (accessed 29 Jan. 2014).

J. Rutenberg (2013) 'Data you can believe in', *Sunday New York Times Magazine*, 20 June, www.nytimes.com/2013/06/23/magazine/the-obama-campaigns-digital-masterminds-cash-in.html?_r=0&gwh=510692AD348 BBB7493715E08892684CA&gwt=pay (accessed 29 Jan. 2014).

S.G. Stolberg (2013) 'Still marching on Washington, 50 years later', *New York Times*,13 Aug., www.nytimes.com/2013/08/14/us/politics/50-years-later-fighting-the-same-civil-rights-battle.html?pagewanted=1&_r=0&nl=todaysheadlines&emc=edit_th_20130814 (accessed 29 Jan. 2014).

P. Taylor, A. Gonzalez-Barrera, J.S. Passel and M.H. Lopez (2012) '*An awakened giant: the Hispanic electorate is likely to double by 2030*' (Washington, DC: Pew Research Hispanic Trends Project), www.pewhispanic.org/2012/11/14/an-awakened-giant-the-hispanic-electorate-is-likely-to-double-by-2030/ (accessed 29 Jan. 2014).

R. Teixeira (2008) *Red, Blue and Purple America: The Future of Election Demographics* (Washington, DC: Brookings Institution).

— (2009) 'The coming end of the culture wars' report (Washington, DC: Center for American Progress), (www.americanprogress.org/wp-content/uploads/issues/2009/07/pdf/culture_wars.pdf (accessed 29 Jan. 2014).

R. Ungar (2012) 'How GOP voter suppression efforts contributed to Obama win', *Forbes*, 9 Nov. www.forbes.com/sites/rickungar/2012/11/09/how-gop-voter-suppression-efforts-contributed-to-obama-win/ (accessed 29 Jan. 2014).

D. Wang (2013) 'The great gerrymander of 2012', *New York Times Sunday Review*, 2 Feb., www.nytimes.com/2013/02/03/opinion/sunday/the-great-gerrymander-of-2012.html?pagewanted=all&_r=0 (accessed 29 Jan. 2014).

R. Wolf (2013) 'From gay marriage to voting law, Kennedy is the key', *USA Today*, 27 June, www.usatoday.com/story/news/politics/2013/06/27/supreme-court-anthony-kennedy-race-voting-abortion-gay-marriage/2161701/ (accessed 29 Jan. 2014).

H. Yen (2013) 'Census: white majority in US gone by 2043', *US News* on *NBC News.com*, 13 June, usnews.nbcnews.com/_news/2013/06/13/18934111-census-white-majority-in-us-gone-by-2043?lite (accessed 29 Jan. 2014).

J.K. White (2002) *The Values Divide: American Politics and Culture in Transition* (Washington, DC: CQ Press).

2. Obama's burden: governing in polarized times[1]

George C. Edwards III

On 31 December 2012, Obama told his base in a video message, 'When I take the oath of office this month, I'll be as determined as ever.' 'Just like four years ago, winning an election won't bring about the change we seek on its own. It only gives us the chance to make that change. What we fought for in 2012, we've got to fight just as hard for in 2013.'[2]

The president was correct. His re-election did little to improve his chances for winning the policy changes he and his supporters desired. From the beginning of his term, he faltered on gun control, sequestration, and other important issues. In this chapter I explain why the president found it so difficult to govern and why his frustrations are unlikely to diminish.

I do so by focusing on the foundation of leadership success, the opportunity structure within which presidents attempt to make policy changes and thus leave their legacy. Rather than the president's rhetorical eloquence or bargaining skills, it is the environment in which he operates that largely determines whether he will succeed or fail in obtaining public and congressional support for his initiatives. Thus, we must approach a presidency from a strategic perspective to evaluate the president's opportunities for change.[3]

Strategic position regarding public opinion

Public support is a key political resource, and modern presidents have typically sought public support for themselves and their policies that they could use as leverage to obtain backing for their proposals in Congress. It is natural for a president, basking in the glow of an electoral victory, to focus on creating, rather than exploiting, opportunities for change. After all, if he convinced voters and party leaders to support his candidacy – and just won the biggest prize in American politics by doing so – why should he not be able to convince the public or members of Congress to support his policies? Thus, presidents may not focus on evaluating existing possibilities when they think they can create their own.

1   At the author's request the main text of this chapter has not been copy-edited.
2   Cited in Simendinger, 'Obama taking campaign-style approach to new goals'.
3   See, for example, Edwards III, *The Strategic President; At the Margins: Presidential Leadership of Congress*; and *On Deaf Ears: The Limits of the Bully Pulpit*.

Yet it is a mistake for presidents to assume they can lead the public. There is nothing in the historical record to support such a belief, and there are long-term forces that work against presidential leadership of the public.[4] Adopting strategies for governing that are prone to failure waste rather than create opportunities,[5] so it is critically important for presidents to assess accurately the potential for obtaining public support.

What is the president's strategic position regarding public opinion? Does it support the direction in which the president would like to move? Is there a mandate from the voters in support of specific policies? Is there a broad public predisposition for government activism? Are opposition party identifiers open to supporting the president's initiatives?

Mandate

New presidents traditionally claim a mandate from the people, because the most effective means of setting the terms of debate and overcoming opposition is the perception of an electoral mandate, an impression that the voters want to see the winner's programs implemented. Indeed, major changes in policy, as in 1933, 1965 and 1981, rarely occur in the absence of such perceptions.

Mandates can be powerful symbols in American politics. They accord added legitimacy and credibility to the newly elected president's proposals. Concerns for representation and political survival encourage members of Congress to support the president if they feel the people have spoken.[6] As a result, mandates change the premises of decision. Perceptions of a mandate in 1980, for example, placed a stigma on big government and exalted the unregulated marketplace and large defense budgets, providing Ronald Reagan a favorable strategic position for dealing with Congress.

When asked about his mandate in his first press conference following his re-election in 2012, the president displayed no note of triumphalism. Instead, he replied in modest and general terms, 'I've got a mandate to help middle-class families and families that are working hard to try to get into the middle class. That's my mandate.' He also noted that the 'clear message' from the campaign was to put our partisan differences aside.[7]

The president had it about right. A *Washington Post*-ABC News poll in December 2012 found that only a third of Americans saw him as having won a broad-based mandate in the November election.[8]

4   Edwards III, *On Deaf Ears; Overreach: Leadership in the Obama Presidency; The Strategic President*, chs. 2–3; and *Governing by Campaigning: The Politics of the Bush Presidency*.

5   See Edwards III, *The Strategic President*, chs. 2, 3, 6.

6   Edwards III, *At the Margins*, ch. 8; Grossback et al., *Mandate Politics*.

7   White House, 'Remarks by the President in a news conference,' 14 Nov. 2012, www.whitehouse.gov/the-press-office/2012/11/14/remarks-president-news-conference (accessed 22 Jan. 2014).

8   *Washington Post*-ABC News poll, 13–16 Dec. 2012.

The basic ingredients for encouraging perceptions of a mandate were missing. Winning 51 per cent is hardly a landslide. Moreover, Obama was the first president since Andrew Jackson in 1832 to be re-elected with a smaller percentage of the vote than in his first election. Republicans increased their share of the presidential vote among a number of important demographic groups, including whites and men (four percentage points), younger voters (six points), white Catholics (seven points) and Jews (nine points). He lost the Independent vote by five percentage points (50 per cent to 45 per cent),[9] which he won 52 per cent to 44 per cent in 2008.

More broadly, Obama ran a hard-edged negative campaign focused on convincing voters that Mitt Romney was unworthy of becoming president. He gave lip service to an agenda, publishing scaled-back and repackaged ideas from his first term in a 20-page pamphlet and often micro-targeting his policy views to elements of the Democratic coalition rather than addressing the broad electorate.

Perhaps equally important, the Republicans retained their majority in the House. They certainly did not see any mandate, and it was their perceptions that mattered most. 'Pretty much everyone in our conference is returning with a bigger margin of victory than the president of the United States', said House Republican Tim Huelskamp. 'He certainly doesn't have a mandate.'[10] Paul Ryan of Wisconsin agreed that the president won no mandate. 'They also re-elected the House Republicans', he noted. Had voters fully embraced the president, and by extension, his call to raise taxes on top earners, 'they would have put Nancy Pelosi in charge of the House of Representatives', Ryan added.[11] (It was convenient for Republicans to ignore the fact that Democrats actually won more votes for House seats than did Republicans).

There was one policy specific on which the president could reasonably claim a mandate, however: increased taxes on the wealthy. As he noted shortly after the election, he spoke incessantly during the campaign about his insistence on eliminating the Bush tax cuts for the wealthiest Americans:

> If there was one thing that everybody understood was a big difference between myself and Mr. Romney, it was when it comes to how we reduce our deficit, I argued for a balanced, responsible approach, and part of that included making sure that the wealthiest Americans pay a little bit more.
>
> I think every voter out there understood that that was an important debate, and the majority of voters agreed with me.[12]

9   2012 National Exit Poll.

10   Quoted in Terris, 'A presidential mandate? How about 435 congressional ones?'

11   Kaplan, 'Ryan: no mandate for Obama in election'. See also Simendinger and Huey-Burns, 'Amid "frank" talks, Obama uses polls as pry bar'.

12   White House, 'Remarks by the President in a news conference', 14 Nov. 2012.

Similarly, in a press conference a week before his inauguration, he proclaimed his intent 'to carry out the agenda that I campaigned on', reminding listeners of his campaigning on the question of tax fairness and a 'balanced' approach to deficit reduction. 'Turns out', he said pointedly, 'the American people agree with me. They listened to an entire year's debate over this issue, and they made a clear decision about the approach they prefer.'[13]

Support for government activism

Democrats, including the president, wish to move policy in a liberal direction. More Americans viewed themselves as conservative than as liberal, however (table 1). In 2012, conservatives outnumbered liberals 39 per cent to 22 per cent. A significantly higher percentage of Americans in most states, even some solidly Democratic ones, called themselves conservative rather than liberal. No state in 2012 had a majority of people who called themselves liberal, and only Massachusetts and Rhode Island (and Washington, DC) had pluralities of liberals.[14] Americans are more than twice as likely to identify themselves as conservative rather than liberal on economic issues: 46 per cent to 20 per cent. The gap is narrower on social issues, but conservatives still outnumber liberals, 38 per cent to 28 per cent.[15]

We can also see the dominance of conservatism if we disaggregate opinion by political party (table 2). While 68 per cent of Republicans in 2012 called themselves conservative, only 38 per cent of Democrats identified as liberal. Thirty-eight per cent of Democrats said they were moderates and another 20 per cent saw themselves as conservative. Among Independents, 30 per cent said they were conservative, and only 22 per cent identified as liberal.[16]

Ideological identification is not determinative, of course, and there is a well-known paradox of the incongruity between ideological identification and issue attitudes.[17] Scholars have long known that only a fraction of the public exhibits

13 White House, 'Transcript of news conference by the President', 14 Jan. 2013.

14 Gallup Poll, 'Alabama, North Dakota, Wyoming Most Conservative States,' 1 Feb. 2013. The analysis is based on telephone interviews conducted as part of Gallup Daily tracking 1 Jan. 1–31 Dec. 2012. The sample includes 211,972 US adults. The margin of sampling error for most states is ±3 percentage points, but is as high as ±6 percentage points for the District of Columbia.

15 Annual Gallup Values and Beliefs Poll, 3–6 May 2012.

16 Gallup Poll surveys conducted Jan.–Sep. 2009.

17 Ellis and Stimson, *Ideology in America*; Treier and Hillygus, 'The nature of political ideology in the contemporary electorate', pp. 679–703; Ellis and Stimson, 'Symbolic ideology in the American electorate', pp. 388–402; Jacoby, 'Policy attitudes, ideology, and voting behavior in the 2008 Election'; Stimson, *Tides of Consent: How Public Opinion Shapes American Politics*; Conover and Feldman, 'The origins and meaning of liberal/conservative identifications', pp. 617–45; Sears et al., 'Self-interest vs. symbolic politics in policy attitudes and presidential voting', pp. 670–84.

Table 1. Self-reported ideology of the public

Year	% Conservative	% Moderate	% Liberal
1992	36	43	17
1993	39	40	18
1994	38	42	17
1995	36	39	16
1996	38	40	16
1997	37	40	19
1998	37	40	19
1999	38	40	19
2000	38	40	19
2001	38	40	20
2002	38	39	19
2003	38	40	20
2004	38	40	19
2005	38	39	20
2006	37	38	21
2007	37	37	22
2008	37	37	22
2009	40	36	21
2010	40	35	21
2011	40	35	21
2012	39	35	22
2013	38	34	23

Source: Gallup Poll

Question: 'How would you describe your political views – very conservative, conservative, moderate, liberal, or very liberal'?

Table 2. Ideological self-identification of party groups

Party ID	% Conservative	% Moderate	% Liberal
Republicans	68	26	5
Independents	30	43	22
Democrats	20	38	38

Source: Pew Research Center, *2012 Values Survey*, 4–15 April 2012

Question: 'Do you think of yourself as _____ '?

the requisite traits of an 'ideologue'.[18] Nevertheless, many more Americans are able to choose an ideological label and use it to guide their political judgments than in previous decades.[19] Scholars have found that ideological self-placements are influential determinants of vote choice,[20] issue attitudes,[21] and views toward government spending.[22]

Many liberal policies require public support for, or at least toleration of, government activism in the form of new programs, increased spending, and additional taxes. When asked whether government should do more to solve problems or is doing too many things better left to businesses and individuals, 43 per cent of voters in 2012 chose the former, but 51 per cent selected the less active government option. Forty-nine per cent disapproved of Obama's Affordable Care Act (ACA), while only 44 per cent approved.[23]

18 Converse, 'The nature of belief systems in mass publics', pp. 206–61.
19 Levitin and Miller, 'Ideological interpretations of presidential elections', pp. 751–71.
20 Huckfeldt et al., 'Accessibility and the political utility of partisan and ideological orientations', pp. 888–911; Knight, 'Ideology in the 1980 election', pp. 828–53; Levitin and Miller, 'Ideological interpretations of presidential elections'; Stimson, 'Belief systems: constraint, complexity, and the 1972 election', pp. 393–417.
21 Goren et al., 'Source cues, partisan identities, and political value expression', pp. 805–20; Federico and Schneider, 'Political expertise and the use of ideology', pp. 221–52; Jacoby, 'Value choices and American public opinion', pp. 706–23; Goren, 'Political sophistication and policy reasoning', pp. 462–78; Goren, 'Core principles and policy reasoning in mass publics', pp. 159–77; Huckfeldt et al., 'Accessibility and the political utility of partisan and ideological orientations'; Jacoby, 'The structure of ideological thinking in the American electorate', pp. 314–35; Jacoby, 'Ideological identification and issue attitudes', pp. 178–205; Feldman, 'Structure and consistency in public opinion', pp. 416–40; Sears et al., 'Self-interest vs. symbolic politics in policy attitudes and presidential voting'.
22 Rudolph and Evans, 'Political trust, ideology, and public support for government spending', pp. 660–71; Jacoby, 'Issue framing and government spending', pp. 750–67; Jacoby, 'Public attitudes toward government spending', pp. 336–61.
23 2012 National Exit Polls.

Showing the difficulty of obtaining support for liberal policy, in April 2013, three years after its passage, only 37 per cent approved of the ACA.[24] Forty-one per cent of Americans did not know the ACA was in place, many thinking Congress had repealed it or the Supreme Court had found it unconstitutional.[25] In March, 67 per cent of the uninsured younger than age 65 – and 57 per cent of the overall population – said they did not understand how the ACA would impact them. Many also continued to hold false impressions of the law: 57 per cent incorrectly believed that the ACA included a public option. Nearly half believed the law provides financial assistance for illegal immigrants to buy insurance. And 40 per cent – including 35 per cent of seniors – still believed that the government would have 'death panels' make decisions about end-of-life care for Medicare beneficiaries.[26]

When asked whether it preferred a smaller government offering fewer public services or a larger government offering more services, the public has chosen the former. Support for larger government was modest when Obama took office, and decreased slightly during his tenure (table 3). Similarly, in September 2012, Gallup found that 54 per cent of the public felt the government was doing too much while 39 per cent thought it should do more to solve the nation's problems.[27]

The public's resistance to government activism should not be surprising. In their sweeping 'macro' view of public opinion, Robert Erikson, Michael MacKuen and James Stimson show that opinion always moves contrary to the president's position. They argue that a moderate public always gets too much liberalism from Democrats and too much conservatism from Republicans. Because public officials have policy beliefs as well as an interest in re-election, they are not likely to calibrate their policy stances exactly to match those of the public. Therefore, opinion movement is typically contrary to the ideological persuasion of presidents. Liberal presidents produce movement in the conservative direction and conservatives generate public support for more liberal policies.[28]

The public continuously adjusts its views of current policy in the direction of a long-run equilibrium path as it compares its preferences for ideal policy with its views of current policy to produce a policy mood.[29] Thus, the conservative policy period of the 1950s produced a liberal mood that resulted in the liberal policy changes of the mid-1960s. These policies, in turn, helped elect conservative Richard Nixon. In the late-1970s, Jimmy Carter's liberal policies

24 Kaiser Health Tracking Poll, 5–10 March 2013.
25 Kaiser Health Tracking Poll Omnibus Supplement, 18–21 April 2013.
26 Kaiser Health Tracking Poll, 5–10 March 2013.
27 Gallup Poll, 6–9 Sep. 2012.
28 Erikson et al., *The Macro Polity*, ch. 9.
29 Ibid., pp. 344, 374.

Table 3. Public support for larger government

Poll dates	% Smaller government, fewer services	% Larger government, more services	% No opinion
12–15 June 2008	50	45	5
13–16 January 2009	53	43	4
18–21 June 2009	54	41	4
12–15 January 2010	58	38	4
22–25 April 2010	56	40	4
29 August–1 September 2011	56	38	6
22–25 August 2012	54	41	5

Source: ABC News-*Washington Post* poll

Question: 'Generally speaking, would you say you favor (smaller government with fewer services), or (larger government with more services)?

paved the way for Ronald Reagan's conservative tenure, which in turn laid the foundation for Bill Clinton's more liberal stances. Negative reaction to the conservatism of George W. Bush encouraged the election of the more liberal Barack Obama. Stuart Soroka and Christopher Wlezien have reached similar conclusions with their thermostatic model of public opinion.[30]

Public polarization

A primary reason for the difficulty of passing major changes in public policy is the challenge of obtaining support from opposition party identifiers among the public. There has been an increase in partisan-ideological polarization as Americans increasingly base their party loyalties on their ideological beliefs rather than on membership of social groups,[31] and they align their policy preferences more closely with their core political predispositions.[32]

30 Soroka and Wlezien, *Degrees of Democracy.*
31 Abramowitz, *The Disappearing Center*; Dancey and Goren, 'Party identification, issue attitudes, and the dynamics of political debate', pp. 686–99; Petersen et al., 'Political parties and value consistency in public opinion formation', pp. 530–50; Levendusky, *The Partisan Sort*; Berinsky, *In Time of War: Understanding American Public Opinion from World War II to Iraq.* See also Fiorina et al., *Culture Wars? The Myth of Polarized America*; Bafumi and Shapiro, 'A new partisan voter', pp. 1–24; Layman et al., 'Party polarization in American politics', pp. 83–110; Jacobson, *A Divider, Not a Uniter: George W. Bush and the American Public.*
32 Garner and Palmer, 'Polarization and issue consistency over time', pp. 225–46.

Partisans are more likely to apply ideological labels to themselves than in earlier decades, a declining number of them call themselves moderate, and the differences in the ideological self-placements of Republicans and Democrats have grown dramatically since the 1980s. This polarization of partisans has contributed to much more ideological voting behavior.[33]

The policy divide between the Democratic and Republican electoral coalitions now encompasses a wide variety of issues including both economic and social issues. Pew found that in 2012 the average difference between the parties on 15 issues was 18 percentage points, the highest in the time series, which began in 1987. The greatest difference, 41 percentage points, was on the social safety net, followed by the environment (39 percentage points), and equal opportunity and the scope and performance of government (33 percentage points each). These issues are at the heart of policymaking in Washington.[34]

Table 4 compares the preferences of Democratic and Republican congressional voters in the 2012 national exit poll on the proper role of government along with four specific policy issues – healthcare reform, taxes, abortion and same-sex marriage. On each issue, a majority of Democratic voters were on the liberal side while a majority of Republican voters were on the conservative side. The divide between supporters of the two parties was especially stark on the issue of healthcare where the question was whether the ACA should be preserved or repealed. The great majority of Democratic voters wanted the law to be kept or expanded while nearly all Republican voters wanted it to be partially or completely repealed.

Partisan polarization extends behind policy disagreements. Republicans and Republican-leaning Independents not only did not support Obama when he initially ran for the presidency. By Election Day 2008, they perceived a huge ideological gulf between themselves and the new president and viewed him as an untrustworthy radical leftist with a socialist agenda. Forty-one per cent of McCain voters judged Obama to be an 'extreme liberal', further left than Republican voters had placed any previous Democratic candidate. Moreover, they placed him further to the left of their own ideologies than they had placed any previous Democratic candidate.[35]

Thus, the Republicans' campaign to brand Obama as a radical socialist[36] out of touch with American values resonated with many McCain voters. An African-American candidate was also likely to exacerbate right-wing

33 McCarty et al., *Polarized America: The Dance of Ideology and Unequal Riches*.

34 Pew Research Center, 2012 Values Survey. Results are based on a national sample of 3,008 adults in the period 4–15 April 2012.

35 Jacobson, 'Legislative success and political failure: the public's reaction to Barack Obama's early presidency', pp. 221–2.

36 Kenski et al., *The Obama Victory: How Media, Money, and Message Shaped the 2008 Election*.

Table 4. The policy divide in public opinion, 2012

	Per cent favoring	
Issue	Democratic voters	Republican voters
Activist government	74	17
Keeping healthcare law	81	14
Raising income taxes	83	44
Same-sex marriage	73	29
Legal abortion	82	43

Source: Alan I. Abramowitz, 'The electoral roots of America's dysfunctional government'. Paper delivered at the Conference on Governing in Polarized Politics, Rothermere American Institute, University of Oxford, 16–17 April 2013, p. 38. Based on 2012 National Exit Poll.

opposition,[37] as was his Ivy League education and somewhat detached manner. The fact that he spent part of his childhood in Muslim Indonesia and that his middle name was 'Hussein' provided additional fodder to those willing or even eager to believe that he was outside the mainstream. Republican voters did not simply oppose Obama; they despised and feared him.

The polarization of the 2008 campaign and the nature of the opposition to Obama laid the groundwork for the intense aversion to Obama and his policies that appeared shortly after he took office. His initial actions of seeking the release of additional Troubled Asset Relief Program (TARP) funds, and promoting an historic economic stimulus bill, confirmed for conservatives that he was indeed a left-wing radical who needed to be stopped at all costs and, along with the president's support of healthcare reform, fueled the emergence of the Tea Party movement.

Partisan polarization reached record levels during Obama's first term.[38] Early on in the Obama presidency, the Democratic political organization Democracy Corps concluded from its focus groups that those in the conservative GOP base believed that Obama 'is ruthlessly advancing a secret agenda to bankrupt the United States and dramatically expand government control to an extent

37 Piston, 'How explicit racial prejudice hurt Obama in the 2008 election', pp. 431–51; Lewis-Back et al., 'Obama's missed landslide: a racial cost?', pp. 69–76; Highton, 'Prejudice rivals partisanship and ideology when explaining the 2008 presidential vote across the states', pp. 6530–5; Tesler, 'The return of old-fashioned racism to white Americans' partisan preferences in the early Obama era', pp. 110–23.

38 Edwards III, *Overreach*, ch. 1; Pew Research Center, 2012 Values Survey, 4–15 April 2012; Abramowitz, *The Polarized Public: Why Our Government Is So Dysfunctional*; Jacobson, 'Partisan polarization in American politics'.

nothing short of socialism.'[39] In August 2010, a national poll found that 52 per cent of the Republican respondents said it was definitely (14 per cent) or probably (38 per cent) true that 'Barack Obama sympathizes with the goals of Islamic fundamentalists who want to impose Islamic law around the world.'[40] It is not surprising, then, that the differences in evaluations of the president between partisans reached record levels in the Obama administration (table 5).

The 2012 election was even more polarized than the election in 2008. Seventy-seven per cent of Republicans characterized Obama as an 'extreme liberal'. Only 7 per cent of Democrats viewed him that way.[41]

An examination of states that deviated from Obama's share of the nationwide vote (about 51 per cent) by ten percentage points or more reveals that there were more 'polarized' states than in any election in generations. A few states (figure 1) – Vermont, Rhode Island, Massachusetts, New York, Maryland, and Hawaii, and the District of Columbia – were polarized in favor of Obama. Most of the polarized states, however, voted for Republican Mitt Romney. The

Table 5. Party differences in presidential public approval

Year of Obama's tenure	Party difference*	Next largest gap	
		Percentage points	President
1st, 2009–10	65	52	Clinton, 1992–3
2nd, 2010–11	68	56	Reagan, 1982–3
3rd, 2011–12	68	59	G.W. Bush, 2003–04
4th, 2012–13	76	76	G.W. Bush, 2004–05

* Differences expressed as percentage points
Source: Gallup Poll.

Question: 'Do you approve or disapprove of the job _____ is doing as president'?

39   Cook, 'Intensity matters'.
40   *Newsweek* poll, 25–26 Aug. 2010.
41   Calculations by Gary C. Jacobson from 2012 Cooperative Congressional Election Study (CCES) data.

Figure 1. Polarized states in 2012 presidential election

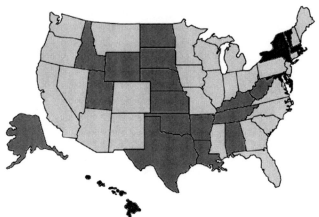

Dark grey = ≤ 10 percentage points below Obama's national average
Black = ≥ 10 percentage points above Obama's national average

majority of these 16 states form a belt stretching from West Virginia, Kentucky, and Tennessee through Alabama, Louisiana and Arkansas over to the states occupying the center of the country: Texas, Oklahoma, Kansas, Nebraska, and North and South Dakota. In addition, Wyoming, Idaho, Utah, and Alaska were strongly in the Republican camp. Given these results, it is not surprising that there were only 35 House districts where the presidential vote was within five percentage points of the national presidential popular vote margin.[42]

Party loyalty in voting hit a record high in 2012. The exit polls found that 92 per cent of Democrats voted for Obama and 93 per cent of Republicans voted for Romney. (There were similar levels of party loyalty in voting for House and Senate candidates.)[43] There was a 26 percentage-point difference in the underlying partisanship of the districts won by Republicans and Democrats in 2012 (as measured by the presidential vote), the highest ever. States are generally more diverse and thus more politically competitive than House districts, but the gap between the Senate parties' electoral constituencies reached a record level of 15 percentage points.[44]

---

42   Silver, 'As swing districts dwindle, can a divided House stand?' Only 14 of these are
     Republican seats.

43   2012 National Exit Poll and 2012 CCES data. Both the Poll and the CCES found that 93
     per cent of partisans reported voting for their party's House candidates and 92 per cent for
     their party's Senate candidate. In the CCES, 95 per cent of the respondents voted for their
     party's presidential nominee. See Jacobson, 'Partisan polarization in American politics', p.
     15.

44   Jacobson, 'Partisan polarization in American politics', pp. 10–11.

As Obama began his second term, this polarization persisted in the underlying partisan and ideological divisions of the country. Many Republicans continued to exhibit a strong antipathy toward Obama. Even after nearly four years in office, many Republicans clung to the views that the president was foreign born (and thus ineligible to be president), a Muslim (which they see in negative terms), or both.[45] Indeed, a majority of Republicans supports impeaching the president.[46] Thus, the president entered his second term with the widest partisan gap in approval of any newly re-elected president ever, 80 percentage points (91–11). George W. Bush was the previous record holder with a 76-percentage point difference.[47]

Contributing to the high levels of polarization was the insulation of the opposition. Sixty-three per cent of Republicans and GOP leaners reported that they received most of their news from Fox News, which is known for its conservative reporting and commentators.[48] Forty per cent of Republicans said they watched Fox regularly.[49] The president's initial actions were grist for commentators on the right, especially those on radio and cable television. They aggressively reinforced the fears of their audiences and encouraged active opposition to the White House.

Summary

In sum, early in the president's second term his strategic position regarding public opinion was not strong. The public remained highly polarized and less than enthusiastic about activist government, and it did not provide Obama with a mandate for governing. Despite criticism from some ill-informed liberal commentators that he was failing to exploit the potential of the bully pulpit,[50] public opinion would continue to present an obstacle to obtaining support from members of Congress not already inclined to support him.

Strategic position regarding Congress

Every president needs support in Congress to pass his legislative proposals. It may seem quite reasonable for a president who has just won the biggest

---

45 Nyhan, 'New surveys show the persistence of misperceptions'; Pew Research Center, Pew Forum on Religion and Public Life, conducted by Princeton Survey Research Associates International, 28 June–9 July 2012. Nearly a third of Republicans said Obama was a Muslim.

46 *Huffington Post*/YouGov poll, 30 Jan.–2 Feb. 2013.

47 For previous presidents, see Jacobson, *A Divider, Not a Uniter*, p. 151. The poll for Obama is from the Gallup Tracking Poll, 21–27 Jan. 2013.

48 Pew Research Media Attitudes Survey, 22–26 July 2009.

49 Pew Research News Consumption Survey, 8–28 June 2010.

50 See, for example, Goldman, 'Cornel West flunks the president'; Reich, 'The empty bully pulpit'; Westen, 'What happened to Obama?'; Dowd, 'No bully pulpit'.

prize in American politics, by convincing voters and party leaders to support his candidacy, to conclude that he should be able to convince members of Congress to support his policies.

As with leading the public, then, presidents may not focus on evaluating existing possibilities when they think they can create their own. Yet, assuming party support in Congress, or success in reaching across the aisle to obtain bipartisan support, is fraught with dangers. There is not a single systematic study that demonstrates presidents can reliably move members of Congress, especially members of the opposition party, to support them.

The best evidence is that presidential persuasion is at the margins of congressional decision making. Even presidents who appeared to dominate Congress were actually facilitators rather than directors of change. They understood their own limitations and quite explicitly took advantage of opportunities in their environments. Working at the margins, they successfully guided legislation through Congress. When these resources diminished, they reverted to the more typical stalemate that usually characterizes presidential-congressional relations.[51]

There are several components of the opportunity for obtaining congressional support. First is the presence or absence of the perception of a mandate for change. Do members of Congress think the public has spoken clearly in favor of the president's proposals? We have already seen that Republicans saw no mandate for the president.

Divided government

The second component is the presence or absence of unified government. Is the president's party in control of the congressional agenda?

The House is the chamber where majority control is most important, because the rules allow the majority to control the agenda and many of the alternatives on which members vote. Republicans control the House in the current 113th Congress (2013–14). Political necessity sometimes forces Republican leaders to allow votes on issues not supported by a majority of the party. Since the 2012 election, Speaker John Boehner has allowed three bills to come to the floor which were opposed by most Republicans but passed with a majority of Democratic votes. The issues were a vote on extending the Bush tax cuts but with higher taxes on the wealthiest taxpayers, federal relief funds for victims of Hurricane Sandy in the north east, and the Violence against Women Act. The public supported these bills, and party leaders felt blocking them would be worse for the party's reputation than allowing them to go forward.

---

51 Edwards III, *The Strategic President*, chs. 4, 5, and *At the Margins*, chs. 9, 10; Bond and Fleisher, *The President in the Legislative Arena*, ch. 8; Fleisher et al., 'Which presidents are uncommonly successful in Congress?'

The president should not expect many other bills to meet this criterion, however. To retain his credibility with his members, many of whom shudder at the idea of finding middle ground with Democrats, Boehner must present a unified front, holding that the House is the last line of defense against the president's progressive agenda. A Democratic majority in the Senate means there will be fewer hearings harassing the administration and, more importantly, that his proposals will arrive on the floor. However, the majority is not large enough to overcome the persistent threat of filibusters, forcing the president to seek Republican support even in a chamber controlled by his party.

Ideology

An important aspect of the opportunity structure is the ideological division of members of Congress. Are they likely to agree with the president's initiatives? Under divided government, is there potential to reach across the aisle and obtain support from the opposition party?

The ideological gap between the parties in the House reached a record high in the 112th Congress (2011–12), and the election did nothing to mitigate the ideological differences between the congressional parties. Keith Poole's prediction for the 113th Congress is that the ideological gap between the House party coalitions will be about the same as in the 112th Congress.[52]

The Senate did gain some likely moderate Democrats (Heidi Heitkamp of North Dakota, Joe Donnelly of Indiana and Angus King, a Maine Independent who organizes with the Democrats, but lost an equal number through retirements, Kent Conrad of North Dakota, Ben Nelson of Nebraska and James Webb of Virginia). Republican departures included three of the party's more moderate members (Scott Brown, Olympia Snowe and Richard Lugar), and all three of its newcomers, Deb Fischer (Nebraska), Ted Cruz (Texas) and Jeff Flake (Arizona) belong to the Tea Party faction. In all, seven of the incoming senators are likely to be more extreme than the incumbents they replaced, and none of the remaining four is likely to be significantly more moderate than their predecessors. Thus, Keith Poole projects the Senate to be even more ideologically polarized than it was in the 112th Congress.[53]

The polarization of party elites has been asymmetrical, with most of it the result of the rightward movement of the Republicans.[54] According to Mann and Ornstein, the Republicans have become ideologically extreme, scornful of

---

52 See his blog, dated 13 Nov. 2012, at voteview.com/blog/?p=609 (accessed 29 Jan. 2014).

53 See his blog, dated 8 Nov. 2012, at voteview.com/blog/?p=602 (accessed 29 Jan. 2014).

54 Kabaservice, *Rule and Ruin*; Jordan et al., 'Polarization and the party platforms, 1944–2012'; Mann and Ornstein, *It's Even Worse Than It Looks*; Jacobson, 'Partisan polarization in American politics', p. 4; Ura and Ellis, 'Partisan moods: polarization and the dynamics of mass party preferences', pp. 1–15.

compromise, contemptuous of facts, evidence, and science, dismissive of the legitimacy of the opposition, and at war with government.[55] It is little wonder that Barack Obama has told aides that a sizable mistake at the start of his administration was his naiveté in thinking he could work with Republicans on weighty issues.[56]

The president was correct. Table 6 shows the average levels of support on contested votes on which the president has taken a stand. In both the House and the Senate, the differences between the support of Democrats and Republicans are the greatest in the past 60 years. The president obtained very little support from Republicans in either chamber, and there is no reason to expect more success in his second term.

Republicans and their constituencies

The president requires Republican support to pass his legislative proposals. Are there constituency cross-pressures to cooperate with President Obama to counter their ideological predispositions to oppose him?

One of the most important political trends in the past half century has been the polarization of the congressional parties' respective electoral bases. The partisan realignment of the South[57] and the sorting of conservatives and liberals outside the South into the Republican and Democratic parties, respectively, has increased the level of consistency between party identification and ideology. In the 2012 election, more than 90 per cent of self-identified liberals and conservatives identified with the 'appropriate' party. Moreover, the relationship between ideology and voting has become much stronger. In 2012, about 90 per cent of self-identified liberals voted for Democrats in the House and Senate elections, while 84 per cent of conservatives voted for Republicans.[58] As a consequence, Democratic and Republican elected officials today represent electoral coalitions with strongly diverging policy preferences across a wide range of issues.

The electoral constituencies of the House Republicans contain relatively few Obama supporters. Not a single Republican won in a Democratic-leaning district.[59] Of the 234 Republicans elected to the House in 2012,

55   Mann and Ornstein, *It's Even Worse Than It Looks*, p. 103.

56   Lee and Langley, 'A more worried Obama battles to win second term'.

57   Black and Black, *Politics and Society in the South*; Frymer, 'The 1994 aftershock: dealignment or realignment in the South', pp. 99–113; Nadeau and Stanley, 'Class polarization among native southern whites, 1952–90', pp. 900–19; Hood III et al., 'Of byrd[s] and bumpers: using Democratic senators to analyze political change in the South, 1960–1995', pp. 465–87; Wattenberg, 'The building of a Republican regional base in the South', pp. 424–31; Bullock III et al., 'The consolidation of the white southern congressional vote', pp. 231–43.

58   2012 National Exit Poll; 2012 CCES data; Jacobson, 'Partisan polarization in American politics', p. 8.

59   Jacobson, 'The Congressional Elections of 2012', p. 7.

Table 6. Presidential support in Congress, 1953–2012

President	President's party	House of Representatives % support*			Senate % support		
		President's party	Opposition party	Difference[†] in support	President's party	Opposition party	Difference[†] in support
Eisenhower	Republican	63	42	21	69	36	33
Kennedy	Democrat	73	26	47	65	33	32
Johnson	Democrat	71	27	44	56	44	12
Nixon/Ford	Republican	64	39	25	63	33	30
Carter	Democrat	63	31	32	63	37	36
Reagan	Republican	70	29	51	74	31	43
G.H.W. Bush	Republican	73	27	44	75	29	46
Clinton	Democrat	75	24	51	83	22	61
G.W. Bush	Republican	84	20	64	86	18	68
Obama (2009–12)	Democrat	85	18	67	94	21	73

* On roll-call votes on which the winning side was supported by fewer than 80 per cent of those voting

[†] Differences expressed as percentage points

just 17 represent congressional districts that Obama also won. Among the House Republicans' electoral constituents – those respondents who said they had voted for a winning Republican – only 12 per cent reported also voting for Obama. The comparable figure for Senate Republican voters was only 9 per cent, the lowest in polling history. (By contrast, the overlap between the electoral constituencies of the president and his partisans in Congress exceeds 90 per cent.)[60]

Most members of the House come from districts where they face little threat of losing their seat to the other party. Charlie Cook calculated that there are only 90 swing seats (districts that fall into the range of five percentage points above the national average for a party).[61] According to Gary Jacobson, only 29 representatives serve districts without a clear partisan tilt.[62] More than 80 per cent of those elected to the House in 2012 won with at least 55 per cent of the vote. Fifty-seven per cent of House Republicans won with 60 per cent of the vote or more. Another 28 per cent won with between 55 and 60 per cent of the vote.[63]

Only one Republican senator (Dean Heller of Nevada) was elected in 2012 in a state Obama carried. The 26 states that voted for Obama in 2012 sent 43 Democrats and just nine Republicans to the Senate. Only four Republican senators serve in the Senate from states that have voted Democrat in each presidential election since 2000: Susan Collins of Maine, Mark Kirk of Illinois, Pat Toomey of Pennsylvania and Ron Johnson of Wisconsin. Of the 13 states where the 14 Republican senators will stand for re-election in 2014 (South Carolina has two, Lindsey O. Graham and Tim Scott), Obama won just one in 2012 – Maine. In the remaining dozen states, he lost all but Georgia by double digits. Indeed, the average margin of victory for Romney across the 13 states was 20 percentage points.

The decline in shared constituencies between the president and Republican members of Congress reflects an increase in party loyalty and thus a falloff in ticket-splitting among voters. As we have seen, in 2012 party-line voting reached its highest level ever for House and Senate elections, with defection rates below 8 per cent for all federal offices. Similarly, 2012 witnessed the lowest incidence of ticket splitting – voting for a Democrat for president and a Republican for US representative or senator, or vice versa – ever, in the range of 7 to 9 per cent.[64]

60   Jacobson, *The Politics of Congressional Elections*, pp. 271–2.

61   Cook, 'The big sort'.

62   Jacobson, 'Partisan polarization in American politics', p. 18.

63   Calculations by Martin Wattenberg, University of California, Irvine.

64   Jacobson, *The Politics of Congressional Elections*, p. 173.

As a result of this individual-level behavior, the proportion of House districts delivering split verdicts – preferring the president of one party, the House candidate of the other – reached a low of only 6 per cent in 2012. Split outcomes are more common in Senate elections because states tend to be more politically heterogeneous and more evenly partisan balanced than congressional districts. Nevertheless, in 2012, only six states delivered split verdicts. In 2013–14, only 21 senators represented states lost by their presidential candidate, a modern low.

The electoral coalitions of the two parties are increasingly divided by race as well as by party and ideology. Eighty per cent of the House Republicans represent districts in which the white share of the voting-age population exceeds the national average, while 64 per cent of House Democrats represent districts in which the minority share of the voting-age population exceeds the national average.[65] Differences in cultural values and attitudes towards government accompany these differences in the racial composition of constituencies, making it more difficult to achieve bipartisan compromises. Few House Republicans have much experience in courting non-white voters – or much electoral incentive to do so.

As a consequence of these differences in constituencies, most congressional Republicans are far more afraid of losing a primary to a more conservative challenger than a general election to a Democrat. The right's demonstrated capacity to punish incumbent Republicans in primaries discourages straying from party orthodoxy. For them, a deal is often more dangerous than no deal.

The potential for such challenges is real, as the Republican primary electorate is very conservative. Republicans in the public are much less likely than Democrats or Independents to want to make compromises to deal with policy issues.[66] We experienced a taste of this inflexibility during a Republican presidential primary debate in Ames Iowa on 11 August 2011, when every candidate rejected the notion of a budget deal that would include tax increases, even if accompanied by spending cuts ten times as large.

In perhaps the most extreme expression of conservative rigidity, the Utah Republican party denied long-time conservative Senator Robert Bennett its nomination for reelection in 2010. Republican Governor Charlie Crist had to leave his party and run for the Senate as an Independent in Florida because he was unlikely to win the Republican nomination against conservative Marco Rubio. Senator Lisa Murkowski lost her renomination in Alaska to a largely unknown candidate on the far right of the political spectrum. The previous year, Republican Senator Arlen Specter of Pennsylvania switched parties, believing there was little chance he could win a Republican primary against

---

65   Brownstein and Bland, 'Stairway to nowhere'.

66   Pew Research Center for the People and the Press poll, 9–13 Jan. 2013.

conservative Pat Toomey. In 2012, Senator Richard Lugar lost the Republican primary in Indiana to a candidate supported by the Tea Party.

Equally important as a curb on compromise is that fact that when elected officials interact with the more politically engaged voters within their re-election constituencies – the voters who are the most attentive to what they are doing, the most likely to influence their friends and neighbors, the most likely to donate money to their campaigns and the most likely to vote in primary elections – the divide between their supporters and their opponents is even greater than it is among rank-and-file voters. Active supporters of Republican-elected officials are generally very conservative.[67]

Compounding the pressure to stay to the right are conservative radio and television commentators who relentlessly incite the Republican base against the president.

Party differences in electoral bases are strongly related to party differences in presidential support and roll call voting.[68] Congressional Republicans are responding rationally to their incentives for re-election when they oppose the president. Thus, the number of Republicans in the 113th Congress who see cutting a deal with the president as politically advantageous is close to zero.

Impact of Republican antipathy

Republican antipathy for Obama was so great that he had to avoid proposing his own immigration bill, because to do so made it more difficult for Republican members of Congress to support it. Because Republicans in Congress come from solidly Republican states or districts, it is easier for them to support an immigration bill that has broad-based support in the business and farming communities (and that also happens to be supported by Obama and the Democratic leadership) than to back a bill so popularly identified with the other side.

After outlining what he wanted in an immigration bill, the president adopted a hands-off approach to designing the legislation, deferring to negotiations among a bipartisan group of senators known as the Gang of Eight. He adopted this strategy soon after his inauguration, as he was preparing to introduce his own bill during a visit to Las Vegas on 29 January. Senator Charles E. Schumer of New York, a Gang of Eight member, told the White House the group was close to reaching consensus on a bill and asked Obama to hold off on announcing his own in order to avoid disrupting the talks. Obama agreed.[69]

Senate Democrats feared that an Obama bill would scare off Republicans like Senator Marco Rubio of Florida, who has presidential ambitions.

67 McCarty et al., *Polarized America*.
68 Jacobson, 'Partisan polarization in presidential support', pp. 8–11.
69 Wilson and Goldfarb, 'With domestic legacy in lawmakers' hands, Obama considers his options'. For a similar example see Woodward, *The Price of Politics*, pp. 255–6.

Indeed, Rubio's office once issued a statement to deny that he was discussing immigration policy 'with anyone in the White House', even as it criticized the president for not consulting Republicans. Indeed, Republican antipathy puts the president in a Catch 22 bind. If he stays aloof from legislative action, Republicans and others accuse him of a lack of leadership. If he gets involved, they complain that they cannot support any bill so closely identified with him without risking the contempt of conservative voters.[70]

Given the broad influences of ideology and constituency, it is not surprising that Frances Lee has shown that presidential leadership itself demarcates and deepens cleavages in Congress. The differences between the parties and the cohesion within them on floor votes are typically greater when the president takes a stand on issues. When the president adopts a position, members of his party have a stake in his success, while opposition party members have a stake in the president losing. Moreover, both parties take cues from the president that help define their policy views, especially when the lines of party cleavage are not clearly at stake or already well established. In early 2010 Republican senators, including the minority leader, Senator Mitch McConnell of Kentucky, demanded that Obama endorse bipartisan legislation to create a deficit-reduction commission. When he did so, they voted against the bill, killing it. When the president supported a deficit reduction plan from the Gang of Six in 2011, Republicans turned to oppose it.[71] This dynamic of presidential leadership further complicates Obama's efforts to win Republican support.

Democrats and their constituencies

The picture on the Democratic side is more mixed. The party in the House is more ideologically coherent. However, this coherence occurred through the resignations, retirements, and primary and general election defeats of 13 members of the moderate Blue Dog coalition, lowering its membership to 14. As recently as 2010, there had been 54 members.[72]

House Democrats are also from secure seats. Ninety-six per cent of House Democrats held seats in districts Obama won in 2012; only nine represented districts won by Romney. Only ten Democrats won Republican-leaning districts in 2012.[73]

Ten Democratic senators represent states Republican presidential candidates have won in each election since 2000. Seven of the 21 Senate Democrats who will stand for re-election in 2014 represent states that Romney won, by double

---

70 Calmes, 'Obama must walk fine line as Congress takes up agenda'.

71 Lee, *Beyond Ideology: Politics, Principles, and Partisanship in the U.S. Senate*, ch. 4. See also Mann and Ornstein, *It's Even Worse Than It Looks*, pp. 18, 51.

72 Wasserman, 'House overview: how House Democrats beat the point spread'.

73 Jacobson, 'The congressional elections of 2012', p. 7.

digits in six of them. Thus, there is a notable group of Senate Democrats who have an incentive to display some independence from the president.

Equally important, by trying to negotiate with Republicans, the president would face resistance from identifiers with his own party. Cuts to education and other major domestic policies including big ticket-items such as Social Security, Medicare and Medicaid benefits and eligibility for the middle class were not popular with the public[74] or Democratic leaders in Congress. House minority leader Nancy Pelosi warned against raising the eligibility age for Medicare from 65 to 67 as a way to shrink federal spending. 'We are not throwing America's seniors over the cliff to give a tax cut to the wealthiest people in America. We have clarity on that', she declared.[75] In response to the president's proposal to make cuts in the growth of Medicare expenditures and change the cost of living measure for Social Security increases, 107 House Democrats – more than half the caucus – signed a letter declaring their 'vigorous opposition to cutting Social Security, Medicare or Medicaid benefits.'[76] A number of Democratic senators, especially those from Republican-leaning states, actively opposed the president's proposals regarding entitlement spending.[77]

The structure of congressional choice

The structure of the choices facing Congress can also help or hinder the president. Which side benefits from a failure to act? Are there broad political incentives to act on an issue?

There can be little doubt that a unique aspect of the 'fiscal cliff' issue was of invaluable aid to the president. The default position, the broad tax increases that would occur if no new policy was enacted, was unacceptable and highly salient to Republicans. Thus, they had incentives to negotiate and pass a bill to avoid being blamed for tax increases and undermining their long-held economic beliefs.

Sequestration was a different story. Once again, policy changes would occur if Congress failed to act. In this case, automatic budget cuts would go into effect for both defense and domestic discretionary (not entitlement) programs unless the Congress and the president could agree on a budget bill. The White House thought the cuts to defense would gain it leverage to obtain Republican support for more revenues and thus prevent the sequestration. The Republicans

---

74 ABC News/ *Washington Post* polls, 13–16 Dec. 2012 and 11–14 April 2013; CBS News poll, 12–16 Dec. 2012; Pew Research Center for the People and the Press poll, 5–9 Dec. 2012; McClatchy-Marist poll, 4–6 Dec. 2012; AP-GfK poll, 29 Nov. –3 Dec. 2012; United Technologies/National Journal Congressional Connection Poll, conducted by Princeton Survey Research Associates International, 29 Nov. –2 Dec. 2012.

75 Quoted in Simendinger and Huey-Burns, 'Amid "frank" talks, Obama uses polls as pry bar'.

76 Montgomery, 'Democrats challenge Obama on Medicare and Social Security cuts'. See also Sonmez, 'Democrats incensed with White House over Social Security, Medicare'.

77 Grim and Siddiqui, 'Red-State Democrats buck Obama on Social Security cuts'.

called the president's bluff, and the budget cuts occurred. The default position was more acceptable to Republican deficit hawks than seeking revenue to pay for discretionary programs. Moreover, the White House could not fully employ its leverage. The president would not risk a government shutdown by demanding a sequester fix out of fear the public would blame Democrats for the shutdown.[78]

Of course, most policies, such as gun control, do not take effect without positive action. Usually, Republicans lack incentives to act. The one exception may be immigration reform. With Mitt Romney winning an anemic 27 per cent of the Latino vote in 2012, and the demographic trends of whites composing a declining percentage of the electorate and Hispanics composing an increasing percentage, many party leaders feel it is time to appeal to Latinos with action on immigration reform.

Calculating political advantage on budgetary issues is difficult. Making progress toward their goal of limiting the size of government provides Republicans with an incentive to strike a bargain with the president. Moreover, such a deal would also provide a measure of political cover because both parties would share responsibility for the pain of cuts to entitlements. On the other hand, resisting the tax increases that would be part of a bargain with the White House would shield Republican incumbents from primary challenges, and deferring unpopular cuts on entitlements could help Republicans win back the Senate in 2014 and the White House in 2016. In theory, the most effective budgetary leverage the Republicans have is a refusal to raise the debt limit. Obama has promised not to negotiate on the debt limit, however, viewing Republicans as having more to lose politically if the public holds them responsible for plunging the country into an economic crisis.

Summary

On the evening of Obama's first inauguration, senior Republicans met to plot their opposition to the new president.[79] Little has changed. As he began his second term, the president faced a Republican majority in the House and a substantial Republican block in the Senate with little or no inclination to support his initiatives. With the exception of a few issues that served their interests, independent of the White House's efforts, the ideology and constituencies of Republicans encouraged vigorous opposition. Moreover, cutting a deal with Republicans would complicate his efforts to keep the Democrats in the fold. Thus, it is no surprise that he lost on gun control and sequestration within the first one hundred days of his second term.

78 Dennis and Newhauser, 'Obama's lost leverage'.
79 This meeting is described in Draper, 'Do not ask what good we do'.

Conclusion

Presidents cannot create opportunities for change. Instead, effective presidents recognize and exploit opportunities that exist in their environments. When these opportunities are few, major change is unlikely to occur. Those who see a pressing need for change are frustrated with the inability of Washington to resolve long-standing issues. Sometimes they take their frustrations out on the president, declaring that he should more effectively move the public and Congress to support his initiatives.

There is little prospect for success in these endeavors, however. The opportunity structure in contemporary US politics is not conducive to liberal change, and there is little the president can do about it. In theory, the electorate could punish extremism and intransigence and reward moderation and compromise at the polls. However, the polarization we see in Washington has its roots in local elections and constituency politics. The public does not seem inclined to support moderation. Those moderates who are elected frequently lose their seats when national tides run against their party. Most of the centrist Democrats elected to the House in 2006 and 2008 – virtually all of them from balanced or Republican-leaning districts – are now gone. Similarly, moderate Republic senators are a dying breed.

Thus, the US has parliamentary-style political parties operating in a system of shared powers, a guarantee for gridlock. Until the political environment changes, policymaking in the US will continue to be anti-deliberative, slow, and reactive, accepting the short-term fix rather than durable long-term solutions.

References

A.I. Abramowitz (2010) *The Disappearing Center* (New Haven, CT: Yale University Press).

— (2012) *The Polarized Public: Why Our Government Is So Dysfunctional* (New York, NY: Pearson).

J. Bafumi and R.Y. Shapiro (2009) 'A new partisan voter', *Journal of Politics*, vol. 71, pp. 1–24.

A.J. Berinsky (2009) *In Time of War: Understanding American Public Opinion from World War II to Iraq* (Chicago, IL: University of Chicago Press).

E. Black and M. Black (1987) *Politics and Society in the South* (Cambridge, MA: Harvard University Press).

J.R. Bond and R. Fleisher (1990) *The President in the Legislative Arena* (Chicago, IL: University of Chicago Press).

R. Brownstein and S. Bland (2013) 'Stairway to nowhere', *National Journal*, 12 Jan, www.nationaljournal.com/magazine/it-s-not-just-partisanship-that-divides-congress-20130110 (accessed 23 Jan. 2014).

C.S. Bullock III, D.R. Hoffman and R.K. Gaddie (2005) 'The consolidation of the white southern congressional vote', *Political Research Quarterly*, vol. 58, pp. 231–43.

J. Calmes (2013) 'Obama must walk fine line as Congress takes up agenda', *New York Times*, 7 April, www.nytimes.com/2013/04/08/us/politics/obama-must-walk-fine-line-as-congress-weighs-agenda.html?_r=0 (accessed 23 Jan. 2014).

P.J. Conover and S. Feldman (1981) 'The origins and meaning of liberal/conservative identifications', *American Journal of Political Science*, vol. 25, pp. 617–45.

P.E. Converse (1964) 'The nature of belief systems in mass publics', in D.E. Apter (ed.), *Ideology and Discontent* (New York, NY: Free Press), pp. 206–61.

C. Cook (2009) 'Intensity matters', *National Journal*, 24 Oct., www.nationaljournal.com/columns/cook-report/intensity-matters-20091024 (accessed 23 Jan. 2014).

— (2013) 'The big sort', *National Journal*, 13 April, www.nationaljournal.com/the-cook-report (accessed 19 Feb. 2014).

L. Dancey and P. Goren (2010) 'Party identification, issue attitudes, and the dynamics of political debate', *American Journal of Political Science*, vol. 54, pp. 686–99.

S.T. Dennis and D. Newhauser (2013) 'Obama's lost leverage', *Roll Call*, 1 March, www.rollcall.com/news/obamas_lost_leverage-222792-1.html (accessed 23 Jan. 2014).

M. Dowd (2013) 'No bully pulpit', *New York Times*, 20 April, www.nytimes.com/2013/04/21/opinion/sunday/dowd-president-obama-is-no-bully-in-the-pulpit.html (accessed 23 Jan. 2014).

R. Draper (2012) *'Do Not Ask What Good We Do'* (New York, NY: Free Press).

G.C. Edwards III (1989) *At the Margins: Presidential Leadership of Congress* (New Haven, CT: Yale University Press).

— (2003) *On Deaf Ears: The Limits of the Bully Pulpit* (New Haven, CT: Yale University Press).

— (2007) *Governing by Campaigning: The Politics of the Bush Presidency*, 2nd edn. (New York, NY: Longman).

— (2009) *The Strategic President: Persuasion and Opportunity in Presidential Leadership* (Princeton, NJ: Princeton University Press).

— (2012) *Overreach: Leadership in the Obama Presidency* (Princeton, NJ: Princeton University Press).

C. Ellis and J.A. Stimson (2009) 'Symbolic ideology in the American electorate', *Electoral Studies*, vol. 28, pp. 388–402.

— (2012) *Ideology in America* (New York NY: Cambridge University Press).

R.S. Erikson, M.B. MacKuen and J.A. Stimson (2002) *The Macro Polity* (New York, NY: Cambridge University Press).

C.M. Federico and M.C. Schneider (2007) 'Political expertise and the use of ideology: moderating the effects of evaluative motivation', *Public Opinion Quarterly*, vol. 71, pp. 221–52.

S. Feldman (1998) 'Structure and consistency in public opinion: the role of core beliefs and attitudes', *American Journal of Political Science*, vol. 32, pp. 416–40.

M.P. Fiorina with S.J. Abrams and J.C. Pope (2011) *Culture Wars? The Myth of Polarized America*, 3rd edn. (New York, NY: Pearson Longman).

R. Fleisher, J.R. Bond and B. D. Wood (2007) 'Which presidents are uncommonly successful in Congress?', in B. Rockman and R.W. Waterman (eds.), *Presidential Leadership: The Vortex of Presidential Power* (New York, NY: Oxford University Press).

P. Frymer (1995) 'The 1994 aftershock: dealignment or realignment in the South', in P.A. Klinkner (ed.), *Midterm: The Elections of 1994 in Context* (Boulder, CO: Westview Press), pp. 99–113.

A. Garner and H. Palmer (2011) 'Polarization and issue consistency over time', *Political Behavior*, vol. 33, pp. 225–46.

A. Goldman (2011) 'Cornel West flunks the president', *New York Times*, 22 July, www.nytimes.com/2011/07/24/magazine/talk-cornel-west.html (accessed 23 Jan. 2014).

P. Goren (2001) 'Core principles and policy reasoning in mass publics: a test of two theories', *British Journal of Political Science*, vol. 31, pp. 159–77.

— (2004) 'Political sophistication and policy reasoning: a reconsideration', *American Journal of Political Science*, vol. 48, pp. 462–78.

P. Goren, C.M. Federico and M.C. Kittilson (2009) 'Source cues, partisan identities, and political value expression', *American Journal of Political Science*, vol. 53, pp. 805–20.

R. Grim and S. Siddiqui (2013) 'Red-State Democrats buck Obama on Social Security cuts', *Huffington Post*, 6 May, www.huffingtonpost.com/2013/05/06/democrats-social-security_n_3224503.html (accessed 23 Jan. 2014).

L.J. Grossback, D.A.M. Peterson and J.A. Stimson (2006) *Mandate Politics* (New York, NY: Cambridge University Press).

B. Highton (2011) 'Prejudice rivals partisanship and ideology when explaining the 2008 presidential vote across the states', *PS: Political Science and Politics*, vol. 44, pp. 6530–5.

M.V. Hood III, Q. Kidd and I.L. Morris (1999) 'Of byrd[s] and bumpers: using Democratic senators to analyze political change in the South, 1960–1995', *American Journal of Political Science*, vol. 43, pp. 465–87.

R. Huckfeldt, J. Levine, W. Morgan and J. Sprague (1999) 'Accessibility and the political utility of partisan and ideological orientations,' *American Journal of Political Science*, vol. 43, pp. 888–911.

G.C. Jacobson (2003) 'Partisan polarization in presidential support: the electoral connection', *Congress and the Presidency*, vol. 30 (Spring).

— (2011) *A Divider, Not a Uniter: George W. Bush and the American Public*, 3rd edn. (New York, NY: Longman).

— (2011) 'Legislative success and political failure: the public's reaction to Barack Obama's early presidency', *Presidential Studies Quarterly*, vol. 41, pp. 221–2.

— (2013) 'Partisan polarization in American politics: background paper for Oxford Conference on Governing in Polarized Politics', Rothermere American Institute, University of Oxford, 16–17 April.

— (2013) 'The congressional elections of 2012', paper presented at the Annual Meeting of the Midwest Political Science Association, Chicago, Illinois, 11–14 April 2013, p. 7.

— (2013) *The Politics of Congressional Elections*, 8th edn. (New York, NY: Pearson).

William G. Jacoby (1991) 'Ideological identification and issue attitudes,' *American Journal of Political Science*, vol. 35, pp. 178–205.

— (1994) 'Public attitudes toward government spending,' *American Journal of Political Science*, vol. 38, pp. 336–61.

— (1995) 'The structure of ideological thinking in the American electorate', *American Journal of Political Science*, vol. 39, pp. 314–35.

— (2000) 'Issue framing and government spending,' *American Journal of Political Science* 44, pp. 750–67.

— (2006) 'Value choices and American public opinion', *American Journal of Political Science*, vol. 50, pp. 706–23.

— (2009) 'Policy attitudes, ideology, and voting behavior in the 2008 election', paper presented at the Annual Meeting of the American Political Science Association.

S. Jordan, C. Webb and B.D. Wood (2013) 'Polarization and the party platforms, 1944–2012', paper presented at the Annual Meeting of the Midwest Political Science Association, Chicago, Illinois, 11–14 April.

G. Kabaservice (2012) *Rule and Ruin: The Downfall of Moderation and the Destruction of the Republican Party, From Eisenhower to the Tea Party* (New York, NY: Oxford University Press).

R. Kaplan (2012) 'Ryan: no mandate for Obama in election', *National Journal*, 14 Nov., www.nationaljournal.com/politics/ryan-no-mandate-for-obama-in-election-20121113 (accessed 23 Jan. 2014).

K. Kenski, B.W. Hardy and K. Hall Jamieson (2010) *The Obama Victory: How Media, Money, and Message Shaped the 2008 Election* (New York, NY: Oxford University Press).

K. Knight (1985) 'Ideology in the 1980 election: ideological sophistication does matter', *Journal of Politics*, vol. 47, pp. 828–53.

G.C. Layman, T.M. Carsey and J.M. Horowitz (2006) 'Party polarization in American politics: characteristics, causes, and consequences', *Annual Review of Political Science*, vol. 9, pp. 83–110.

C.E. Lee and M. Langley (2012) 'A more worried Obama battles to win second term', *Wall Street Journal*, 31 Aug., http://online.wsj.com/news/articles/SB10000872396390443864204577621424114535022 (accessed 23 Jan. 2014).

F.E. Lee (2009) *Beyond Ideology: Politics, Principles, and Partisanship in the U.S. Senate* (Chicago, IL: University of Chicago Press).

M. Levendusky (2009) *The Partisan Sort* (Chicago, IL: University of Chicago Press).

T.E. Levitin and W.E. Miller (1979) 'Ideological interpretations of presidential elections', *American Political Science Review*, vol. 73, pp. 751–71.

M. Lewis-Back, C. Tien and R. Nadeau (2010) 'Obama's missed landslide: a racial cost?', *PS: Political Science and Politics*, vol. 43, pp. 69–76.

N. McCarty, K.T. Poole and H. Rosenthal (2006) *Polarized America: The Dance of Ideology and Unequal Riches* (Cambridge, MA: MIT Press).

T.E. Mann and N.J. Ornstein (2012) *It's Even Worse Than It Looks* (New York, NY: Basic Books).

L. Montgomery (2013) 'Democrats challenge Obama on Medicare and Social Security cuts', *Washington Post*, 14 March, www.washingtonpost.com/business/economy/senate-democrats-budget-challenges-obama-on-medicare-social-security-cuts/2013/03/13/b17a39c2-8c12-11e2-b63f-f53fb9f2fcb4_story.html (accessed 23 Jan. 2014).

R. Nadeau and H.W. Stanley (1993) 'Class polarization among native southern whites, 1952–90', *American Journal of Political Science*, vol. 37, pp. 900–19.

B. Nyhan (2012) 'New surveys show the persistence of misperceptions', Huffpost Pollster, *Huffington Post*, 30 July, www.huffingtonpost.com/brendan-nyhan/new-surveys-show-the-pers_b_1718794.html (accessed 23 Jan. 2014).

M.B. Petersen, R. Slothuus and L. Togeby (2010) 'Political parties and value consistency in public opinion formation', *Public Opinion Quarterly*, vol. 74, pp. 530–50.

S. Piston (2010) 'How explicit racial prejudice hurt Obama in the 2008 election', *Political Behavior*, vol. 32, pp. 431–51.

R. Reich (2011) 'The empty bully pulpit', *The American Prospect*, 27 July, www.huffingtonpost.com/robert-reich/the-empty-bully-pulpit_b_913346.html (accessed 23 Jan. 2014).

T.J. Rudolph and J. Evans (2005) 'Political trust, ideology, and public support for government spending', *American Journal of Political Science*, vol. 49, pp. 660–71.

D.O. Sears, R.L. Lau, T.R. Tyler and H.M. Allen (1980) 'Self-interest vs. symbolic politics in policy attitudes and presidential voting', *American Political Science Review*, vol. 74, pp. 670–84.

N. Silver (2012) 'As swing districts dwindle, can a divided House stand?', *New York Times*, 27 Dec., http://fivethirtyeight.blogs.nytimes.com/2012/12/27/as-swing-districts-dwindle-can-a-divided-house-stand/ (accessed 23 Jan. 2014).

A. Simendinger (2013) 'Obama taking campaign-style approach to new goals', *RealClearPolitics*, 3 Jan., www.realclearpolitics.com/articles/2013/01/03/obama_taking_campaign-style_approach_to_new_goals_116581.html (accessed 23 Jan. 2014).

A. Simendinger and C. Huey-Burns (2012) 'Amid "frank" talks, Obama uses polls as pry bar,' *RealClearPolitics*, 14 Dec., www.realclearpolitics.com/articles/2012/12/14/amid_frank_talks_obama_uses_polls_as_pry_bar_116425.html (accessed 23 Jan. 2014).

F. Sonmez (2011) 'Democrats incensed with White House over Social Security, Medicare', *Washington Post*, www.washingtonpost.com/blogs/2chambers/post/democrats-incensed-with-white-house-over-social-security-medicare/2011/07/08/gIQAHmMm3H_blog.html (accessed 23 Jan. 2014).

S.N. Soroka and C. Wlezien (2010) *Degrees of Democracy* (New York, NY: Cambridge University Press).

J.A. Stimson (1975) 'Belief systems: constraint, complexity, and the 1972 election', *American Journal of Political Science*, vol. 19, pp. 393–417.

— (2004) *Tides of Consent: How Public Opinion Shapes American Politics* (New York, NY: Cambridge University Press).

B. Terris (2012) 'A presidential mandate? How about 435 congressional ones?', *National Journal*, 16 Nov., www.nationaljournal.com/magazine/a-presidential-mandate-how-about-435-congressional-ones-20121115 (accessed 23 Jan. 2014).

S. Treier and D.S. Hillygus (2009) 'The nature of political ideology in the contemporary electorate', *Public Opinion Quarterly*, vol. 73, pp. 679–703.

M. Tesler (2013) 'The return of old-fashioned racism to white Americans' partisan preferences in the early Obama era', *Journal of Politics*, vol. 75, pp. 110–23.

J.D. Ura and C.R. Ellis (2011) 'Partisan moods: polarization and the dynamics of mass party preferences', *Journal of Politics*, vol. 74, pp. 1–15.

D. Wasserman (2012) 'House overview: how House Democrats beat the point spread', *Cook Political Report*, 9 Nov., http://cookpolitical.com/articles/38 (accessed 23 Jan. 2014).

M.P. Wattenberg (1991) 'The building of a Republican regional base in the South: the elephant crosses the Mason-Dixon Line', *Public Opinion Quarterly*, vol. 55, pp. 424–31.

D. Westen (2011) 'What happened to Obama?' *New York Times*, 6 Aug., www.nytimes.com/2011/08/07/opinion/sunday/what-happened-to-obamas-passion.html?pagewanted=all (accessed 23 Jan. 2014).

S. Wilson and Z.A. Goldfarb (2013) 'With domestic legacy in lawmakers' hands, Obama considers his options', *New York Times*, 13 April, www.washingtonpost.com/politics/with-domestic-legacy-in-lawmakers-hands-obama-considers-his-options/2013/04/13/9067a1e4-a38b-11e2-9c03-6952ff305f35_story.html (accessed 23 Jan. 2014).

B. Woodward (2012) *The Price of Politics* (New York, NY: Simon & Schuster).

3. The Obama administration, Congress and the battle of the budget

Tim Hames

The story of the Obama administration has been one of a bitter, continuous and deeply partisan struggle over the US federal budget, and not what the president expected would unfold when he began his term of office in January 2009. He and his supporters thought then, and with some reason, that the theme of his tenure would be economic recovery in the short term and economy reconstruction thereafter. For a brief period this did indeed appear to be the national political narrative. That upbeat script was soon overtaken, however, by the ever-darker shadows of a deepening economic crisis, the battle over healthcare reform, and then – following the Republican party's House of Representatives victory in the 2010 elections – the explosive dispute over the very character of the federal government itself. The federal budget has hence proved to be the principal battleground for that epic and, in many ways, enduring conflict.

The numbers that set the context for this contest, as set out below in table 1, are dramatic in nature. The backdrop to these figures is that in the late 1990s a strong domestic economy, combined with considerable spending constraint, had led to consistent budget surpluses in the last years of the Clinton administration. The election of George W. Bush alongside a Republican Congress in 2001 and again from 2003–07 had, though, triggered a substantial package of income tax cuts. These were theoretically temporary rather than permanent, but politicians had preferred to continue on that basis rather than anchor them fully into law or risk the unpopularity of letting them lapse. When combined with a huge increase in military and national security spending in the aftermath of the terrorist attacks on the United States of 11 September 2001, the subsequent deployment of US troops to Afghanistan, and the further decision to invade and then administer Iraq from March 2003, had seen a sharp return to considerable fiscal deficits, although the impact was mitigated by a contentious decision to keep much of the expenditure on Afghanistan/Iraq 'off budget'. An improving economy (and this accounting decision) then saw the federal budget deficit ease back until the very last year of the Bush administration when the near collapse of the US economy in late 2008 was witnessed.

Table 1. US federal budget deficit 2007–14 (2014–15 projected)

Fiscal year*	Deficit	% of GDP**	% Ratio of debt to GDP
2007	$161 billion	1.1	36.3
2008	$459 billion	3.2	40.5
2009	$1.413 trillion	10.1	54.0
2010	$1.294 trillion	9.0	62.9
2011	$1.299 trillion	8.7	67.8
2012	$1.090 trillion	7.0	72.6
2013	$642 billion ***	4.0	72.5
2014****	$560 billion	3.4	73.6
2015****	$378 billion	2.1	72.1

Source: Congressional Budget Office (CBO)

*US fiscal years start on 1 October of a calendar year; **GDP is Gross Domestic Product; ***CBO estimate and ****CBO projection

Barack Obama was thus elected and assumed office in completely different economic circumstances to those pertaining when he launched his candidacy for the Democratic nomination, and hence the Oval Office (February 2007), or even when he accepted the Democratic nomination (August 2008) and went on, assisted by the economic collapse of late 2008, to beat John McCain.

Act One. Enter Obama

The Obama administration took office having rather vaguely promised to do something about the state of the economy in the short term and with somewhat grander (if again not very precise) plans to modernise it thereafter. The early weeks of his first term were thus dominated by deciding what doing something would actually mean. As the president did not have an especially specific blueprint the Democratic leadership in the House and the Senate who commanded robust majorities in each chamber set about drawing up a blueprint themselves, with the House of Representatives preferring a larger fiscal stimulus and the Senate, as it typically does, proving more cautious and centrist. The ultimate compromise within Congress, and between it and the president, was for a stimulus package which would cost a substantial $787 billion, but which was open to the charge of being less a programme that had been carefully thought through than a vast wish list to which politically savvy and institutionally powerful figures had added favours to their preferred constituencies and voters. Despite this, and not unreasonably from his standpoint, the president claimed the stimulus outcome as a victory and insisted that it would have a significant impact on rapidly rising unemployment.

Whether or not it did is debatable. The package certainly did have an impact on the federal deficit, but was hit by a truck in 2009 and 2010. Those years saw the cumulative impact of the continuation of the 'temporary' Bush tax cuts, the $787 billion stimulus, overdue changes in budget rules which meant that spending in Afghanistan and Iraq could no longer be hidden off budget and, above all else, the full impact of the economic crisis which had started with the mismanaged collapse of Lehman Brothers in September 2008 (arguably the worst public policy mistake made in a major democracy since appeasement). The federal deficit increased by almost a trillion dollars in 12 months from $459 billion to $1.413 trillion. It tripled as a percentage of GDP in that period from 3.2 per cent to 10.1 per cent and the ratio of debt to GDP surged by almost a third from 40 per cent to 54 per cent, once again in a single year.

These were astonishing numbers. They were the sort of increase in a deficit and debt which would normally be associated with a nation in the second year of fighting a massive international war. They had virtually no relevant precedent in peacetime. And there was little if anything that the president or Congress could do about it without the risk of making matters worse by undermining an economy which was only being saved from repeating the Great Depression by a Federal Reserve Board absolutely determined to hold interest rates at virtually nothing and engage in a variety of highly unorthodox techniques with which to prop up the banking system and save the economy. Without that determination, Barack Obama could have found himself an accidental Herbert Hoover.

Act Two. Enter the House Republicans

In November 2010 the Democrats lost control of the House of Representatives in a seismic fashion. The Republican party seized more than 60 seats to hold a comfortable majority, a margin made more secure by the fact that the party was in one respect more ideologically coherent than its rival. There were comparatively few moderate, let alone liberal, Republicans who might defy their leaders. The Republicans were, though, divided between those who were conservative, very conservative and very, very conservative. The numbers in the last camp had been swollen by the arrival of the so-called Tea Party movement inside the Republican party as a whole and courtesy of the 2010 mid-term elections within the House of Representatives itself (but scarcely at all in the Senate).

Although the Tea Party was not and is not a monolith, its mission was to restore the notion of limited government that a strict reading of the US constitution implies to be appropriate. Tea Party congressmen believed that taxes in the United States remained too high and that federal spending on almost anything except defence and national security was not only spectacularly excessive but a threat to the proper constitutional order of the country. They had come to Washington to cut spending and the existence of an epic, seemingly out of control, federal budget deficit added even greater urgency to the matter. They were determined to hold the line on taxes and then to institute sweeping cuts in discretionary domestic expenditure (excluding defence) and they would not permit their leadership, and Speaker of the House John Boehner in particular, to stray from that objective.

At first it did not seem that much resistance to their agenda would be encountered. The new Speaker won an early skirmish over the 2011 fiscal year (FY) budget by cutting current spending by $38 billion. Although a tiny reduction in the context of the overall federal budget, it was a symbolic triumph in that spending had not been cut in this manner since 1995 under Speaker Newt Gingrich.

Emboldened by this outcome and sensing that the Obama White House would buckle, the Republican leadership decided to go for broke and look for a huge multi-year reduction in federal spending centred on Medicaid and Medicare, but with reductions across the board (bar defence). They chose to wield the weapon of linking their demands to the pressing if coincidental need to raise the debt ceiling. In the United States the total stock of debt which might legally be held by the federal government is set in law and can only be raised or not by the approval of Congress. The US Treasury may (and often will) employ extraordinary measures to avoid breaching the ceiling and defaulting on its debts, but in the end requires the support of Congress to avoid that catastrophic outcome.

Congress, in the form of the House, was holding a gun to the president's head. The White House wobbled badly and nearly offered the sort of deal which would have satisfied most Republicans. The threat to default if a bargain was not struck backfired with neither the markets nor the American public expressing any enthusiasm or endorsement for this strategy. Both sides shifted position. The House belatedly realised that the pistol was now pointing at its own head. There was an urgent need to find an interim solution which would allow the House Republican leadership to claim at least a partial triumph and permit it to relent on the debt ceiling without political humiliation. That interim solution was the hastily assembled Budget Control Act (BCA) of 2011. It ended the immediate crisis but was not sufficient to offset the reputational harm that had been done to the United States by having appeared to play politics with the debt ceiling and hence the repayment of debt. The credit rating agency Standard and Poor ended the US's AAA rating in August 2011.

This was taken as a stinging act of commentary on the ability of American governing institutions to perform in a fashion that would strike the wider world as compelling or convincing. It was, it should be noted, a bold even reckless decision which no other agency came close to choosing to emulate.

Act Three. The Budget Control Act 2011

For those with long memories in Washington the politics of the BCA 2011 had more than a hint of the Gramm-Rudman-Hollings Act of 1985, passed when the federal budget deficit was exploding in the later Reagan years. The deal finalised on 31 July 2011 covered both the debt limit and the federal deficit. In relation to the debt limit it permitted an increase in two stages. It was raised instantly by $900 billion from $14.3 trillion to $15.2 trillion and allowed for an additional rise by a further $1.2 trillion to $16.4 trillion in January 2012. This had the political impact of pushing the deadline for re-addressing the issue beyond the November 2012 elections, although how far to go beyond that point would depend on the size of the federal deficit as it was this that was driving overall national debt levels up towards its legal ceiling.

Turning to the federal deficit itself, the BCA called for $2.4 trillion in spending cuts over ten years (including $300 billion arising from reduced debt service cuts – hence, not a spending budget cut). Some $900 billion of those were identified immediately and laid out. A bipartisan congressional supercommittee was established to find a formula for implementing the remaining $1.2 trillion in cuts. If no such plan was agreed then the cuts would simply be imposed automatically with 50 per cent coming from non-exempt defence spending and 50 per cent from non-exempt non-defence spending. The deadline for the axe to fall was 1 January 2013 (after the 2012 elections) and neither the president nor Congress could stop these cuts except by coming up with an alternative scheme, a process known as sequestration. Simultaneously, the 'temporary' Bush-era tax cuts were again allowed to continue on an interim basis until the same date of 1 January 2013, after which they would expire if not enacted properly or would once more be offered another temporary lease of life.

Entirely predictably, in November 2011, the bipartisan congressional supercommittee announced that it had failed to reach an agreement. It would have been a miracle on the scale of the loaves and the fishes if they had. The whole saga was effectively punted the other side of the November 2012 elections. Tax cuts would or would not expire and sequestration would or would not occur in 2013.

Act Four. Obama and the House on taxation

After a tough and tense competition in which the economy had been pivotal, Barack Obama defeated Mitt Romney by a modest margin in the popular vote but one amplified in the Electoral College. The Republicans held the House of Representatives, performing about as well as might be anticipated in the circumstances. In the Senate, by contrast, where they had real hopes of making gains and even snatching control of that chamber they went backwards, losing a net two seats. That underwhelming outcome was largely blamed on the selection of Tea Party candidates in a few key states where the GOP might otherwise expect to be strong – Indiana and Missouri were prominent – who proved to be too doctrinaire for even the relatively conservative electors of those locations. Democrats won upset victories instead. The same had happened in 2010 when similarly hard-line (and politically inept) Tea Party contenders in Delaware and Nevada had blown races which a more mainstream contender would surely have won. The occasional Tea Party affiliate did make it to the Senate in 2012 – Ted Cruz of Texas would prove to be such a counter example – but on the whole the Republican caucus in the Senate retained more diversity of opinion and more pragmatism in instinct than was true for their counterparts in the House, who held the majority in that chamber.

The election was barely over before the (outgoing) Congress had to return to the budget. The main focus this time was on what to do with the temporary Bush-era tax cuts which were finally due to end on 1 January 2013 unless Congress acted to retain them. During the presidential election, the incumbent had insisted that income tax rates should rise on all Americans earning $250,000 or more, as should other taxes mostly paid by the wealthy, while 'loopholes' exploited by the rich to avoid tax should be closed. Mr Romney and the Republicans, to the contrary, asserted that all of the Bush-era tax cuts should be rendered permanent and mused as to what further taxes could be cut once spending had been reduced to the level where both the deficit and taxation could be curtailed.

A titanic political stand-off between the White House and Congress duly occurred. It raged through the Christmas holidays and then the New Year celebrations. The Bush-era tax cuts very briefly and really rather technically expired. On 4 January 2013 an understanding was announced. The House Republicans were obliged to abandon their 'not one cent of an increase' stance on taxation. It was agreed that while the Bush-era tax cuts would finally be declared permanent for the vast majority of Americans, income tax increases would occur for individuals earning $400,000 or more (the sum was $450,000 for households). This was the first increase of its kind since 1993 or for two decades. The rate for capital gains tax and dividends tax also increased from 15 to 20 per cent. In an additional symbolic victory for the Oval Office, unemployment insurance benefits were extended for another 12 months. It proved impossible to reach an accord on spending so sequestration was deferred from 1 January to 1 March to allow for additional negotiations. In public relations terms, this package was a clear win for the president. In policy terms, as will emerge, matters were less certain.

The net impact of the January settlement was to raise taxes by $660 billion over the next ten years. In 2013, this would represent a negative impact on the economy (or 'fiscal withdrawal') of an estimated $240 billion or 1.4 per cent of GDP – although this assessment is far from absolutely forensic. It was thought that the recovering US economy could withstand such a headwind regardless.

As noted, the media deemed this a political coup for the president. He had forced his opponents to blink due to several factors including:

- the proximity of the 1 January deadline to his own re-election in November

- the unexpectedly strong Democratic performance in the Senate elections

- public opinion which, while wary of tax increases, would permit them to be imposed on the wealthy

- the fear in Republican circles that brinkmanship would lead to the full withdrawal of the Bush tax cuts leading to them absorbing the blame for such a result

- the concern in the business community and in the markets that such a sharp tax increase would derail the economic recovery

- the absence of any linkage this time to the debt ceiling which would not be reached again for some months

- a major strategic split between the Republicans in the Senate (who cared more about the deficit than absolute philosophical purity on tax) and their Republican brothers and sisters in the House (for whom the reverse was true)

- the fact that the vote on the tax programme was cast in the last few hours of the outgoing Congress allowed some retiring or defeated members to vote for it

In policy content terms, the tax accord looked rather different. The $660 billion raised over ten years by this set of increases was somewhat less than the $900 billion that had already been agreed in spending cuts back in July 2011, let alone the extra $1.2 trillion in cuts that either had to be agreed in Washington or would be enforced via sequestration. At least 95 per cent of the Bush-era tax cuts had now been set in legislative stone (some thought 98 per cent or even 99 per cent had been). Few if any of the president's targeted 'loopholes' had actually been closed. The path to deficit reduction was one in which spending reductions of some form would be more important than tax increases. At first glance this would seem to be a rather more Republican than Democratic way of proceeding. Or, put another way, it seemed to have some similarity to the deficit reduction approach seen in the United Kingdom under a Conservative-led government which had put the emphasis on spending control.

Act Five. Sequestration

For the next two months the Republicans licked their wounds and the clock ticked on sequestration. Some fairly half-hearted negotiations took place to find an alternative to a system of automatic cuts which almost everyone (albeit for their own reasons) considered to be blunt, crude and damaging but which were now locked in to law unless a means could be found of replacing them. Yet sequestration was proving to be, as was said of a similar set of measures required by Gramm-Rudman-Hollings almost 30 years previously, 'a bad idea whose time has come'. There was no alternative deal out there on which the House of Representatives, Senate and president could agree.

On 1 March the long dance, begun almost two years earlier, finally ended and sequestration was enacted. It meant $492 billion in non-exempt defence cuts over ten years (or 9.4 per cent of all spending in that area) and the same $492 billion in non-exempt, non-defence discretionary spending over a decade (or 8.2 per cent of spending here). This was a tough settlement. Optimists hoped it would prove only temporary. Realists suspected it would prove no less temporary than the Bush tax cuts.

Although there was political pain on all sides it was widely accepted that the agony was more intense for the White House. The president had lost in March for the mirror reasons he had won in January. The impact of his re-election was fading. The surprise result in the Senate was now priced in. The public were, at least in the abstract, sympathetic to the argument that federal spending was excessive and should be cut back. The business community and the markets also sang from the same hymn-sheet. The economy appeared to be strong enough to deal with the negative impact of the cuts. The Republicans in the House and Senate were relatively united on this issue and determined to swallow defence spending cuts they did not care for in order to secure discretionary domestic spending cuts that they actively favoured. There was no brinkmanship on the debt ceiling (which was still a few months away from being reached), as there had been in 2011, nor was there the threat to close down the federal government that there had been in 1995/1996 (and would be again later in 2013), nor did the Tea Party appear to be in the driving seat. This was instead largely old-fashioned fiscal conservatism, even if it was being framed by a sequestration procedure which lacked any sense of subtlety.

Sequestration had become the new orthodoxy. The politics and practice of the federal budget would be largely shaped by it for months, if not years, to come.

Act Six. Shutdown and the debt ceiling (revisited)

In a straight repeat of 2011, the Republican leadership, having won a key strategic victory early in the year, sought a much bigger one a few months later. The sequestration process was now in place. The only issue for some congressional Republicans was whether they could force a further round of spending cuts on the White House. For others this ideal chimed with another one, defunding the expenditure necessary to make the Patient Protection Act and Affordable Care Act 2010 (almost universally known as 'Obamacare') effective. Obamacare had passed through the Senate and the House of Representatives via a complex parliamentary technique known as reconciliation when the death of Senator Edward Kennedy, and unexpected election of Republican Scott Brown in his place, had meant that the Democrats no longer had the 60 votes in the Senate needed to block a filibuster of healthcare legislation. Not one Republican in either chamber had backed it. It had survived a Supreme Court challenge to its constitutional legitimacy in July 2012 in the case of *National Federation of Independent Business v. Sebelius* by a 5–4 vote and only because Chief Justice John Roberts had clearly acted against his own instincts to protect the non-partisan image of the Court in backing the law, employing an argument which might politely be described as tortured (he, alone among the nine justices, deemed it to be a tax increase which Congress was entitled to impose). If Mitt Romney had won the 2012 elections, then Obamacare would probably have been repealed.

He was not the one sitting in the White House. While President Obama was in place and backed by a 55–45 advantage in the Senate, the House of Representatives could rage against Obamacare, and vote against it and to repeal it all they liked (more than 40 times in fact), but there was no direct means of derailing it. The one indirect device would be to deny it the money that it needed in order to function. A faction in the Republicans started demanding that they do so.

By law, the federal government has to have a budget by 30 September in any given year. This means that the 13 distinct appropriations bills which fund the various institutions of government should have been enacted annually by that date. In the real world, this has virtually never happened. The norm is for some of those bills to be passed by Congress and signed by the president and for others to wait for longer. In the meantime, the government is financed by means of a continuing resolution which allows departments to carry on spending as they have been doing until a further set date. Without a continuing resolution at that time the departments affected should shut down. This is the norm, not the novelty of Washington budgetary politics. Some House Republicans wanted to take Obamacare hostage by declining to fund the government unless healthcare reform was defunded.

The Republican leaders were initially highly reluctant to take the risks involved with this approach. They could not see how either the Senate or the president would accept it. The public seemed to have little appetite for Obamacare but even less for closing down the government over it. Although strictly speaking completely separate as an issue, the debt ceiling had still not been addressed and it was about to be hit on 17 October. There was the horrible political risk that the Republicans in the House would appear to be holding both the federal government and the reputation of the United States as a credit-worthy country hostage in a kamikaze attempt to cut Obamacare off at the knees. Senate Republicans sent off distress flares. The Speaker and his leadership team agonised. Yet the pressure of internal party sentiment proved irresistible. In a partial compromise the House leadership resolved for the slightly less dangerous approach of deferring expenditure on Obamacare for a year as their price for accepting a continuing resolution and funding the government.

That switch in tactics did little for them. September saw a stand-off and then stalemate followed by the shutdown. The federal government partially closed on 1 October, remaining so for two long weeks. This meant that the shutdown was indeed becoming entangled with the debt ceiling issue and the Republicans were back in the same place as in 2011 (worse, in fact, because the federal government did not come anywhere near to being shut down then). The international markets reacted in disbelief at the prospect of a US default and the public recoiled at the shutdown. Utterly predictably, the Republicans were taking virtually all the heat in the polls. The Senate sought a bipartisan solution which left Obamacare alone, while an increasingly ragged Republican leadership in the House cast about for something, anything, which they could successfully attach to either a continuing resolution or the debt ceiling to claim as a political victory. The clock was against them. Raising the debt ceiling was an imperative. The US could not default on the world economy.

In the late hours of 16 October and the early hours of the following day the Republicans relented. The Senate had folded first, despite a somewhat surreal 21-hour speech by the Tea Party Texan Senator Ted Cruz intended as a filibuster against Obamacare in the spirit of Senator Strom Thurmond's extraordinary 24-hour-plus oration which attempted to defeat the Civil Rights Act of 1957 (except that Cruz looked less dignified and was even less successful). The House, through gritted teeth, finally caved in. A conventional continuing resolution was enacted which would keep the federal government open until 15 January 2014 (a long enough period of time to deal with the appropriations process) and the debt ceiling was raised until 7 February 2014. The crucial link with defunding Obamacare was broken and plainly would not be restored. In political terms this was a far bigger victory for the president than had been true in January in the struggle over tax increases. Implementing Obamacare would remain an awesome challenge but it would not be defunded.

Act Seven. Sequestration amended yet entrenched

The deal described above bought all parties but particularly the Republicans some time. In theory it offered the opportunity for a 'grand bargain' to be struck on spending (and possibly taxation) which could be approved before 15 January 2014 and displace the sequestration procedure. In practice, such an overarching settlement was never very likely. It would have required further deep cuts in social spending enacted in the name of 'entitlements reform' alongside an increase in federal revenues triggered by an ambitious 'tax reform' which disposed of many so-called 'loopholes'. There were few incentives for either side to surrender their principles in late 2013.

There was, nonetheless, the opportunity for some minor amendments to sequestration which would restore some military spending and a little social spending but in return for further reductions elsewhere. House Republicans serving on the Armed Services and Appropriations Committees, in particular, had an interest in such an adjustment if it could be reconciled with deficit reduction. If it strayed from that objective, then other Republicans in the Senate, if not the House, would revolt.

The leaders of the House and Senate Budget Committees started exploring whether they could make some minor and modest moves in this direction. The two key players were Representative Paul Ryan, Republican Chairman of the House Budget Committee, and Senator Patty Murray, Democrat from Washington, who was his counterpart in the Senate. That Ryan had been the vice presidential candidate for Mitt Romney a mere year earlier and was assumed to have ambitions to put himself forward in his own right, made most Washington observers believe that he would offer nothing to the Democrats and be content with a political stalemate. This was to underestimate Ryan. Although a radical in terms of his own personal preferences for budgetary policy, he was capable of making incremental changes if he was convinced that he could carry his colleagues with him. He also had a professional working relationship with Senator Murray and understood what she could accept.

In early December, therefore, a decidedly incremental but not insignificant Ryan/Murray deal was put forward, both amending and entrenching sequestration. It proposed that for the period up to 30 September 2015, a total of $63 billion in spending on the military and certain social disbursements be added to the tallies permitted under the original version of sequestration.

Those sums would then be frozen at the new level from September 2015 for another eight years (hence the 'entrenchment' of the BCA 2011). In order to compensate for this additional $63 billion in spending over the short term, an extra $83 billion would be saved in the longer term, mostly by extending a 2 per cent cut to Medicare providers from 2021 to 2023 and by raising fees on airline tickets to offset the costs involved in airport security. This was the closest that Ryan would offer to anything akin to a tax increase (although it enraged some of his fellow conservatives). The overall reduction in the deficit would be increased by $23 billion over the entire ten-year period.

It cannot be said that anyone was hugely enthused by this package but it soon won some traction. Democrats were more enthusiastic than Republicans because the short-term increase in spending was 'real', whereas who knew what might happen by the end of the ten-year period? This was reflected in the votes cast in the House of Representatives and the Senate. The House passed the changes by a lopsided margin of 332–94. The House Republican caucus split 169–62 in favour, the Democratic caucus backed it by the proportionately more emphatic 163–32. The Senate, while being much more centrist than the House as consistently noted here, took more convincing as it is also more hawkish in terms of fiscal discipline. Senator Marco Rubio (Florida), a prospective rival to Ryan in 2016, denounced the details almost before they were known. Others in the party leadership were also distinctly cool about the whole idea. Senate Democrats, by contrast, were united in support of Senator Murray and this proved crucial. After a longer debate than had taken place in the House, the Senate finally approved the measure by 64–36 (with all Democrats and nine Republicans backing the bargain). A few other Republicans initially opted to permit the vote to take place (thus rejecting the option of a filibuster which would have proved fatal to the proposition) before then casting their votes against the measure when it did take place. This is quite standard senatorial procedure. As much out of exhaustion and relief that the battle of the budget would not be resumed until after September 2015 than any hope and faith in the amended sequestration that had been endorsed, Congress sent the legislation to the president who signed it in a similar low-key spirit.

Insofar as absolute purity on spending levels in the 2013–15 period had been compromised, it could be argued that the Republicans had conceded a little territory to their opponents. They had done so, however, for three rational reasons. First, having lost out in the politics of the budget battle in both July/August 2011 and September/October 2013, the party leadership had no reason whatsoever to risk another public relations disaster in January/February 2014 – an election year. Second, no sooner had the Republican attempt to castrate Obamacare ended than it became clear that those seeking to implement it for the president were doing so in a fashion that served Republican rather than

Democratic interests. The sheer complexity of reforming a sector which is one-sixth of the entire US economy was becoming apparent. Websites, which were supposed to ease the burden of registration, crashed. The presidential promise that patients who were happy with their current medical arrangements could maintain them exactly as they were was rapidly proving to be suspect. Even those committed to Obamacare started to wonder if it might collapse under its own weight. Republicans finally realised that their best strategy was not to seek to repeal or defund Obamacare but to state to the president: 'This is your scheme. It is up to you to make it function.'

Finally, and very much as a consequence of the difficulties of Obamacare, Republican prospects in the senatorial contests of 2014 suddenly seemed much brighter. If they could avoid making highly public mistakes in terms of public relations in Washington and avoid again nominating neophyte candidates in key contests (a big ask in the light of the Tea Party's influence), then the notion of securing an additional six extra Senate seats, and hence control of the chamber in the November 2014 elections, suddenly seemed much less daunting than had been true a few weeks earlier. In this context, a two-year budget ceasefire was more likely to help Republican candidates than hinder them. If the party strengthened its command over the House of Representatives in 2014 and took over the Senate, then it would be in a strong position then to reduce spending by more than the $63 billion increase which it had accepted as part of amending the sequestration procedure.

This process of the Republicans being in orderly political retreat was completed in February 2014 when the debt ceiling question again had to be considered. It has been an article of faith for the House Republican leadership, especially the Speaker of the House personally, that any increase in the national debt must be offset by a detailed plan to reduce spending. No such formula was attempted this time. Instead the Speaker and the House Majority Leader voted (as did 26 other colleagues) to allow a 'clean' increase in the debt ceiling (with no reference to spending cuts or any other conditionality), which passed that chamber with the support of virtually the entire House Democratic caucus. In the Senate, Senator Cruz insisted that 60 votes would be required in order that the measure could next be placed before that chamber for settlement by majority sentiment. Mitch McConnell, Senate Republican leader, was one of 12 from his party to elect to allow a vote on the debt ceiling before the vote itself took place. This initial vote split along party lines and thus sent the measure to the president. The Republicans had, in effect, conceded the political fight for now and deferred it for another year.

Ten observations on Obama, Congress and the battle of the budget

As stated right at the outset of this chapter, the struggle over the size and shape of the US Federal Budget has been absolutely central to the story of the Obama presidency. Despite the modest adjustments agreed at the end of 2013 and the sense of a ceasefire until 30 September 2015, few would not anticipate the issue being revisited before Barack Obama leaves office. The lessons of what has been witnessed in Washington should be significant, if not seminal. The following ten observations suggest that they do indeed frame much of the US domestic politics of our time.

One, this whole struggle was meant to be about reducing the federal budget deficit. Yet that deficit is falling rapidly anyway. In FY 2013 it will be less than half the size that it was four years earlier, having dropped from 10.1 per cent to 4 per cent of GDP. It is predicted to decline again to 3.4 per cent in 2014 and 2.1 per cent in 2015. The tax increases secured in January 2013 and the spending cuts obtained through sequestration in March 2013 are assisting this trend but they are far from the only factors at work here. The deficit is being driven down in the short term because of enhanced taxation revenues from a more buoyant economy, slower entitlement spending and enhanced repayments from Fannie Mae and Freddie Mac, the two giant federal sponsors of mortgages which had to be rescued from outright collapse in 2008. In a sense, the federal deficit, crisis what crisis?

Two, the United States does not really face a truly serious fiscal crisis until the middle of the next decade, the point at which demographic factors suggest a great increase in Medicare spending on an ageing population at precisely the same time as the tax base starts to shrink. Even here, though, demanding drastic action now seems improbable and unnecessary. As the writer Dean Baker tartly noted on theguardian.com website on 14 October, as the battle of the budget reached its height, panic over the medium-term deficit 'makes as much sense as arguing that someone driving west in New Jersey risks falling into the Pacific Ocean. People driving west in New Jersey invariably turn or park their cars before ending up in the Pacific Ocean and the United States has always taken measures to reduce deficits long before they posed a fundamental threat to the economy.'[1]

Three, the real potential problem in public finances concerns not the level of the deficit but the scale of US national debt. The ratio of that debt to national income doubled in five years between FYs 2007 and 2012 from 36.3 per cent to 72.6 per cent. That is astounding. Although the deficit is

1   Baker, 'Republicans are delusional about US spending and deficits', 14 Oct. 2013, www. theguardian.com/commentisfree/2013/oct/14/shutdown-republicans-government-spending-delusions (accessed 22 Jan. 2014).

projected to fall sharply in the near future, that ratio of debt to national income is predicted to remain stable at around 70 per cent for the foreseeable future. That debt has to be serviced and the age of exceptionally low interest rates, which makes the current cost of interest repayments acceptable and restrains the policy opportunity cost of repaying debt, will not last forever. The stock of debt could only be sent back towards the same level it reached in 2007 should the US be capable of running budget surpluses in future years on the scale of the supersized deficits seen in the aftermath of the financial crisis. Utah will vote for a Democratic presidential candidate and Washington, DC will back a Republican one before surpluses of that magnitude are witnessed.

Four, the United States is a relatively low taxation economy by international standards and is likely to remain so. The January 2013 agreement locks in more than 95 per cent of the Bush-era tax cuts on a permanent basis. Tax increases are likely to be a relatively mild element in deficit reduction. This is a remarkable outcome for a period in which the Democrats held the White House and the Senate.

Five, the United States is a comparatively low spending nation on non-defence discretionary domestic expenditure and seems certain to remain so. Despite this parsimony, it is exactly this aspect of the federal budget that is destined to be hit hardest to achieve deficit reduction. This is again a notable outcome for a period in which the Democrats held the White House and Senate. As the liberal economist Paul Krugman protested in a *New York Times* column, 'the actual numbers show that we have been living through an era of unprecedented government downsizing. Government employment is down sharply; so is total government spending (including state and local governments) adjusted for inflation, which has fallen by almost 3 per cent since 2010 and around 5 per cent per capita.'[2]

Six, the politics of the federal budget process is essentially the politics of the sequestration process. That the original blueprint was amended a little in December 2013 does not alter this fact. This is not an apartisan outcome. As Fred Barnes sagely observed in the *Wall Street Journal* in an attempt to find some crumbs of comfort in the budget climbdown for fellow conservatives: 'For Republicans eager to corral federal spending – and that's most of them – the sequester is a gift that keeps on giving.'[3] They should have recognised this rather than seeking to defund Obamacare as well.

Seven, the above is doubly true because the defence cuts which many Republicans oppose would probably have happened anyway. The United States

2   Krugman, 'The biggest losers', 12 Dec. 2013, www.nytimes.com/2013/12/13/opinion/krugman-the-biggest-losers.html?_r=0 (accessed 22 Jan. 2014).

3   Barnes, 'The upside of the GOP shutdown defeat', 21 Oct. 2013, http://online.wsj.com/news/articles/SB10001424052702303448104579149741045522708 (accessed 22 Jan. 2014).

is now well out of Iraq and basically out of Afghanistan as well. As the response of the Obama administration to the Syrian civil war shows, it is not looking to become involved in any more (costly) conflicts. The War on Terror continues but has changed its character in the Obama years with the emphasis increasingly placed on technological rather than human solutions. The assassination of key opponents by unmanned drones might well be brutal and controversial but it is also effective and comparatively cheap. It would be particularly hard to argue that the Pentagon requires the sort of funding today that it won during the Bush presidency. There is almost certainly a better way to cut defence spending than by crass sequestration, as was belatedly acknowledged in the amended budget package accepted at the end of 2013, but a reduction in expenditure on the sort of scale that sequestration would deliver has a logic to it.

Eight, the stimulus package enacted in 2009 was seen as a political triumph for the president and the Democrats at the time (largely because they had done something) but in retrospect it does not appear a wise investment. There has been no coherence to the spending, and unemployment remained above the peak of the Bush period for the entire duration of the Obama first term (if it had not nudged below 8 per cent in late 2012, then his second term would have been imperilled). In retrospect, a conventional tax cut or rebate aimed squarely at the poor would have been better politics and policy for the Democrats and would have had more chance of enhancing the economy.

Nine, despite all of the above the decision of Standard and Poor to downgrade the United States from its triple AAA rating was far more poor than standard. It was close to madness. As President Obama said at the time 'we are, always have been and remain a triple A nation'.[4] Despite the appearance of almost compulsive brinkmanship, the prospect of the US Government walking away from its financial obligations via breaking through the debt ceiling was always minimal. Markets persistently fail to understand the nature of politics but S & P should have known better.

Ten, the most bewildering aspect of all this is that the Republican party has conspired to lose 90 per cent of the politics of this story while basically winning 90 per cent of the policy. In substance, the Bush-era tax cuts – which were extremely bold and barely affordable even at that time – are now set in stone for 19 out of 20 Americans, possibly 98 out of a hundred. Federal spending will almost certainly be lower on the day that President Obama leaves office than it was when he arrived. Government spending declined for the past two fiscal years in a row for the first time in five decades. The deficit reduction strategy is predominantly a spending cuts one.

4   President Obama speech, 8 Aug. 2011, www.reuters.com/article/2011/08/08/
      idUS74221581220110808 (accessed 22 Jan. 2014).

Despite this, the Republicans have consistently allowed their agenda to be driven by their most doctrinaire supporters and so have conceded the centre ground to the Democrats in general and the president in particular. This may not cost them much in the 2014 elections (let alone 2016) but it is still striking. The party lost the story of the battle of the budget because it kept on overreaching. Only by the end of 2013, and having endured two outright defeats in the court of public opinion, as well as something of a roasting in terms of the international image of the Republicans, did leading figures within the party come to appreciate that a more subtle and sophisticated strategy would be in their better interests electorally and also in terms of future influence over the policy debate itself. It will be intriguing to see whether such political realism can be maintained after the 2014 ballot.

Conclusion

The essence of the US budget is now set until 30 September 2015 in that total sums for spending and taxation have been set in law. The Republican defeat (politically) in October 2013 rendered it unlikely that the House would want to take Obamacare on via the threat or execution of a federal government shutdown again, and a third attempt to link domestic politics with the debt ceiling would be absolutely toxic. House Republicans eventually concluded that they should pocket the advance that sequestration offered them and await the perhaps unavoidable difficulties that introducing a change as profound as Obamacare will bring for the White House and the Democrats. At the same time, they should lower their own rhetorical volume with the ambition of obtaining more seats in the Senate in 2014 and even retaking that chamber. They might then hope to regain the White House, retake the Senate by 2016, if they have not done so two years earlier, and retain their majority in the House of Representatives throughout. The Democrats can use the power of veto in the interim to maintain their policy position. The politics of all this to the majority of Americans and to the rest of the world probably seems all but inexplicable. The sole superpower in the world looks ungovernable in a variety of foreign capitals. In Washington, DC, this politics is as nitrogen is to air. It is nature itself.

References[5]

---

5   Since this chapter only cites a few references, these appear in full in the footnotes and are not listed here.

4. Beast of burden: the weight of inequality and the second Obama administration

Steven Pressman

*One makes an economy work not by rewarding the rich but by rewarding
all who contribute to its success* (J.K. Galbraith, 1967, p. 124)

*The outstanding faults of the economic society in which we live are its
failure to provide for full employment and its arbitrary and inequitable
distribution of wealth and income* (J.M. Keynes (1936, p. 372)

Since President Obama's re-election, politicians, political pundits and
the general public have been obsessed with problems of sequestration,
debt ceilings and the so-called fiscal cliff. Taxes were raised in January
2013 by $180 billion to avoid the cliff. Between March and September 2013,
$85 billion in government expenditures was sequestered. Although Congress
appropriated the money, it cannot be spent.

This focus on debt and deficits is unfortunate for two related reasons. First,
it directs attention to a phoney issue and then proposes a bad solution as its
remedy. Second, it ignores the more pressing problems facing the US, such as
enormous income inequality. As the above quotes suggest, income inequality
has negative microeconomic and macroeconomic effects. Section 2 of this
chapter summarises the problem of this rising imbalance in the US, while
Section 3 briefly discusses its costs. President Obama's proposed solution to
this complication is then outlined and critiqued. The chapter concludes by
setting forth an alternative strategy to reduce income inequality in the US.

Rising inequality in the US

The facts about rising income inequality in the US are now well-known. It fell
from the 1930s to the 1970s and began to rise in the 1980s. Using income
tax data, economists Thomas Piketty and Emmanuel Saez have established
that this mounting inequity in the US story is about more and more income
flowing to the wealthy.[1] The share of income going to the top 10 per cent has

---

1   Piketty and Saez, 'Income inequality in the United States, 1913–1998'; 'How progressive is
     the U.S. federal income tax system?'; 'Top incomes and the great recession'.

Figure 1: Shares of income received by the top decile

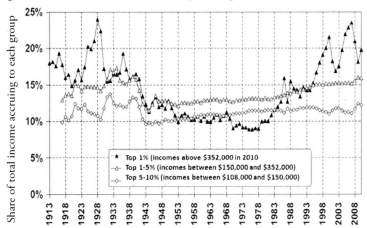

Source: Picketty & Saez (2012)

Note: Income is defined as market income including capital gains (excludes all government transfers).

risen from around one-third to approximately one-half of all income. Since the late 1970s, they have received 58 per cent of aggregate income gains in the US and a whopping 65 per cent during the Bush expansion of 2002–07.[2]

Figure 1,[3] makes this more precise by breaking down the percentage of income received by the top 10 per cent of earners into three subgroups – the top 1 per cent, the top 1–5 per cent and the top 5–10 per cent. Over the past 30 years, the main change in US income distribution is the larger fraction of total US income going to the top one per cent. In fact, the largest gains have been concentrated at the very top, the richest 0.1 per cent or those making more than $1.5 million.

These facts are not in dispute; however, the main cause of these changes remains controversial. The two most popular economic explanations for rising income inequality are globalisation and technical change.

The technological change story has its historical origins in the work of Jan Tinbergen,[4] co-winner of the first Nobel Prize in Economics.[5] It has been revived more recently by two University of Michigan economists, John Bound and George Johnson.[6] The main plot line is relatively simple – improvements in technology favour skilled workers, adept at using the new technology, and

2　Table 2 from Piketty and Saez, 'Top incomes and the great recession'.
3　Ibid., Table 1C.
4　Tinbergen, *Income Distribution: Analysis and Policies*.
5　See Pressman, *Fifty Major Economists*.
6　Bound and Johnson,'Changes in the structure of wages in the 1980s'.

hurt unskilled workers, who are not. As a result, wages of skilled workers rise and those for workers lacking the skills to work with new technology fall, and income inequality increases.

The globalisation story has been told recently in academic terms by Oxford economist Adrian Wood[7] and in popular terms by *New York Times* reporter and columnist Thomas Friedman.[8] Its theme is that greater world trade, increased capital mobility, and increased flows of labour across national borders all generate income inequality. Globalisation means that US businesses can set up production facilities wherever labour is cheapest in the world. This reduces the demand for US workers, exerting downward pressure on their wages. More production abroad also increases US imports, exerting downward pressure on the price of goods made in the US that must now compete with cheaper goods from abroad. This, in turn, puts further downward pressure on the wages of US workers producing these goods.

While these stories have a certain verisimilitude, we should remain sceptical about their actual truth. The big problem is that time-series and cross-sectional studies provide no empirical support for them. Since technical change and globalisation have an equal impact on all developed countries, both should impact income distribution to approximately the same extent in each of those nations (after all, that is what globalisation is all about). Yet the inequality problem became much worse in the US than in the UK and much worse in the UK than in Continental Europe. In addition, both globalisation and technical change have progressed rather steadily since the end of World War Two. Yet, overall income inequality in the US (using the statistical dispersion measure, the Gini coefficient) fell during the 1950s and 1960s, remained constant during the 1970s, and began its sharp upward trajectory in the 1980s.

The costs of rising inequality

While the causes of rising income inequality remain a matter of contention, the consequences are less controversial. It has negative economic effects as well as negative political and social consequences.

On the economic side, the macroeconomic effects are the most important. John Maynard Keynes noted that an unequal distribution of income leads to less consumption, and that lower consumption slows economic growth and increases unemployment.[9] When lots of income goes to those at the very top of the distribution, with low spending propensities, and too little goes to middle-income households, economic growth will be sluggish and unemployment will

---

7   Wood, *North-South Trade, Employment and Inequality.*
8   Friedman, *The World is Flat.*
9   Keynes, *The General Theory of Employment, Interest and Money*, p. 95.

be high. In contrast, when incomes are distributed more equally, spending and growth are higher.

Slow growth also increases government budget deficits. Tax revenues fall as national income declines, and government spending on automatic stabilisers (such as unemployment insurance and aid to the poor) rises. This puts pressure on governments to reduce spending and/or raise taxes – both of which only worsen macroeconomic problems.

Another negative economic consequence of inequality concerns productivity growth, the main determinant of rising living standards over time. Traditional economic analysis holds that inequality is necessary for productivity growth. This works two ways. People work in order to reap the rewards of their output. Large income incentives cause employees to work harder and increase their output. On the other hand, income taxes and the availability of government benefits reduce incentives for some people to work (or work hard), and increase inducements to collect benefits and not find employment.

This analysis works well for small firms run by entrepreneurs, where individual effort determines individual gain. But in a world of large corporations, where people work in teams, traditional economics does rather badly. In this situation, the relative distribution of pay within a firm determines employee behaviour. According to Harvey Leibenstein, worker productivity is a variable controlled by the individual worker.[10] He coined the term 'x-efficiency' to indicate that much worker effort is discretionary. Workers who feel that too much income goes to top executives will tend to work more slowly.

Large pay differentials may also increase employee turnover,[11] which is known to lower productivity or to lead to increases in vandalism, absenteeism, strikes and other forms of sabotage against the firm.[12] Perhaps most important of all, large pay differentials create disincentives for cooperation. Employees focus only on their own performance, to the detriment of organisational performance. Substantial research has found that when productivity depends upon team effort, unequal rewards hurt productivity.[13]

Figure 2 gives this alternative hypothesis some empirical support at the aggregate level. Productivity growth in the US was greatest during the 1950s and 1960s when income equality was greatest; then there was a miniboom in productivity growth during the 1990s when income inequality fell slightly.

10 Leibenstein, 'Allocative efficiency vs. x-efficiency'.

11 Gerhart and Milkovich, 'Employee compensation'.

12 Crosby, 'Relative deprivation in organizational settings'.

13 See Bloom, 'The performance effects of pay dispersion'; Pfeffer and Langton, 'The effect of wage dispersion on satisfaction, productivity, and working collaboratively'; Cowherd and Levine, 'Product quality and pay equity between lower-level employees and top management'; Bloom and Michel, 'The relationships among organizational context, pay dispersion, and managerial turnover'.

Figure 2: US annual productivity growth in manufacturing

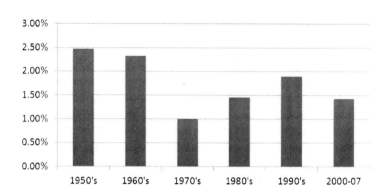

Income inequality also complicates the political economy of macroeconomic policy, perhaps the most important hurdle President Obama faces. When lots of money goes to very few people, these individuals are able to exert undue political influence using their vast wealth to support their own political positions, which surveys show are not the same as those of the general public.[14] Extreme wealth enables some people to buy up media outlets, which then exert great influence on the general public. Wealthy individuals can contribute large sums of money to their favoured candidates seeking election or re-election. They can establish phoney grassroots organisations and have them to apply pressure on politicians. All this makes it harder to pass legislation that might help reverse the trend towards rising inequality.

Compounding this problem, US elections are expensive; prohibitively so over the past several decades. Spending for the 2012 presidential election was $2 billion, around $1 billion by each candidate plus the Super Political Action Committees (Super PACs) supporting each candidate. Part of the enormous cost stems from the importance of TV advertising.[15] Another factor is the length of political campaigns. One standard joke is that the 2016 presidential election began on 6 November 2012 at around 11.15 pm when the networks declared Barack Obama winner of the 2012 presidential election. Finally, US elections take place fairly frequently – every two years for House races and every four years at the presidential level.

All this makes candidates heavily dependent on money. Politicians must constantly seek funds, bestowing a great deal of power on those who can

14 Page et al., 'Democracy and the policy preferences of wealthy Americans'.
15 Hacker and Pierson, *Winner-Take-All Politics*.

contribute large amounts of money to campaigns. But there is a quid pro quo. For their quid, the very wealthy can get legislation passed that serves their economic interests, but not those of the majority of Americans. Failure to support the economic interests of the wealthy not only means inadequate financial resources when running for re-election, it also increases the chances that some other candidate will get this financial aid, possibly even a primary fight to get their party's nomination. Such a battle inevitably damages the incumbents and increases their chances of losing in a general election. Since this outcome is not desired by incumbent politicians, the result is legislation that favours the very wealthy at the expense of everyone else. Put rather sarcastically, the US seems to have the best Congress money can buy.

Another difficulty is the reverse political business cycle, the traditional theory of which holds that economic business cycles are determined, in part, by political election cycles.[16] Stimulative macroeconomic policies get enacted a year or so before presidential elections, ensuring a low unemployment rate around election day. After the election, as inflation rises, politicians pass contractionary policies that lower inflation but push up the unemployment rate. However, knowledge can be a dangerous thing; it can be used for malevolent purposes as well as to improve economic performance. Politicians can use their knowledge of how the economy works to hurt the election chances of their political opponents, so that their party is more likely to win the next election. As we get closer to it, the benefits of opposing appropriate policies will increase and the less likely it is that necessary economic policies will get enacted.

Finally, there are many negative social consequences to rising inequality. Richard Wilkinson, an epidemiologist at Nottingham University, devoted his career to identifying and documenting them. His most recent work shows that greater income inequality is associated with mistrust, more crime, less giving to charity, worse school performance by children, more teen pregnancies, a greater incidence of obesity, more mental illness, increased drug addiction and reduced social mobility.[17] This is true for one country over time, across countries and within countries (for example, states in the US).

Although the US has an inequality problem, there is a window of opportunity to tackle it because the president does not have to run for re-election and worry about wealthy campaign donors. Now is also a good time to try to address this difficulty because public opinion polls in the US indicate substantial public support for higher taxes on the very wealthy.[18] The Obama administration

16 Tufte, *Political Control of the Economy*.

17 Wilkinson and Pickett, *The Spirit Level*.

18 'Post-ABC poll: support for reducing the nation's Budget deficit, Nov, 20–25, 2012', *Washington Post*, 28 Nov., www.washingtonpost.com/politics/polling/postabc-poll-support-reducing-nations-budget/2012/11/28/083a0a26-3952-11e2-9258-ac7c78d5c680_page.html (accessed 21 Jan. 2014).

seems to have recognised this and has set forth several proposals that would reduce income inequality in the US.

Solving the inequality puzzle – the Obama solution

As is fairly well-known, President Obama strives to be the grown-up in the room – the Aristotelian compromiser and the voice of reason. His instincts are to seek out a middle position and then, using logical arguments, convince others to go there. Rationality, rather than hardball politics, is how Obama seeks to win the day on all issues, including inequality.

The president's State of the Union address of February 2013 proposed two policies to deal with the problem of income inequality. His short-run solution was to increase the minimum wage; his long-run solution was to put greater emphasis on pre-school education.

From a *purely economic* perspective these are good solutions. Despite some critics who argue that the benefits of increasing the minimum wage will go to teenagers with rich or middle-class parents, most of them go to those at the bottom of the income distribution. In addition to giving more income to those making the current minimum wage, raising it also pushes up the wages of those earning slightly more than the minimum.

The real minimum wage in the US has declined substantially from its peak in 1968 (see figure 3). Because Congress has failed to index it, ensuring increases every year with inflation, its purchasing power falls continuously – unless Congress legislates an increase in the nominal minimum wage, which happens infrequently.

In contrast to most conservative business critics, the academic literature[19] finds that minimum wage hikes do *not* significantly increase unemployment (as long as the increase is kept within limits similar to past increases). To understand why this might be so, we can frame the minimum wage debate in terms of basic economic analysis – income and substitution effects. Increasing it makes employers less likely to hire new workers (the substitution effect), but it also causes demand to grow (for reasons cited by Keynes), requiring employers to hire more workers (the income effect). The empirical question is which of these two forces is greater.

A 'natural experiment' enabled economists to examine this issue more closely. New Jersey raised its minimum wage on 1 April 1992 (from $4.25 to $5.05 per hour), but the neighbouring state of Pennsylvania did not. David Card and Alan Krueger surveyed fast food establishments in one New Jersey

19 See Addison et al., 'The effects of minimum wages on labor market outcomes'; Card and Krueger, *Myth and Measurement: The New Economics of the Minimum Wage*; Doucouliagos and Stanley, 'Publication bias in minimum-wage research?'; Dube et al., 'Minimum wage effects across state borders'; Schmitt, 'Why does the minimum wage have no discernible effect on employment?'

Figure 3. Federal minimum wage's real value, 1968–2012 (in 2012 dollars)

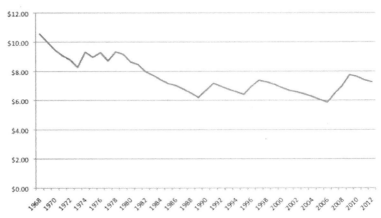

Source: National Employment Law Project Analysis of Consumer Price Index (CPI-U)

county and a similar county just over the border in Pennsylvania.[20] They found no impact on employment in New Jersey due to the higher minimum wage. Following this approach, many subsequent studies have come to the same conclusion (see footnote 19).

The literature on the benefits of pre-school education is even more conclusive. Many natural experiments involving pre-school have been undertaken over the years. These studies randomly divided a sample of young children into two groups and provided pre-school to one of them only. Among the most famous of these experiments was one that took place in Ypsilanti, Michigan. The Perry Elementary School began enrolling three- and four-year-olds in pre-school in 1961. The study found that these youngsters were less likely to skip school or repeat a grade and were more likely to stay out of prison and graduate from high school when compared to a control group. In their 40s, their salaries were 25 per cent higher. Each dollar spent on this programme returned seven in future tax revenues.[21] This is a massive return on investment; it is hard to think of any other form of spending that might yield such a high rate of return.

Head Start is slightly more controversial. Part of President Johnson's War on Poverty, it provides pre-school to three- and four-year-olds from low-income households with the goal of ensuring these children do not begin school far behind fellow pupils because of having grown up in poor families.

Research consistently finds that Head Start raises school performance and IQ scores. The average gain is one-half a standard deviation or around eight IQ points, although estimates are wide-ranging – from 25 IQ points in Milwaukee

20   Card and Krueger, *Myth and Measurement*.
21   Kirp, *Kids First*.

to zero in Syracuse.[22] An eight-point increase in IQ scores may not sound like much, but a one-standard deviation increase in test scores raises earnings by 16 per cent.[23] Half a standard deviation should raise earnings by 8 per cent a year. The only controversial issue concerns whether these IQ gains persist into adolescence. The mixed results on this question may be due to the fact that Head Start children often attend schools of poor quality later on.[24]

In sum, the president advanced two *reasonable economic solutions* to the problem of income inequality. But good economics and good politics frequently do not mix. In this case, there is little chance that a large rise in the minimum wage will become law. Congress may pass a small increase that takes effect several years in the future, but this is unlikely to restore the purchasing power of the minimum wage to its late-1960s peak. That would require a 50 per cent hike in the current US minimum wage – to around $11 an hour (compared to the current $7.25 per hour). Recent increases have averaged around 20 per cent spread out over two years. A similar rise now would bring the minimum wage up to almost $9 an hour, still far short of the large hike needed to return it to its peak.

More money for pre-school will also improve income equality, if the empirical literature is correct; however, it will take decades to achieve this end. Another difficulty with this proposal is that higher taxes will be required now to finance the additional pre-school provision, and this is not likely to be forthcoming from Congress.

Finally, while these two policies address the problem of inequity at the bottom of the distribution, they do not touch that of sharply rising incomes at the top of the distribution, which was identified in the work of Piketty and Saez and is the main factor contributing to rising US income inequality.

President Obama took a more daring approach in April 2013 when he delivered his 2014 budget to Congress. He proposed reducing the US budget deficit partly through cuts in the Social Security retirement programme – but only if the Republicans agreed to a large tax increase on the wealthy. Benefit cuts would come mainly from using the chain-weighted Consumer Price Index (CPI)[25] to measure inflation and determine annual cost of living adjustments for Social Security recipients. The chained CPI yields a slightly smaller inflation measure (around 0.3 per cent per year) and would slow the annual growth of benefits for the elderly. Obama held this carrot out to Republicans worried

---

22 McKey et al., *The Impact of Head Start on Children, Families, and Communities.*

23 Krueger, 'Economic considerations and class size'.

24 See Lee and Loeb, 'Where do Head Start attendees end up?'; Currie and Thomas, 'Does Head Start make a difference?'

25 The chained CPI takes into account changes in spending propensities when the price of a good rises. So if the apple crop gets destroyed and people substitute other fruits for apples, inflation is not calculated by assuming that everyone still buys high-priced apples.

about deficits and the future solvency of Social Security. He would slow the growth of social expenditures by using a chained CPI if they agreed to a tax hike on wealthy Americans.

Many Obama supporters felt betrayed by this proposal, believing the president had reneged on a campaign promise. They indicated that it would substantially reduce benefits for the very old, those most likely to have exhausted their savings. They also pointed out the unfairness of changing the rules and not honouring government promises made during a lifetime of paying Social Security taxes while working. For me, much of this criticism seems beside the point. A proposal involving a large tax hike for the very wealthy will never be accepted by Republicans in Congress. It was a bluff, designed to make Republicans look bad when they refused to compromise, rather than a serious proposal by the president.

These reflections indicate that another approach is needed to address the income inequality problem facing the US. The remainder of this chapter looks at two particular issues – tax policy and income support programmes. It focuses on the US system of supporting families with children and provides some practical solutions for the Obama administration that can then be generalised.

Solving the inequality puzzle – some suggested alternatives

(i) Tax reform

This is an important issue since the US tax code is riddled with tax expenditures, which the US Budget and Impoundment Act of 1974 defines as 'revenue losses attributable to provisions of the federal tax laws which allow a special exclusion, exemption, or deduction from gross income, or which provide a special credit, a preferential tax rate, or a deferral of tax liability.'

The Joint Committee on Taxation (2013) is required to make estimates of tax expenditures each year and to forecast them over the next five years. According to their estimates, tax expenditures for both individuals and corporations will exceed $1 trillion in the 2012–13 FY, around 7 per cent of US GDP, or greater than the US budget deficit for the year. The vast majority of these tax breaks go to individuals rather than corporations. In terms of lost tax revenues, the biggest tax expenditures in the 2012–13 FY were for medical care (mainly employer-paid insurance that is not taxed, around $160 billion), various retirement plans ($117 billion), mortgage interest ($70 billion), state and local tax payments ($46 billion) and charitable contributions ($40 billion). These tax breaks are just like direct government expenditures. For example, the government provides Pell Grants to low-income college students to help them pay their tuition and tax breaks to high-income households saving for their children's education. Little practical difference exists between the two.

The problem with tax expenditures is that they are upside-down subsidies. They benefit the wealthy but do little to help anyone else. One drawback is that most low-income and middle-class households don't itemise deductions when they file their income taxes and so get no benefits at all. Another is that wealthy taxpayers are in high tax brackets and so get back proportionately more than anyone else. Consider the mortgage deduction. The US tax code allows households to deduct the interest paid on their home mortgages, reducing their taxable income and their tax payments for the year. Households that owe no income taxes or take the standard deduction on their income tax returns (rather than itemising) get no tax benefit. Households in the 10 per cent tax bracket get back only 10 cents from the government for each dollar of mortgage interest they pay during the year. In contrast, taxpayers in the top tax brackets get back more than 30 cents for each dollar paid. The nature of these concessions means that the main beneficiaries are those households in the top income brackets, the very wealthy.

The Congressional Budget Office (CBO) has recently estimated that more than half of tax expenditures go to households in the top income quintile and 17 per cent go to the top one per cent.[26] For some tax expenditures, such as reduced rates for dividends and capital gains, the mortgage interest deduction and the deduction for charitable contributions, more than three-fourths of the gains go to the richest quintile and more than one-third goes to the top one per cent. In addition, tax expenditures provide other benefits to wealthy families. To take one personal example, I can deduct museum memberships on my income tax return, saving me between $20 and $25 when I go to a museum in New York. After my tax break, I come out slightly ahead on my third visit. But I also get other benefits as well. I can bring guests into the museum for a few dollars, and I get a discount when eating at the café there or purchasing something at its gift shop.

In his April 2013 budget, President Obama sought to limit deductions taken by the wealthy, capping the maximum allowable rate at 28 per cent. While a step in the right direction, this proposal doesn't go nearly far enough. Wealthy households would still get to deduct a larger fraction of their mortgage interest payments (28 per cent) than other households (0, 10, 15 or 25 per cent). And, as with the president's other proposals to reduce inequality, the plan is bad politics; it will never make it through the US Senate, where it will be filibustered, or the House, where it will be opposed by Republicans, who have the majority of votes there. The proposal is a tax hike on wealthy

26 Congressional Budget Office, *The Distribution of Major Tax Expenditures in the Individual Income Tax System.*

Americans and on the American public in general. This will not garner either Republican or popular support.

However, it is a step in the right direction because it limits the ability of wealthy households to reduce their tax obligations through various loopholes. A better strategy would be to take the next logical step – convert tax expenditures into a refundable tax credit. Politically, this should garner considerable support since it would not be a tax increase for the entire nation. In addition, it means that all citizens benefit proportionately from tax breaks, including those without tax liabilities, so this proposal should receive broad public support.

The CBO suggested in 2009 that the mortgage interest deduction could be converted into a 15 per cent refundable tax credit, estimating that such a change would result in no revenue loss to the federal government.[27] Accounting for likely behavioural changes, Eric Toder et al. calculated that replacing the mortgage interest deduction with a 16.3 per cent refundable credit would be revenue neutral for the government.[28] Overall, such a change would increase taxes for those in the top income quintile, especially the top one per cent, but would result in lower taxes for everyone else, including gains of a few hundred dollars (around 0.3 per cent of income) for the middle and fourth income quintiles.

This approach, which can easily be applied to other tax expenditures, has a number of important advantages. It retains incentives for certain desirable activities – such as making charitable contributions, purchasing a home, and saving for college – at the same time as broadening the array of citizens who receive such incentives. It will appeal to the American notion of equality and fairness. Why should the rich get a *proportionately bigger* tax benefit than everyone else for paying interest on their mortgages or for making charitable contributions? Since the wealthy have more money, I can accept giving them a proportionately *smaller* tax break, but it is hard to justify giving them a larger one.

Finally, and most importantly, converting tax expenditures into refundable tax credits would not raise taxes in the aggregate, and would not raise marginal tax rates, the main conservative argument against increasing taxes. However, it would make the US tax system more progressive and it would make income distribution more equal because it shifts the tax burden from low-income and middle-class households to wealthy households. As Sam Pizzigati argues, progressive taxation was mainly responsible for building the US middle class.[29] It took income from those at the very top of the distribution and used it to finance benefits for those at the middle and bottom of the distribution. This

27 Congressional Budget Office, *Budget Options*, vol. 2.

28 Toder et al., *Reforming the Mortgage Deduction*.

29 Pizzigati, *The Rich Don't Always Win*.

money went to mass education, the social safety net and other programmes that provided benefits to the large majority of the population. Tax expenditure reform is also viable politically. Republican House Speaker John Boehner proposed raising $800 billion in revenues (over a ten-year period) in this manner on 3 December 2012 when negotiating with President Obama about the impending fiscal cliff. And congressional Republicans have put out a proposal with several options to limit tax expenditures.[30]

(ii) Benefit reform

The size and structure of government spending is another factor contributing to income inequality in the US. Relative to most other developed countries, government spending in the US is a much lower percentage of GDP. Furthermore, considering the high percentage of spending focused on national defence, this means spending on social programmes in the US is low compared to other developed nations.

Table 1 compares public social expenditures relative to GDP for the US and other developed countries. This is mainly government spending on retirement

Table 1. Public social expenditures as % GDP, 2011

Australia	18.1
Canada	18.3
Finland	28.6
France	32.1
Germany	26.2
Italy	27.6
Netherlands	23.7
Norway	22.6
Sweden	27.6
United Kingdom (UK)	23.9
United States (US)	19.7
OECD-34	21.7
EU21	24.9

Source: OECD (2012) Social Expenditure database (www.oecd.org/social/expenditure/)

---

30 Committee for a Responsible Federal Budget, 'Raising revenue from higher earners through base broadening'.

benefits for the elderly, unemployment and disability insurance, and benefits that help families with children. The most recent comparable data (for 2012) from the Organisation for Economic Cooperation and Development (OECD) show that US social public expenditures were below 20 per cent of US GDP, far below the EU21 average (24.9 per cent), the UK figure (23.9 per cent), and the rate for the Nordic countries (close to 30 per cent). These numbers are surprising on purely economic grounds because the US has around the highest per capita income level in the world. Public goods become more important than private goods with higher income levels and nations with higher average incomes are able to afford more public goods.[31] So, we should expect to see *higher* levels of public social expenditure in the US than elsewhere.

The US falls short of other countries in many ways, so I will focus on only two – child allowances and paid parental leave. These policies are designed to help families raise their children and keep them out of poverty; but they also mitigate income inequality because they provide benefits to all families. Child allowances and paid parental leave also provide a good contrast with what President Obama has proposed to aid young children. Like pre-school, these two government spending programmes should be seen as a form of investment in the future of the nation. Their absence means that families have inadequate support to both work and raise their children.

It is worth considering child allowances first because of their connection to tax exemptions for children. Unlike other developed countries, the US aids families with children primarily through its tax system. Households get a tax exemption for each child, reducing their taxable income and lowering the income tax the owe. Although *not* officially counted by the US government as a tax expenditure, it probably should be.[32]

As noted previously, there are two problems with such a policy. First, since the value of the exemption is not refundable, these exemptions are pretty worthless for low-income households. Second, since low-income households are in the lowest tax bracket, they get back less from the government than households in higher brackets. In 2013, each child exemption reduced family taxable income by $3,900. The value of this was nearly $1,560 for married couples in the top (39.6 per cent) tax bracket (with a taxable income greater than $450,000), but only $390 for someone in the bottom (10 per cent) tax bracket (married couples with taxable incomes of $17,850 or less) and $585 for those with taxable incomes between $17,850 to $72,500 (in the 15 per cent tax bracket).[33]

31   Galbraith, *The Affluent Society*.

32   See Pressman, 'Policies to reduce child poverty: child allowances versus tax expenditures for children'.

33   Because of income exclusions (i.e., tax expenditures) these figures should be increased 10–20% to get actual incomes.

In contrast to the US, most nations have some form of child allowance programme. Child or family allowances are regular payments made to families on behalf of their children.[34] Their purpose is to raise household income and help families support their offspring. Like tax exemptions for children, this policy keeps families from being penalised economically if they have a large number of children.

Typically, all households receive equal payments for each child. Some countries, however, do make lower payments to households with higher incomes. For example, in Canada, in 2008, the basic benefit was $2,813 (both US and Canadian dollars) for a family with two children, but rose to $6,630 for low-income families.[35] In Italy, a family with two children is eligible for a monthly benefit of €250.48 ($359 US) if household income is below €11,989.56 ($17,189). Those with incomes between €29,066.61 ($41,673) and €31,911.40 ($45,764) receive only €38.73 ($56); those making more than €46,142.56 ($66,150) get nothing. Payments can also vary according to the number of children or the age of the child. For example, Finland provides a

Table 2A. The impact of child allowances on child poverty

Country	Child poverty rates	Child poverty rates less child allowances	Impact of child allowances on child poverty
Australia	14.7%	27.1%	-12.4
Canada	19.5%	25.1%	-5.6
Denmark	5.1%	9.3%	-4.2
Finland	5.5%	13.3%	-7.8
Germany	12.9%	22.6%	-9.7
Italy	24.5%	28.2%	-3.7
Luxembourg	17.1%	28.5%	-11.4
Norway	6.3%	11.3%	-5.0
Sweden	6.7%	11.0%	-4.3
UK	16.9%	23.4%	-6.5
US	26.3%	26.4%	-0.1
Averages (unweighted)	14.1%	20.6%	-6.5

Source: Author's computations from the Luxembourg Income Study database

34 See Macinol, *The Movement for Family Allowances, 1918–45*; Vadakin, *Family Allowances and Children, Poverty, and Family Allowances*.

35 Waldfogel, 'The role of family policies in antipoverty policy'.

basic annual allowance of €1,200 ($1,721) for one child and €2,526 ($3,623) for two, with a €439 ($630) per child supplement for single-parent families.[36]

Tables 2A and 2B show the extent to which child allowances reduce child poverty and increase the fraction of middle-class families with children. It uses the Luxembourg Income Study (LIS) for these calculations. Poor households are those with an adjusted household income that is below half of the median adjusted household income while middle-class households are those where that figure falls between 75 per cent and 150 per cent. In order to keep living standards equivalent as families get bigger and bigger, household income is adjusted for family size using the original OECD recommendations.[37] On average (including the US), child allowances reduce child poverty close to seven percentage points and increase middle-class families by more than five points. Converting tax exemptions for children into child allowances would greatly benefit low-income households. It would be paid for by reducing the tax benefits received by wealthy households.

Table 2B. The impact of child allowances on middle-class children

Country and year	Percentage of children who are middle class	Percentage of middle-class children without family allowances	Change due to family allowances
Australia (2003)	48.3%	41.5%	6.8
Belgium (2000)	59.3%	52.4%	6.8
Canada (2004)	45.3%	42.7%	2.6
Denmark (2004)	70.7%	64.1%	6.6
Finland (2004)	62.4%	53.9%	8.5
Germany (2004)	51.8%	42.3%	9.5
Italy (2004)	38.1%	36.9%	1.2
Luxembourg (2004)	46.9%	35.8%	11.1
Norway (2004)	50.5%	45.5%	5.0
Sweden (2005)	62.6%	54.9%	7.7
UK (2004)	42.6%	39.3%	3.3
US (2004)	39.2%	39.2%	0
Averages (unwtd)	52.1%	46.1%	6.0

Source: Author's computations from the Luxembourg Income Study database

36 Figures come from LIS institutional data, available from www.lisproject.org/.

37 To keep incomes equivalent for households of different sizes, additional adults are assumed to require 70% of the income of the household head, and children are assumed to require 50% of the income of the household head.

Paid parental leave replaces lost wages around the time of birth or adoption, enabling families to care for a new child. It enables mothers *and fathers* to take time off from paid employment to care for a new child without suffering a large loss of income. It also helps new parents seeking to balance the demands of work and the fresh challenges they face in the home. Table 3 summarises

Table 3. Paid parental leave and baby bonuses, 2003–06

Country	Benefits policies
Australia	Lump-sum birth grant of Au$3,000
Denmark	Up to 3,203 kroner per week for up to 52 weeks
Finland	70% of daily earnings up to €28,403 + 40% of earnings between €28,404–43,698 + 25% of earnings above €43,698 for 105 work days
Germany	100% of earnings for 3 months
Norway	100% of earnings for 43 weeks or 80% of earnings for 53 weeks
Sweden	100% of income for 390 days + 60 kroner per day for an additional 90 days
UK	90% of earnings for 6 weeks + £108.85 for 30 weeks + 1 or 2 weeks at £108.85 for spouse
US	None

Source: Vera Brusentev and Wayne Vromah, 'Compensating for birth and adoption'. Paper presented at Canadian Economic Research Forum, Halifax, June 2007

paid leave benefits (and the closely related policy of baby bonuses, a lump sum payment at the birth of a new child) in several developed nations.

Until fairly recently, few women worked for pay outside the home or family business, especially those with children. It was not until the latter part of the 20th century that female labour force participation was the norm rather than the exception. Some reasons for this are psychological and sociological. Others are economic – extra income raises living standards. In the US, the percentage of mothers working in the paid labour force increased sharply from 17 per cent in 1948 to 40 per cent in the early 1970s and then to 70 per cent in the 1990s. By the start of the 21st century, the labour force participation rate for married women with infants, whose husband's earnings were in the middle three income quintiles, was 64 per cent.[38] What is true of the US is likewise true of other industrial nations. Women now comprise close to half the labour force in most developed countries; they are just as likely to work as men.

This creates difficulties when a child is born. For health reasons women need to take some time off from work before they give birth. Studies have

38 Cohany and Suk, 'Trends in labor force participation of married mothers of infants'.

consistently found that when women return to work shortly after giving birth, their health is adversely affected; they suffer from increased fatigue, depression and anxiety.[39] While paid leave was originally thought of as a way to aid mothers who might damage their health by working immediately before and after giving birth, over time concern has shifted from the mother to the children. A large literature has demonstrated that maternal employment during the first year following the birth of a new child has many negative consequences.[40] Paid parental leave thus has many advantages.

First, children benefit from the reduced stress on them during and after pregnancy, which has been linked to slower learning, reduced attention and worse motor skills.[41] Second, maternal employment has been linked to behavioural problems in children at age four and to lower scores on language and cognitive skills tests, possibly because it harms the social bonding or attachments between mother and child.[42] Finally, public health officials strongly recommend that infants be breastfed because of the health benefits to children; but this may be difficult to do at work, leading some new mothers to take time off.[43]

What does paid parental leave do for families with young children? Tables 4A and 4B provide this information focusing on young children (two and under), the main beneficiaries of this programme. Paid parental leave greatly reduces the poverty of households with young children, on average by around 8–9 percentage points. It increases the size of middle-class families with young children by around 11 percentage points (when excluding the US).

Paid parental leave also empowers women and makes motherhood socially acceptable in a world where work is necessary. It says that it is OK to have children and that this activity is valued by the nation – not only with words, but with action. And, like child allowances, it lessens the great inequality plaguing the US. Even with overwhelming evidence that it provides a positive return over a generation, funding it would be controversial, especially now, when politicians are unwilling to undertake programmes that add to the federal deficit. However, there are three simple ways to incorporate paid parental leave into the US Social Security system, financing the programme with payroll taxes.

39 Hock and DeMeis, 'Depression in mothers of infants: the role of maternal employment'.

40 Brooks-Gunn et al., 'Maternal employment and child cognitive outcomes in the first three years of life'; Waldfogel et al., 'The effects of early maternal employment on child cognitive development'.

41 Boyce, 'Stress and child health'.

42 Belsky and Eggebeen, 'Early and extensive maternal employment and young children's socioemotional development'.

43 Blau et al., 'Infant health and the labor supply of mothers'; Roe et al., 'Is there competition between breast-feeding and maternal employment?'; Ryan and Martinez, 'Breast-feeding and the working mother'.

Table 4A. The impact of paid parental leave on child poverty

Country and year	Poverty rate of young children	Poverty rate of young children less parental leave & baby bonuses	Change due to these policies
Australia (2003)	16.7%	23.6%	-6.9
Denmark (2004)	8.9%	14.2%	-5.3
Finland (2004)	10.4%	26.5%	-16.1
Germany (2004)	19.0%	23.4%	-4.4
Norway (2004)	10.1%	22.9%	-12.8
Sweden (2005)	9.2%	25.9%	-16.7
UK (2004)	22.4%	22.6%	-0.2
US (2004)	34.6%	34.6%	0
Averages (unwtd)	16.4%	24.2%	-7.8
Averages (w/out US)	13.8%	22.7%	-8.9

Source: Author's calculations from Wave 6 of the Luxembourg Income Study

Note: In this analysis young children are aged from 0–2

First, paid parental leave, covering 100 per cent of earnings over 12 weeks for new mothers, could be funded by a 0.3 percentage point increase in the Social Security payroll tax. Paying 75 to 80 per cent of previous earnings seems a reasonable alternative, given work-related costs (commuting, food eaten at work and work clothes), childcare expenses and higher marginal tax rates for couples with two earners. This would put a US programme more in line with the replacement rates for those in Europe. It would also lower the needed tax increase proportionately, or it would allow for a proportionately longer period of leave at a similar cost.

Alternatively, 12 weeks of paid leave at 100 per cent of previous earnings could be funded by increasing the wage level to which Social Security taxes apply. Raising the Social Security wage base by around 10 per cent (to $125,000 from the 2013 limit of $113,700) would accomplish this. Again, replacing only 75 to 80 per cent of previous earnings would reduce the needed base increase or allow for longer periods of paid leave.

Third, delaying the date at which people can collect full Social Security benefits if they take paid parental leave could also fund the system. Twelve weeks of paid leave for any one parent could require both parents to work an extra six weeks in order to collect their full Social Security benefit upon retirement. For a family with two children, each parent would need to work an

Table 4B. The impact of paid parental leave on middle-class children

Country and year	Percentage of families with young children that are middle class	Percentage of middle-class families without paid parental leave and birth grants	Change due to these policies
Australia (2003	48.2%	45.2%	3.0
Denmark (2004)	67.9%	59.3%	8.6
Finland (2004)	57.2%	42.1%	15.1
Germany (2004)	49.5%	44.2%	5.3
Norway (2004)	65.0%	44.1%	20.9
Sweden (2005)	60.2%	38.9%	21.3
UK (2004)	40.5%	39.8%	0.7
US (2004)	36.7%	36.7%	0
Averages (unwtd)	50.6%	44.9%	7.6
Averages (w/out US)	55.5%	44.8%	10.7

Source: Author's calculations from Wave 6 of the Luxembourg Income Study

Note: In this analysis young children are aged from 0–2

extra 12 weeks or three months to collect full benefits. Parents could still retire at their normal retirement age and collect lower monthly benefits. By either delaying retirement or accepting slightly smaller benefits at retirement, they would effectively shift the time they pay for parental leave far into the future so they can have valuable time at home with a young child.

Conclusion

The various solutions set forth by President Obama to deal with the problem of income inequality make good economic sense; politically, however, they are non-starters. For this reason a different approach is necessary. This chapter has advanced two suggestions. On the tax side, it advocates reforming tax expenditures so they no longer constitute a large subsidy to the wealthy. On the spending side, it recommends two policies that focus on children. These programmes are easy to finance in the short run with just a few simple changes to the US tax system. They are also long-term investments that will more than pay for themselves.

Such an approach does not require a tax hike or any increase in marginal tax rates, something that is always anathema to conservative economists and to Keynesian economists while the country is in the midst of a great economic slump. The American public is likely to regard this approach as fair because these are policies involving everyone in it together all benefiting equally from government tax and spending programmes equally, regardless of income. Finally, the policies advocated here are investments that can easily be paid for now and that will yield large dividends later on. This means the future revenue stream will provide endless amusement as we watch Democrats and Republicans battle over whether these monies should be used for tax cuts or for more generous government spending programmes.

References

J. Addison, M. Blackburn and C. Cotti (2012) 'The effects of minimum wages on labor market outcomes: country-level estimates from the U.S. restaurant and bar sector', *British Journal of Industrial Relations*, vol. 50, pp. 412–35.

J. Belsky and D. Eggebeen (1999) 'Early and extensive maternal employment and young children's socioemotional development: children of the national longitudinal survey of youth', *Journal of Marriage and the Family*, vol. 53, pp. 1083–98.

D. Blau, D. Guilkey and B. Popkin (1996) 'Infant health and the labor supply of mothers', *Journal of Human Resources*, vol. 31, pp. 90–139.

M. Bloom (1999) 'The performance effects of pay dispersion on individuals and organizations', *Academy of Management Journal*, vol. 42, pp. 25–40.

M. Bloom and J. Michel (2002) 'The relationships among organizational context, pay dispersion, and managerial turnover', *Academy of Management Journal*, vol. 45, pp. 33–42.

J. Bound and G. Johnson (1992) 'Changes in the structure of wages in the 1980s: an evaluation of alternative explanations', *American Economic Review*, vol. 82, pp. 371–92.

T. Boyce (1985) 'Stress and child health: an overview', *Pediatric Annals*, vol. 14, pp. 539–42.

J. Brooks-Gunn, W. Hun and J. Waldfogel (2002) 'Maternal employment and child cognitive outcomes in the first three years of life: the NICHD study of early child care', *Child Development*, vol. 73, pp. 1052–72.

D. Card and A. Krueger (1995) *Myth and Measurement: The New Economics of the Minimum Wage* (Princeton, NJ: Princeton University Press).

S. Cohany and E. Suk (2007) 'Trends in labor force participation of married mothers of infants', *Monthly Labor Review*, vol. 130, pp. 9–16.

Committee for a Responsible Federal Budget (2012) 'Raising revenue from higher earners through base broadening', Working Paper, Nov., http://crfb.org/document/report-raising-revenue-high-earners-through-base-broadening (accessed 14 April 2012).

Congressional Budget Office (2009) *Budget Options*, vol. 2 (Washington, DC: CBO).

— (2013) *The Distribution of Major Tax Expenditures in the Individual Income Tax System* (Washington, DC: CBO).

D. Cowherd and D. Levine (1992) 'Product quality and pay equity between lower-level employees and top management: an investigation of distributive justice theory', *Administrative Science Quarterly*, vol. 37, pp. 302–20.

F. Crosby (1984) 'Relative deprivation in organizational settings', in B. Staw and L. Cummings (eds.), *Research in Organizational Behavior*, vol. 6 (Greenwich, CT: JAI Press), pp. 51–93.

J. Currie and D. Thomas (1995) 'Does Head Start make a difference?', *American Economic Review*, vol. 85, pp. 341–64.

H. Doucouliagos and T. Stanley (2009) 'Publication bias in minimum-wage research? A meta-regression analysis', *British Journal of Industrial Relations*, vol. 47, pp. 406–28.

A. Dube, T.W. Lester and M. Reich (2010) 'Minimum wage effects across state borders: estimates using contiguous counties', *Review of Economics and Statistics*, vol. 92, pp. 945–64.

T. Friedman (2005) *The World is Flat* (New York, NY: Farrar, Straus & Giroux).

J.K. Galbraith (1958) *The Affluent Society* (Boston, MA: Houghton Mifflin).

— (1967) 'Let us begin: an invitation to action on poverty', in L. Thurow (ed.), *American Fiscal Policy: Experiment for Prosperity* (Englewood Cliffs, NJ: Prentice-Hall), pp. 123–30.

B. Gerhart and G. Milkovich (1992) 'Employee compensation: research and theory', in M. Dunnette and L. Hough (eds.), *Handbook of Industrial and Organizational Psychology*, 2nd edn., vol. 3 (Palo Alto, CA: Consulting Psychologists Press), pp. 481–569.

J. Hacker and P. Pierson (2010) *Winner-Take-All Politics* (New York, NY: Simon & Schuster).

E. Hock and D. DeMeis (1990) 'Depression in mothers of infants: the role of maternal employment', *Developmental Psychology*, vol. 26, pp. 285–91.

Joint Committee on Taxation (2013) *Estimates of Federal Tax Expenditures for Fiscal Years 2012–2017* (Washington, DC: GPO).

J.M. Keynes (1936) *The General Theory of Employment, Interest and Money* (London: Macmillan).

D. Kirp (2011) *Kids First* (New York, NY: Public Affairs).

A. Krueger (2003) 'Economic considerations and class size', *Economic Journal*, vol. 113, pp. F34–F63.

V. Lee and S. Loeb (1995) 'Where do Head Start attendees end up? One reason why preschool effects fade out', *Educational Evaluation and Policy Analysis*, vol. 17, pp. 62–82.

H. Leibenstein (1966) 'Allocative efficiency vs. x-efficiency', *American Economic Review*, vol. 56, pp. 392–415.

J. Macinol (1980) *The Movement for Family Allowances, 1918–45* (London: Heinemann).

R. McKey, L. Condelli, H. Ganson, B. Barrett, C. McConkey and M. Plantz (1985) *The Impact of Head Start on Children, Families, and Communities* (Washington, DC: US Department of Health and Human Services).

B. Page, L. Bartels and J. Seawright (2011) 'Democracy and the policy preferences of wealthy Americans', paper presented at the American Political Science Association meetings.

J. Pfeffer and N. Langton (1993) 'The effect of wage dispersion on satisfaction, productivity, and working collaboratively: evidence from college and university faculty', *Administrative Science Quarterly*, vol. 38, pp. 382–407.

T. Piketty and E. Saez (2003) 'Income inequality in the United States, 1913–1998', *Quarterly Journal of Economics*, vol. 11, pp. 1–39.

— (2007) 'How progressive is the U.S. federal income tax system? A historical and international perspective', *Journal of Economic Perspectives*, vol. 21, pp. 3–24.

— (2012) 'Top incomes and the great recession: recent evolutions and policy implications', 13th Jacques Polak Annual Research Conference.

S. Pizzigati (2012) *The Rich Don't Always Win* (New York, NY: Seven Stories Press).

S. Pressman (2011) 'Policies to reduce child poverty: child allowances versus tax expenditures for children', *Journal of Economic Issues*, vol. 45, pp. 323–32.

— (2013) *Fifty Major Economists*, 3rd edn. (London and New York, NY: Routledge).

B. Roe, L. Whittington, S. Fein and M. Teisl (1999) 'Is there competition between breast-feeding and maternal employment?', *Demography*, vol. 36, pp. 157–71.

A. Ryan and G. Martinez (1989) 'Breast-feeding and the working mother: a profile', *Pediatrics*, vol. 83, pp. 524–31.

J. Schmitt (2013) 'Why does the minimum wage have no discernible effect on employment?', Center for Economic and Policy Research, Working Paper.

J. Tinbergen (1975) *Income Distribution: Analysis and Policies* (Amsterdam: North Holland).

E. Toder, M. Turner, K. Lim and L. Getsinger (2010) *Reforming the Mortgage Deduction* (Washington, DC: Tax Policy Center, Urban Institute and Brookings Institution).

E. Tufte (1978) *Political Control of the Economy* (Princeton, NY: Princeton University Press).

J. Vadakin (1958) *Family Allowances* (Miami, FL: University of Miami Press).

— (1968) *Children, Poverty, and Family Allowances* (New York, NY: Basic Books).

J. Waldfogel (2009) 'The role of family policies in antipoverty policy', *Focus*, vol. 26, pp. 50–5.

J. Waldfogel, W. Han and J. Brooks-Gunn (2002) 'The effects of early maternal employment on child cognitive development,' *Demography*, vol. 39, pp. 369–92.

R. Wilkinson and K. Pickett (2010) *The Spirit Level* (New York, NY: Bloomsbury Press).

A. Wood (1994) *North-South Trade, Employment and Inequality: Changing Fortunes in a Skill Driven World* (Oxford: Clarendon Press).

5. The Affordable Care Act: cure or train wreck?[1]

Daniel Béland and Alex Waddan

The first 15 months of President Barack Obama's time in office saw significant and highly controversial legislative activity. Two laws in particular stand out, which were championed by the administration's supporters and scorned by its opponents.

The American Recovery and Reinvestment Act (ARRA), passed soon after Obama's inauguration, was a hugely contentious stimulus package containing proposals totalling $787 billion designed to reinvigorate the economy.[2] Under normal circumstances, such a massive government intervention in the economy would dominate the politics of the congressional cycle. But the second law, enacted in March 2010, was an even more wide-ranging mix of social and economic policy and proved even more controversial. This complex law, the Patient Protection and Affordable Care Act (known as the Affordable Care Act – ACA), put forward a major reform of the US healthcare system, which generated much sound and fury through the legislative process; and it is highly likely to be remembered as the landmark piece of legislation from the Obama era. This is due not only to the potential long-term impact of the law but also the sustained political conflict that it set in play.

In late March 2010, on the day that President Obama signed the law, triumphant administration supporters and congressional Democratic leaders were keen to celebrate the reform, after what had proved to be a traumatic law-making episode. Perhaps most memorably, Vice President Biden, in a remark not intended for public consumption, was overheard to say, 'Mr. President, this is a big [expletive] deal.' The President himself declared that the bill contained 'the core principle that everybody should have some basic security when it comes to their health care.' He added that the ACA 'will set in motion reforms that generations of Americans have fought for and marched for and hungered to see.' One other victorious advocate was Senator Max Baucus from Montana who, as chair of Senate Finance Committee, had been one of the central figures in the legislative process. He urged Republican opponents to

1   Daniel Béland acknowledges support from the Canada Research Chairs Program.
2   Morgan, 'The quest for renewed economic prosperity', p. 76.

accept that healthcare reform was a reality: 'Now it is a fact. Now it is law. Now it is history.'[3] Yet, more than three years later, Republicans had far from given up their fight against what they labelled 'Obamacare'. They were also fond of quoting another of Baucus's statements in relation to the proposed health legislation, 'I just see a huge train wreck coming down'.[4]

In fact, with public opinion polls showing majorities opposed to the ACA, the Republican leadership was keen to continue pressing the issue as an electoral concern, even as central aspects of the ACA were scheduled to come into effect in the fall of 2013. A series of polls conducted in September 2013 (as aggregated by the Real Clear Politics website) found an average of 52 per cent disapproval of the ACA as against 38.7 per cent approval.[5] In August 2013, the Kaiser Health tracking poll, which had sometimes suggested a less hostile public perspective on the ACA than polls conducted for news organisations, still found unfavourable opinion about the law outstripping favourable opinion by 42 per cent to 37 per cent.[6] Given these numbers, it was hardly surprising that Republican leaders wished to keep the ACA on the political front burner. For example, appearing on an episode of NBC's 'Meet the Press' in May 2013, Republican Senate Minority Leader Mitch McConnell from Kentucky predicted that 'Obamacare', which he described as 'the single worst piece of legislation that's been passed in modern times in this country', would be the 'biggest' issue in the 2014 mid-term congressional elections.[7] On 1 October 2013, a federal government shutdown of non-essential services began, as House Republicans demanded that any continuing resolution to keep government funded be accompanied by a delay in the implementation of the ACA. Senate Democrats and the White House refused to negotiate as major aspects of the ACA actually came into effect on the same day. When the

3   Quotations from the signing ceremony reproduced in Stolberg and Pear, 'Obama signs health care overhaul bill, with a flourish'.

4   Baucus made this statement at a Senate Budget Committee hearing in April 2013 when expressing his anxiety to Kathleen Sebelius, Secretary of Health and Human Services, that there was not enough information in the public domain about how the new law was to work. See Kertscher, 'In context: Obamacare "train wreck"'.

5   See www.realclearpolitics.com/epolls/other/obama_and_democrats_health_care_plan-1130.html (accessed 19 Feb. 2014). The polls concerned, with the disapproval rating margin shown in parentheses were: CBS News/*New York Times* (12); Rasmussen Reports (10); ABC News/*Washington Post* (10); CNN/Opinion Research (18); Fox News (19); NBC News/ *Wall Street Journal* (13); *U.S.A. Today*/Pew Research Center (11). These poll numbers do not distinguish between people who disapproved of the ACA because they felt it would involve too much government intervention and those who considered it did not go far enough in reforming the prevailing healthcare arrangements.

6   See Kaiser Health Tracking Poll, Aug. 2013: The Henry J. Kaiser Family Foundation, kff.org/health-reform/poll-finding/Kaiser-health-tracking-poll-august-2013/ (accessed 29 Jan. 2014).

7   See http://uneditedpolitics.com/mitch-mcconnell-on-meet-the-press-obamacare-will-be-focus-of-2014-midterm-51913/#.UukpqqNFDL8 (accessed 29 Jan. 2014).

government shutdown ended on 16 October, Democrats appeared to have won a political battle against the Republican opponents of ACA.

The purpose of this chapter is to examine the factors that shaped the ACA's format, particularly in the light of the economic inequalities apparent in American society highlighted elsewhere in this volume. In this context, the nature of the intense political conflict that the law generated is reflected upon here, which was to continue years even after its passage.

In order to do this, it is important to start by laying out the problems that the ACA was designed to resolve. It is also vital to understand how the legislative process itself shaped the ACA: what were the assumptions of the central political actors about what they could achieve? And, drawing upon insights gleaned from historical institutionalist analysis, how did policy legacies, potential legislative veto points and the behaviour of political parties frame the ACA?

A system in crisis

Back in the early 1990s, when Governor Bill Clinton was campaigning for the presidency, he promised to reform a set of arrangements that 'leaves 60 million Americans without adequate health insurance and bankrupts our families, our businesses, and our federal budget.'[8] Whatever view is taken of Clinton's subsequent attempt to bring about change, the critique he made of the prevailing system was compelling. In 1993, 39.7 million Americans, constituting 15.3 per cent of the population, were uninsured.[9] In addition, millions more were underinsured. Yet with over 13 per cent of GDP devoted to healthcare expenditure, the US spent a higher proportion of GDP on healthcare than any other industrialised nation.[10] In the wake of the failure of Clinton's reform effort and the perception that this had been a step too far in the direction of 'Big Government' liberalism, neither Al Gore nor John Kerry, the next two (losing) Democratic presidential candidates, placed health reform at the centre of the political agenda in the manner that Clinton had done.[11] By the end of the 2000s, however, the evidence showed that the problems evident in the early 1990s, which had persuaded Clinton of the need to act, had worsened. In short, the system cost too much as it placed a major burden

---

8   Clinton and Gore, *Putting People First: A Strategy for Change*, p. 107.

9   See 1996 section of United States Census Bureau, *Statistical Abstract of the United States, 1995–2000*, p. 120.

10 Patel and Rushefsky, *Health Care Politics and Policy in America*, p. 162.

11 On the demise of Clinton's efforts see Hacker, *The Road to Nowhere: The Genesis of President Clinton's Plan for Health Security* and Skocpol, *Boomerang: Health Care Reform and the Turn Against Government*.

on both private business and government, yet simultaneously many millions of Americans were excluded from regular access to healthcare.[12]

The US is far from unique in facing rising healthcare costs. In fact, the level of healthcare spending as a percentage of GDP has risen steadily over time in nearly all industrialised nations, but that trajectory has been especially pronounced in the US. In 1980, spending accounted for 9 per cent of the country's GDP. By 2000, that proportion had risen to 13.4 reaching 16 per cent in 2008. This placed the US as an outlier at the top of the health-spending league. For example, the comparable percentage of GDP figures for France in 2008 were 11.2, Germany 10.5 and the United Kingdom 8.7. The numbers look even starker when expressed as per capita spending. Using the OECD's measure of purchasing power parity (PPP) calculated in US dollars, per capita health expenditure in the US in 2008 was 7,771 $US PPP. The next highest figure for an OECD country was 5,246 $US PPP in Norway, with the respective numbers for the UK, Germany, and France being 3,274 $US PPP, 3,973 $US PPP, and 3,764 $US PPP.[13]

Unsurprisingly, therefore, the call to 'bend the curve' on healthcare spending had been a regular refrain among US policymakers since the 1980s but no long-term solution had been found, and both government and corporate America were increasingly feeling squeezed. In January 2010, as the ACA was still in the legislative process, the Congressional Budget Office (CBO) warned:

> The biggest single threat to budgetary stability is the growth of federal spending on health care – pushed up both by increases in the number of beneficiaries of Medicare and Medicaid (because of the aging of the population) and by growth in spending per beneficiary that outstrips growth in per capita GDP.[14]

For the federal government, this spending was mainly on the Medicare programme, which provides health insurance for America's seniors, and the Medicaid programme, which is run in partnership with the states and provides coverage for some low-income households. In addition to the costs incurred by the federal government, there was growing evidence that state governments were becoming increasingly distressed about paying their share of Medicaid costs, with state officials apparently being forced to make uncomfortable choices between Medicaid and other areas of important social spending.[15] In addition, healthcare costs were also hurting American businesses, as employers

---

12   Béland and Waddan, 'The Obama presidency and health insurance reform', pp. 319–30.

13   OECD Directorate for Employment, Labour and Social Affairs, OECD Health Data for 2013, http://stats.oecd.org/Index.aspx?DataSetCode=SHA (accessed 29 Jan. 2014).

14   Congressional Budget Office, *The Budget and Economic Outlook: Fiscal Years 2010 to 2020.*

15   Orszag, 'How health care can save or sink America', pp. 42–56. See also Goldstein and Balz, 'Governors differ on extent of flexibility for Medicaid'.

were forced to balance the value of offering insurance to their workers against the rising cost of doing so. By the mid-2000s, for example, Starbucks was spending more money on providing insurance for its employees than it did on coffee beans.[16] These pressures partially helped explain the long-term decline in the extent of the employer-based model of insurance.[17] In 2000, 65.1 per cent of Americans had employment-based insurance but this had declined to 56.1 per cent in 2009.[18]

That the US spends more of its GDP on healthcare than other nations is not in itself problematic, since access to healthcare is a desirable good and there is a correlation between a country's wealth and its proportionate expenditure on health. What is troubling, however, is that the US level of spending remains beyond what might be expected and the outcomes generated by that spending do not appear to justify the excess expenditures. For example, a detailed study of healthcare spending and its benefits, conducted during 2006 by the McKinsey Global Institute, found that, in that year, the US spent $2.1 trillion on healthcare, which amounted to 'nearly $650 billion more ... than peer OECD countries, even after adjusting for wealth.' In return, the US did have 'some of the best hospitals in the world. Cutting edge drugs are available earlier, and waiting times to see a physician tend to be lower'.[19] But set against these positive attributes were some more discouraging statistics, with health outcomes in the US – as measured by life expectancy and infant mortality – no better than peer OECD nations spending considerably less. The aggregate effect was to create the well-known paradox whereby the US spent more money on healthcare than any other nation yet, in 2008, 14.9 per cent of the population was uninsured.[20] Furthermore, many millions more were underinsured, leaving the prospect of potentially crippling medical bills should illness strike. About three-quarters of people filing for bankruptcy and citing medical costs as primary cause reported that they had some form of insurance.[21]

It is also important to look beyond these aggregate data to investigate how different parts of the country and diverse population groups were able to access health insurance. This information makes it clear that when Obama came to office there were wide discrepancies, both in geographical terms and also in racial and ethnic terms. First, the ratio of the uninsured varied widely from state to state. In 2008, eight states plus the District of Columbia had rates of

16 Morris, *Apart at the Seams: The Collapse of Private Pension and Health Care Protection.*
17 Gottschalk, 'Back to the future? Health benefits, organized labor, and universal health care', pp. 923–70.
18 United States Census Bureau (2012) Health Insurance Historical Tables, Table HIB-1.
19 McKinsey Global Institute, *Accounting for the Cost of U.S. Health Care.*
20 United States Census Bureau, Health Insurance Historical Tables, Table HIB-4.
21 Thorne and Warren, 'Get sick, go broke', pp. 66–87.

uninsurance that were below 10 per cent. Massachusetts, with 5 per cent of its population lacking health insurance, had the lowest rate of uninsurance. In contrast, six states had uninsurance rates above 19 per cent. At the head of that dubious table were New Mexico, where 22.8 per cent of the population were without health insurance in 2008, and Texas where the number of uninsured reached 24.5 per cent.[22]

Second, it is crucial to take inequities along racial and economic lines into account. Long-term data comparing the life expectancy of white Americans and African Americans show that

> In 1990, blacks achieved the life expectancy that whites had in 1950 but in 2007, there was still a 5-year gap between the two groups. Although health outcomes have been tied to income and social economic status, there are black-white differences in life expectancy of at least 3 years at every level of income.[23]

Clearly multiple factors account for these inequalities and the relatively high number of premature deaths and excess illnesses among not just African Americans but other minorities as well. One study by the Institute of Medicine found that minorities would often get worse treatment than white Americans even when they had the same level of health insurance and the same capacity to pay for care as their white counterparts.[24] This type of data suggests how hard it will be to smooth out racial and ethnic health inequalities since they are not based on income alone, but clearly and perhaps more straightforwardly access to care was highly unequal. In its report, commissioned by Congress, the Institute of Medicine reflected:

> There are wide differences between racial and ethnic groups in access to health care and the availability of health insurance. Minorities, especially Hispanic and African-American families, are less likely than whites to have private health insurance. Or if they have insurance, minorities are more likely than whites to be enrolled in health plans that place tight limits on the types of services that patients may receive. Also, the best quality health care services and providers are not always found in minority communities.[25]

That report was produced in 2002 and the disparities persisted when President Obama took office. For example, in 2008, the rate of health uninsurance amongst white, non-Hispanic Americans, was 10.4 per cent. Among those

22 United States Census Bureau, Health Insurance Historical Tables, Table HIB-4.
23 Devi, 'Getting to the root of America's racial health inequalities'.
24 Institute of Medicine, 'Unequal treatment: confronting racial and ethnic disparities in health care'.
25 Ibid., p.1.

described by the Census as 'black alone', 18.4 per cent were uninsured and, for people of Hispanic origin, that number was higher still at a remarkable 29.8 per cent. These numbers reflect the fact that African Americans and Hispanics were significantly less likely to have access to employer-related insurance. In 2008, 58.9 per cent of Americans had some sort of employer-related insurance. For white Americans, the figure was above that average, at 65 per cent, but for African Americans and Hispanics, it was significantly below the average, at 48.8 per cent and 41 per cent respectively.[26] These data are perhaps unsurprising, as it would seem to be highly likely that health insecurities and inequalities reflect wider economic disparities in American society.

The road to reform

Given this array of problems arising from the manner in which healthcare was supplied and consumed in the US, it is hardly surprising that health policy wonks had long been debating how to bring order to the prevailing mess. Yet, from a political perspective, it was not necessarily obvious that candidates for national office in the late 2000s would automatically embrace plans for comprehensive reform.

On the Republican side, there was simply no demand for candidates to take such a policy position. President Nixon had in fact advanced significant reform plans, but these had made little progress[27] and, 20 years later, the Nixonian wing of the Republican party was no longer ascendant. In the heat of the battle over Clinton's reform effort in 1993, the highly influential conservative strategist Bill Kristol had articulated the political calculations, as well as GOP policy concerns, in a memo distributed among Republican members of Congress. Kristol, based at a think tank called the Project for a Republican Future, was adamant that there should be no attempt to broker a compromise agreement with President Clinton, as any intervention by government, perceived to be successful, would in turn give credibility to the idea that government should be providing more collective protection against economic risk.[28] There did, of course, remain Republicans more moderate in their view than Kristol, but the rightward movement of the GOP that gained impetus during the 1980s continued to do so throughout the 1990s and 2000s.[29] In 2003, the George W. Bush administration did aggressively push a law through Congress that added a prescription drug programme to Medicare, but this pre-empted an issue that Democrats hoped to increase their support amongst seniors, while advancing a number of pet conservative preferences such as expanding the availability

26 United States Census Bureau, Health Insurance Historical Tables, Table HIB-1.

27 Blumenthal and Morone, *The Heart of Power: Health and Politics in the Oval Office.*

28 Johnson and Broder, *The System: The American Way of Politics at Breaking Point*, p. 234.

29 Hacker and Pierson, *Winner-Take-All Politics.*

of Health Savings Accounts.[30] Overall, the national Republican party of the 2000s was not a vehicle for ideas about how to dramatically reduce the number of uninsured. Even among conservatives exploring ways to correct the flaws in the healthcare marketplace, there was little appetite for extending government intervention.[31]

On the Democratic side the story was more complex, as comprehensive healthcare reform had long been a goal for the party's liberal wing, but the legislative debacle that unfolded through 1993 and 1994 – with the Democratic-controlled Congress making no progress in advancing the administration's Health Security Act (HSA) – also illustrated that there was little consensus within the party about what reform should actually mean, and whether it should prioritise cost-containment or expanding insurance coverage. In addition, the Clinton experience had suggested that while health care was generally an issue where Democrats polled better than Republicans, it was possible for the party to overreach and lose public support to dramatic effect.[32] On the other hand, the problems of cost and uninsurance had become more acute through the 2000s,[33] although it is perhaps ironic that it was Hillary Clinton, mocked for her part in devising the 'Hillary-care' plan in 1993, who during 2007 and 2008 raised the bar for Democratic candidates for the party's presidential nomination by embracing the notion of comprehensive reform in a manner clearly appealing to the party's activist base. In fact, as health reform became one of the key issues during the Democratic party's presidential primary battle with Senator John Edwards, as well as Clinton's pressing for comprehensive reform, some of her high-profile supporters, notably the *New York Times* columnist and renowned economist Paul Krugman, expressed scepticism about Senator Obama's commitment to the health reform cause.[34]

---

30 Jaenicke and Waddan, 'President Bush and social policy: the strange case of the Medicare prescription drug benefit', pp. 217–40.

31 As is often the case in the US there are important regional differences to take into account. Most notably, in 2006, the Republican Governor of Massachusetts, Mitt Romney, signed into law 'An Act providing Access to Affordable, Quality, Accountable Health Care', a state health reform plan that contained many elements later partially emulated in the ACA. At the time Romney reflected that the law would constitute 'a big part of the legacy I will have personally for my four years' service as governor' (quoted in Belluck and Zezima, 'Massachusetts legislation on insurance becomes law'). Massachusetts, however, is hardly a template for the national GOP and his actions in the state later proved awkward for Romney, as a candidate for the Republican presidential nomination in 2012, when denouncing 'Obamacare' became an article of unshakeable faith for the party's activists.

32 Peterson, 'The politics of health care policy: overreaching in an age of polarization', pp. 181–229.

33 Peterson, 'It was a different time: Obama and the unique opportunity for health care reform', pp. 429–36.

34 Krugman, 'Clinton, Obama, insurance'.

Crucially, however, when he entered the White House, Obama did choose to place health reform at the top of the agenda. Perhaps unsurprisingly, this in turn antagonised Republicans, who declared that the new president should focus on the economic situation (though few of them went along with his solutions on that front either). More interestingly, the choice to 'do' both health reform and economic stimulus immediately also went against the advice of Vice-President Biden and Chief-of-Staff Rahm Emmanuel. Both feared that pushing for healthcare reform and a massive stimulus package simultaneously would prove too crowded an agenda that might lead to legislative failure on both fronts. But Obama was influenced more by arguments from high-profile congressional champions of health reform, including Senators Max Baucus and Ted Kennedy, a long-time champion of a national health insurance system, who was suffering from increasingly poor health himself. In addition to arguments about improving access to insurance for millions of Americans, the new president was convinced any long-term plan to bring down the deficit necessitated government getting a tighter grip on health spending and that economic growth was hindered by the growth of costs on businesses.[35]

As it was, the decision to move ahead with health reform at the start of the presidency was vital, as the institutional alignment through 2009 and, critically, the numbers in Congress, were as good as could be hoped for from a reformer's perspective. As the reform process got underway in 2009, the Democrats had a 257 to 178 Democratic majority in the House and, importantly, by the summer of 2009, a 60 to 40 majority in the Senate, which meant that, if all the caucus could stick together, then the Democrats had a filibuster-proof majority.[36] But simply having unified government, even with sizeable majorities in Congress, had not historically meant that presidents were able to act in harmony with Congress. President Obama could look back to the time when his predecessor, George W. Bush, had been unable to persuade the Republican-controlled Congress to make serious legislative headway on his plan to partially privatise the Social Security system in 2005. And, more pertinently, one factor in the downfall of the Clinton-era effort at healthcare reform was that the Republicans were ultimately much more united in their opposition to the administration's proposals than the Democrats were united behind them. The left of the Democratic party did support the HSA, but

35 Jacobs and Skocpol, 'Hard-fought legacy: Obama, congressional Democrats, and the struggle for comprehensive health care reform', pp. 60–3.

36 This majority did not materialise until the summer since Al Franken from Minnesota was not formally sworn into the Senate until July 2009 after winning his November 2008 Senate contest by only 312 votes. The defeated Republican incumbent, Senator Norm Coleman, challenged the result and it was not until June 2009 that the Minnesota Supreme Court finally ratified it. Furthermore, the majority also depended on Arlen Specter switching parties at the end of April 2009. Finally, the total of 60 included two formally Independent senators, Bernie Sanders from Vermont and Joe Lieberman from Connecticut.

with limited enthusiasm, as their preferred policy option of a single-payer plan had been passed over in favour of so-called 'managed competition'. More significantly, many more conservative and centrist Democrats, clustered in an organisation called the Democratic Leadership Council which had embraced Clinton's bid for the presidency, felt that, through the HSA, the president had abandoned his commitment to a new style of Democratic politics and assumed a big government persona.

In fact, by the time Obama took office, mirroring to some extent longer-term shifts on the Republican side, the nature of the Democratic party had changed. As described below, the liberal wing did not prevail in their demand for the single payer plan, but the conservative forces within the congressional party were diminished. Rhodes Cook, a distinguished commentator on US political affairs, stated in February 2009:

> In January 1993, Southern Democrats comprised nearly one-third of the party's number in the House and more than one-quarter in the Senate. Nowadays, the Southern component of the Democratic majority is less than one-quarter in the House and barely 10 per cent in the Senate. The Democrats have made up for their Southern losses by gaining congressional seats in the party's liberal beachheads on the two coasts.[37]

On the other hand, choosing to go ahead with reform in what was a plausibly favourable institutional environment was quite different from achieving it and did not explicitly answer questions about what reform would look like. So, while the congressional numbers were more promising for Obama than they had been for Clinton, there remained significant obstacles and many potential roadblocks to successfully accomplishing reform. Notably, the legislative process remained laden with potential veto points and there were many separate issues, which might in fact be tangential to the main thrust of reform, such as access to abortion,[38] which could trigger any given group of legislators to activate those veto points. One feature that quickly became clear was that, for all the administration's talk of a bipartisan approach, any reform was going to rely on Democratic votes as the possibility of there being any from the Republicans was almost non-existent. There was certainly no group within the party willing to cede that Obama had a mandate and give the new president political leeway in the manner, for instance, in which some congressional Democrats had been willing to compromise to enable President Reagan to pass significant economic reforms in 1981. In addition, through the spring and summer of 2009, the emergence of the Tea Party as an active force in US politics reinforced the

37   Cook, 'Not your father's Democratic Congress'.
38   Connolly, 'How we got there'.

positioning of the congressional GOP as a party institutionally opposed to the Obama agenda.

As it became clear that few if any Republicans would support a reform bill, this meant that the situation in the Senate was especially delicate, with the need to secure all 60 Democratic votes. In this context, while the congressional Democrats were more ideologically coherent in 2009 than they had been 16 years earlier, this did not mean they were united around a particular health reform plan. The liberal wing of the party still championed a single-payer scheme but that was a non-starter for many other Democrats, and there is no evidence that the Obama administration considered this to be a valid policy option.

The differences within Democratic ranks, and the manner in which these differences threatened to invoke a veto point, were well illustrated by the argument over the so-called 'public option'. This might be regarded as single-payer 'lite', as it was a plan to allow the federal government to sell health insurance directly to individuals, in competition with private insurers.[39] In the end, the House version of reform did contain a minimal 'public option' provision but, in the Senate, the objections of some Democrats, and critically of the Independent Joe Lieberman of Connecticut, killed off this notion. President Obama did express support for the principle but proved willing to sacrifice the idea to secure passage of a bill through the Senate.[40]

This episode is highly revealing, as it shows the importance of the pivot points in the legislative process, with so much depending on the actions of a small number of lawmakers. In addition, it illustrates that some Democrats remained greatly uneasy about extending the role of government too far when intervening in the healthcare marketplace.

Yet, reforming the existing healthcare system by building on that system rather than replacing it inevitably meant that reform was going to be extraordinarily complex, requiring an intricate policy design that might prove vulnerable through the implementation process.[41] One rationale for compromising the scope of the reform effort was that the organised interests, such as the health insurers, the Chamber of Commerce and the National Federation of Independent Business, which had so vociferously lobbied against the Clinton plan, had not gone away and were still acutely aware of any perceived threat to their perceived economic interests. As it was, reform advocates were always unlikely to win over those two groups. Yet, the administration thought it important to mute the opposition of doctors' groups and the pharmaceutical

39 Brasfield, 'The politics of ideas: where did the public option come from and where is it going?', pp. 455–9.

40 Personal interview with Democratic congressional staffer by Daniel Béland, Aug. 2010.

41 Béland et al., 'Implementing health reform in the United States: the dilemmas of institutional design', unpublished paper.

industry, and so was willing to cut deals with those interests in a manner that perhaps facilitated the political process, but which left unchallenged fundamental aspects of what might be termed the existing medical-industrial complex.

In the end, the Obama administration and its allies in the Democratic leadership in Congress did manage to negotiate their way past the various constraining factors in order for the president to sign the ACA into law. The legislative endgame, however, proved to be a messy affair after the Democrats lost their (60-seat) filibuster-proof Senate majority in January 2010, when Republican Scott Brown won a special election in Massachusetts to replace Senator Kennedy, who had died the previous summer. By the end of 2009, both chambers of Congress had passed reform legislation but there had been no opportunity to send the bills to conference committee to iron out the differences between them. In fact, it briefly appeared as if the whole process had stalled.[42] A consistent theme of Brown's campaign was that he would provide the 41st vote that would sustain a filibuster-blocking, comprehensive health reform. In the immediate aftermath of the Massachusetts election, Senate Minority Leader Mitch McConnell answered 'I sure hope so' when asked if the healthcare reform effort was now over.[43] Faced with the prospect of yet another failed effort at major health reform, the administration and leading congressional Democrats chose to move ahead by getting the House of Representatives to pass the Senate's version of reform. This was followed by a controversial legislative manoeuvre, with a series of amendments being made to the Senate bill to remove elements that no-one had seriously anticipated would be part of the final legislation. These changes were pushed through Senate via the reconciliation process that prevented the use of the filibuster.[44]

Thus President Obama was able to sign the ACA into law and succeed where predecessors Truman, Nixon and Clinton had failed; but the decision to embrace the Senate bill, albeit with few other viable options, was not without consequence. In particular, compared to the final ACA, the House version of reform had contained some more liberal aspects including 'a (limited) public option, more generous benefits, more extensive national administration, and higher taxes on the privileged'.[45] These elements may not have survived through a conference committee between House and Senate but, as it turned out, it was not even possible to consider inserting them into the final law.

42 This apparent collapse of the reform process was welcomed not just by conservative opponents, as some liberals, unsatisfied with the compromises made through 2009, thought it might be a blessing in disguise. See, for example, Kuttner, *A Presidency in Peril*, p. 233.

43 Stolberg and Herszenhorn, 'Obama weighs paring goals for health bill'.

44 See Jacobs and Skocpol, *Health Care Reform and American Politics*, for details of the debate between administration and congressional leaders that led to this strategy choice.

45 Jacobs and Skocpol, *Reaching for a New Deal*, pp. 72–3.

Nevertheless, the ACA was certainly the most significant public policy reform of the US healthcare system since at least the mid-1960s, and advocates could point to estimates from the CBO that predicted the law would significantly reduce the number of Americans without health insurance, while slowing down healthcare inflation.[46]

A cure?

The underlying objective of the ACA was to resolve the contradiction that the US paid more for its healthcare arrangements, by any conceivable measure, than any other country, yet was the only nation in the industrialised world to leave a significant proportion of its population lacking institutionalised health coverage. One consequence of this contradiction was that the distribution of healthcare was highly unequal. In order to remedy these problems, the ACA built upon elements of existing arrangements, by adding new regulatory frameworks for insurers, employers and individuals, as well as creating some new institutions and attempting to change the incentive structures for some healthcare providers.

One fundamental aspect of the US healthcare system left unchallenged by the ACA was that most Americans should get their health insurance through their employer. In fact, the law introduced changes designed to encourage employers to offer insurance to their employees and hence reverse the decline in employer-provided insurance apparent in the previous few years.[47] As it was enacted, the ACA would impose fines on large firms that did not provide insurance, while smaller businesses would receive subsidies to help them pay for insurance.[48] In order to help households without employer-provided insurance, the ACA proposed both to significantly expand an existing programme and to create a new set of institutions.

First, eligibility for the Medicaid programme was to be extended to everyone with an income below 138 per cent of the poverty line, without regard to their family or household status. In those states with more restrictive pre-ACA eligibility criteria, this move had potentially transformative implications. When the ACA was passed, the CBO estimated that expanding Medicaid in this fashion would provide access to health insurance coverage for an extra 16 million Americans.[49]

Second, the ACA called for the states to establish health insurance exchanges that would be regulated insurance markets offering a choice of private health

46 Congressional Budget Office, 'H.R. 4872, Reconciliation Act of 2010 (Final Health Care Legislation)'.
47 Gottschalk, 'Back to the future?'
48 Simon, 'Implications of health care reform for employers'.
49 Congressional Budget Office, 'H.R. 4872, Reconciliation Act of 2010'.

plans aimed at low-income households.[50] People getting their insurance through these exchanges would be eligible for a subsidy from the federal government, on a sliding scale, with incomes up to 400 per cent of the poverty level. Again, according to CBO estimates, 24 million Americans would be insured through these exchanges by 2019.[51]

Further to these measures, the ACA also placed a series of new regulations on insurance companies. For example, children were to be allowed to remain covered by their parent's insurance up to the age of 26.[52] In addition, insurers could no longer refuse to cover people with pre-existing illnesses, nor could they maintain annual or lifetime caps on insurance plans. Another particularly controversial rule introduced in the ACA was that everyone would have to buy available insurance or face paying a fine.[53] This so-called 'individual mandate' would help collectivise the insurance risk pool by making the young and relatively healthy take out insurance, so providing some compensation to insurers who were no longer allowed to reject high-risk individuals.

As well as reducing the number of Americans without health insurance, the ACA was also designed to slow the growth of health spending in the US. With regard to government spending, the CBO's initial estimate was that the ACA would result in a net saving of $143 billion for the federal budget.[54] That meant that the extra spending incurred would be more than offset by savings and new revenues generated elsewhere. The latter included an increase in the Medicare payroll tax for people earning over $200,000, a new tax on unearned income of over $200,000, and various taxes and fees on medical providers. On the spending side, payments to private insurers in the Medicare Advantage programme were to be reduced, as were the annual updates of Medicare's fees for service payments. The law also created a new body to be called the Independent Payment Advisory Board (IPAB), which will have the power to recommend limits to Medicare spending.

In order to reduce the overall burden of healthcare inflation on the economy, the ACA set out to institutionalise incentive structures for medical providers, such as hospitals and doctors, to encourage greater attention to promoting efficiency and integration. Other measures were aimed at reducing alleged extravagant use of care. For example, the so-called 'Cadillac tax' intended to

---

50 The idea behind the public option was that there would be a government-backed plan competing on these exchanges.

51 Congressional Budget Office, 'H.R. 4872, Reconciliation Act of 2010'.

52 This manoeuvre was introduced very quickly and deemed to be successful. See Langmaid, 'CDC: health reform extends coverage to young Americans'.

53 By 2016, the penalty was $695 or 2.5% of income, whichever was the higher.

54 Congressional Budget Office, 'H.R. 4872, Reconciliation Act of 2010'.

start in 2018 imposed penalties on insurance plans with high premiums.[55] Some of these measures, notably the role of IPAB and the Cadillac tax, were unpopular even among supporters of reform but, according to proponents, the overall package of measures would bring about significant cost savings in the long term.[56]

A train wreck?

While some of the measures described above were implemented quite quickly after the passage of the ACA, many of the more significant aspects were not scheduled to start until 2014. As that date approached, opponents of the original law continued to maintain that 'Obamacare' would prove to be a highly unpopular recipe for the administrative chaos that would unravel during the implementation process and act as a drag on the faltering economic recovery. Importantly, opponents of the law were sometimes in a position to make some of these prophecies self-fulfilling. This was true because the design of the ACA meant that the effective implementation of the law depended on the cooperation of state governments – often not forthcoming in states controlled by Republicans.[57]

The depth of opposition to the ACA among state officials was illustrated by the fact that more than half the state governments across the US joined challenges to the constitutionality of the law in the aftermath of its enactment in early spring 2010. The primary thrust behind the legal challenges was that the individual mandate was unconstitutional. After some contradictory rulings in lower courts, the case was expedited to the Supreme Court. In June 2012, in the case of the *National Federation of Independent Business v. Sebelius*, the Court ruled the mandate as constitutional, provoking an immediate interpretation that the administration had triumphed, if by an unexpected rationale. This was because, in a 5 to 4 majority, Chief Justice Roberts ruled the mandate to be a legitimate form of taxation rather than pointing to the federal government's power to regulate through the Commerce Clause.[58] Thus the mandate survived, but the Court in fact gave more consideration than many had expected to a further challenge to the ACA concerning the Medicaid expansion.[59]

---

55 The premiums at which the Cadillac tax kicked in were as shown at: www.kaiserhealthnews. org/Stories/2010/March/18/Cadillac-Tax-Explainer-Update.aspx (accessed 29 Jan. 2014).

56 Cutler et al., 'The impact of health reform on health system spending'.

57 Béland et al., 'Implementing health reform in the United States'.

58 Mariner et al., 'Reframing federalism – the Affordable Care Act (and Broccoli) in the Supreme Court', pp. 1154–8.

59 Thompson, *Medicaid Politics*; Waddan, 'Health care reform after the Supreme Court', pp. 139–43.

Critically, the Court ruled that the ACA's condition that states engage with the expansion or lose their existing Medicaid funding from federal government constituted unacceptable levels of 'economic dragooning'.[60] Thus, states could now simply continue to operate their Medicaid programmes as they already did, without sanction if they chose not to join in the expansion. And, in the immediate aftermath of the Court's decision, that is exactly what Texas governor Rick Perry declared his state would do, despite the fact that it had the nation's highest rate of uninsurance.[61] Perry remained steadfast in his opposition, proclaiming in summer 2013: 'Texas will not be held hostage by the Obama administration's attempt to force us into this fool's errand of adding more than a million Texans to a broken system'.[62] The fiscal incentives for states to participate in the expansion in fact remain strong, as they would benefit from a considerable influx of federal dollars, but if only Texas, Florida, Georgia and North Carolina remained resolute in their refusal then that would exclude over three million Americans from gaining access to insurance in the way the ACA initially proposed.

Further to the ambivalent attitudes towards Medicaid expansion, about half of state governments also refused to cooperate in the effort to set up health insurance exchanges. Unlike in the case of Medicaid, the ACA did leave scope for the federal government to step in and organise the exchange on a state's behalf, but so many states decided to let the federal authorities coordinate it that they were left thinly resourced, which in turn contributed to the widespread difficulties that occurred when the exchanges opened for business on 1 October 2013. Obama administration officials maintained that the problems people had accessing the online exchanges showed just how much demand there was for affordable insurance, but conservatives retorted that it was another example of the ACA collapsing under its own weight. To support the latter interpretation, critics pointed to other evidence that the law was proving impossible to implement coherently. For example, as early as the summer of 2011, more than 1,400 waivers had been granted, allowing health plans to vary from the minimum standards mandated in the ACA.[63] Then in July 2013 the administration unilaterally delayed the enforcement of the so-called employer mandate by a year to 2015, which amplified conservative calls for a delay in the individual mandate. On the other hand, despite the highly publicised problems that many people encountered when trying to register

60 Supreme Court of the United States, *National Federation of Independent Business et al. v. Sebelius, Secretary of Health and Human Services et al.*, www.supremecourt.gov/opinions/11pdf/11-393c3a2.pdf, p. 51 (accessed 29 Jan. 2014).

61 Fernandez, 'Perry declares Texas' rejection of health care law "intrusions"'.

62 Kennedy, 'Medicaid expansion gap could leave poor shortchanged'.

63 Pear, 'Program offering waivers for health law is ending'.

for insurance via the newly created exchanges in October 2013, by the end of the first period of open enrolment (end of March 2014) the total number of people who had signed up in this way had exceeded the administration's initial projections.

Conclusion

In the fall of 2013, as the roll-out of major aspects of the ACA began, supporters and critics of the law were engaged in furious competition to legitimise their narrative of what was unfolding. According to the former, the teething problems for people trying to access the online health exchanges would be resolved and the ACA would go on to offer affordable care to millions of Americans previously in effect denied access to health insurance. The latter protested that the ACA was doomed to be a failed big government project that would cause major economic collateral damage. Beyond these immediate arguments, however, remained the question of whether the law, even if largely implemented, would meet its own objectives.

Because the law looked to build on rather than replace the existing mix of private and public healthcare provision, its impact will inevitably be constrained by the inefficiencies and inequities inherent in those arrangements. After the enactment of the ACA, some commentators reflected on how the law was a major act of economic redistribution.[64] In one early assessment of the likely implications of the ACA, political scientists Larry Jacobs and Theda Skocpol maintained that the law was 'one of the most important pieces of social legislation since Social Security, Civil Rights, and Medicare. It promised to put the United States on a new path – toward affordable health care for all Americans.'[65] Jacobs also stressed the aggregate re-distributive effects the bill could have in helping low-income households, especially in terms of providing health, and therefore economic, security to millions of poor minority families.[66] But these comments came before the Supreme Court ruling gave state governments, such as those in Texas, Georgia and Florida, the opportunity to manifest their ideological opposition to the law by refusing to participate in the Medicaid expansion, despite their large numbers of poor, uninsured residents.

On the other hand, with the expansion going ahead in other large states that have significant numbers of uninsured people, such as California, then the law will make government-funded healthcare available to millions. In addition, the health exchanges, if fully implemented, promise to offer low-cost insurance cover to many Americans who were previously effectively excluded from the health insurance market. Hence the ACA has the potential to reduce, but far

64   Leonhardt, 'In health bill, Obama attacks wealth inequality'.
65   Jacobs and Skocpol, *Health Care Reform and American Politics*, p. 120.
66   Jacobs, 'America's critical juncture: The Affordable Care Act and its reverberations', pp. 625–31.

from end, some of the inequalities present in the system in place when Obama entered the White House. This is true in part because the ACA is not even designed to bring about genuine universal coverage, as millions of Americans are set to remain without health insurance.

On the other hand, if the measures to reduce the number of Americans living without access to health insurance should have a quantifiable impact, it is less clear how the efforts at cost control will take effect. The decision to accommodate rather than explicitly challenge the interests of healthcare providers may have been politically astute, but it meant that the most direct means of putting downward pressure on costs, which would have involved some form of price control, was passed over.[67]

Overall, it is unwise to attempt to predict the future in the extraordinary world of American healthcare politics and policy. The ACA was certainly the most significant public policy intervention in that world in nearly half a century, but judgment on whether it was a successful intervention is likely to remain highly contested for a considerable period.

References

D. Béland and A. Waddan (2012) 'The Obama presidency and health insurance reform: assessing continuity and change', *Social Policy & Society*, vol. 11, no. 3, pp. 319–30.

D. Béland, P. Rocco and A. Waddan (2014) 'Implementing health reform in the United States: the dilemmas of institutional design', *Health Policy*, www.sciencedirect.com/science/article/pii/S0168851014000232 (accessed 29 April 2014).

P. Belluck and K. Zezima (2006) 'Massachusetts legislation on insurance becomes law', *New York Times*, 13 April, www.nytimes.com/2006/04/13/us/13health.html?pagewanted=print&_r=0 (accessed 30 Jan. 2014).

D. Blumenthal and J. Morone (2009) *The Heart of Power: Health and Politics in the Oval Office* (Berkeley, CA: University of California Press).

J. Brasfield (2011) 'The politics of ideas: where did the public option come from and where is it going?', *Journal of Health Politics, Policy and Law*, vol. 36, no. 3, pp. 455–9.

W.J. Clinton and A. Gore (1992) *Putting People First: A Strategy for Change* (New York, NY: Times Books).

Congressional Budget Office (2010) *The Budget and Economic Outlook: Fiscal Years 2010 to 2020* (Washington, DC: Congress of the United States),

---

67 Gusmano, 'Do we really want to control health care spending?', pp. 495–500.

www.cbo.gov/sites/default/files/cbofiles/ftpdocs/108xx/doc10871/01-26-outlook.pdf (accessed 29 Jan. 2014).

— (2010) 'H.R. 4872, Reconciliation Act of 2010 (Final Health Care Legislation)', 18 March, www.cbo.gov/ftpdocs/113xx/doc11355/hr4872.pdf (accessed 29 Jan. 2014).

C. Connolly (2010) 'How we got there', in *Washington Post* staff, *Landmark: The Inside Story of America's New Health-Care Law and What It Means for Us All* (New York, NY: Public Affairs).

R. Cook (2009) 'Not your father's Democratic Congress', Sabato's Crystal Ball, 19 Feb., www.centerforpolitics.org/crystalball/articles/frc2009021901/ (accessed 30 Jan. 2014).

D. Cutler, K. Davis and K. Stremikis (2010) 'The impact of health reform on health system spending' (The Commonwealth Fund and the Center for American Progress), www.americanprogress.org/issues/2010/05/pdf/system_spending.pdf (accessed 29 Jan. 2014).

S. Devi (2012) 'Getting to the root of America's racial health inequalities', *The Lancet*, vol. 380, issue 9847, 22 Sep., www.thelancet.com/journals/lancet/article/PIIS0140-6736(12)61584-0/fulltext (accessed 30 Jan. 2014).

M. Fernandez (2012) 'Perry declares Texas' rejection of health care law "intrusions"', *New York Times*, 9 July, www.nytimes.com/2012/07/10/us/politics/perry-says-texas-rejects-health-law-intrusions.html (accessed 30 Jan. 2014).

A. Goldstein and D. Balz (2011) 'Governors differ on extent of flexibility for Medicaid', *Washington Post*, 27 Feb., www.washingtonpost.com/wp-dyn/content/article/2011/02/27/AR2011022703688.html?wpisrc=nl_politics (accessed 30 Jan. 2014).

M. Gottschalk (2007) 'Back to the future? Health benefits, organized labor, and universal health care', *Journal of Health Policy, Politics and Law*, vol. 32, pp. 923–70.

M. Gusmano (2011) 'Do we really want to control health care spending?', *Journal of Health Politics, Policy and Law*, vol. 36, no. 3, pp. 495–500.

J. Hacker (1997) *The Road to Nowhere: The Genesis of President Clinton's Plan for Health Security* (Princeton, NJ: Princeton University Press).

J. Hacker and P. Pierson (2010) *Winner-Take-All Politics: How Washington Made the Rich Richer – And Turned Its Back on the Middle Class* (New York, NY: Simon & Schuster).

Institute of Medicine (2002) 'Unequal treatment: confronting racial and ethnic disparities in health care', www.iom.edu/Reports/2002/Unequal-

Treatment-Confronting-Racial-and-Ethnic-Disparities-in-Health-Care. aspx (accessed 29 Jan. 2014).

L. Jacobs and T. Skocpol (2010) *Health Care Reform and American Politics: What Everyone Needs to Know* (New York, NY: Oxford University Press).

L. Jacobs (2011) 'America's critical juncture: The Affordable Care Act and its reverberations', *Journal of Health Politics, Policy and Law*, vol. 36, no. 3, pp. 625–31.

— (2011) 'Hard fought legacy: Obama, congressional Democrats, and the struggle for comprehensive health care reform', in T. Skocpol and L. Jacobs (eds.), *Reaching for a New Deal: Ambitious Governance, Economic Meltdown, and Polarized Politics in Obama's First Two Years* (New York, NY: Russell Sage Foundation).

D. Jaenicke and A. Waddan (2006) 'President Bush and social policy: the strange case of the Medicare prescription drug benefit', *Political Science Quarterly*, vol. 121, no. 2, pp. 217–40.

H. Johnson and D. Broder (1997) *The System: The American Way of Politics at Breaking Point* (Boston, MA: Little, Brown and Company).

K. Kennedy (2013) 'Medicaid expansion gap could leave poor shortchanged', *USA Today*, www.usatoday.com/story/news/politics/2013/09/05/100-percent-medicaid/2749143/ (accessed 30 Jan. 2014).

T. Kertscher (2013) 'In context: Obamacare "train wreck"', 6 Aug., www.politifact.com/wisconsin/article/2013/aug/06/context-obamacare-train-wreck/ (accessed 30 Jan. 2014).

P. Krugman (2008) 'Clinton, Obama, insurance', *New York Times*, 4 Feb., www.nytimes.com/2008/02/04/opinion/04krugman.html?_r=0 (accessed 30 Jan. 2014).

R. Kuttner (2010) *A Presidency in Peril: The Inside Story of Obama's Promise, Wall Street's Power, and the Struggle to Control Our Economic Future* (White River Junction, VT: Chelsea Green Publishing).

T. Langmaid (2011) 'CDC: health reform extends coverage to young Americans', CNN, 14 Dec., http://edition.cnn.com/2011/12/14/health/health-insurance/index.html?hpt=hp_t1 (accessed 30 Jan. 2014).

D. Leonhardt (2010) 'In health bill, Obama attacks wealth inequality', *New York Times*, 23 March, www.nytimes.com/2010/03/24/business/24leonhardt.html (accessed 30 Jan. 2014).

McKinsey Global Institute (2008) *Accounting for the Cost of U.S. Health Care: a new look at why Americans spend more*, www.mckinsey.com/insights/health_systems_and_services/accounting_for_the_cost_of_us_health_care (accessed 30 Jan. 2014).

W. Mariner, L. Glantz and G. Annas (2012) 'Reframing federalism – The Affordable Care Act (and Broccoli) in the Supreme Court', *The New England Journal of Medicine*, 367, pp. 1154–8.

I. Morgan (2013) 'The quest for renewed economic prosperity', in J. Dumbrell (ed.), *Issues in American Politics: Polarized Politics in the Age of Obama* (Abingdon: Routledge).

C. Morris (2006) *Apart at the Seams: The Collapse of Private Pension and Health Care Protection* (New York, NY: The Century Foundation Press).

P. Orszag (2011) 'How health care can save or sink America', *Foreign Affairs*, vol. 90, no. 4, pp. 42–56, www.foreignaffairs.com/articles/67918/peter-r-orszag/how-health-care-can-save-or-sink-america (accessed 30 Jan. 2014).

K. Patel and M. Rushefsky (1999) *Health Care Politics and Policy in America* (Armonk, NY: M.E. Sharpe).

R. Pear (2011) 'Program offering waivers for health law is ending', *New York Times*, 17 June, www.nytimes.com/2011/06/18/health/policy/18health.html (accessed 30 Jan. 2014).

M. Peterson (1998) 'The politics of health care policy: overreaching in an age of polarization', in M. Weir (ed.), *The Social Divide, Political Parties and the Future of Activist Government* (Washington, DC: Brookings Institution Press).

— (2011) 'It was a different time: Obama and the unique opportunity for health care reform', *Journal of Health Politics, Policy and Law*, vol. 36, no. 3, pp. 429–36.

K. Simon (2010) 'Implications of health care reform for employers: an analysis of the Patient Protection and Affordable Care Act' (Washington, DC: Center for American Progress), www.americanprogress.org/issues/2010/05/pdf/health_employers.pdf (accessed 29 Jan. 2014).

T. Skocpol (1996) *Boomerang: Health Care Reform and the Turn Against Government* (New York, NY: W.W. Norton and Company).

S.G. Stolberg and D. Herszenhorn (2010) 'Obama weighs paring goals for health bill', *New York Times*, 20 Jan., www.nytimes.com/2010/01/21/health/policy/21health.html (accessed 30 Jan. 2014).

S.G Stolberg and R. Pear (2010) 'Obama signs health care overhaul bill, with a flourish', *New York Times*, 23 March, www.nytimes.com/2010/03/24/health/policy/24health.html?gwh=6C5FC44F64D39C9CCFA6B553BF DF6617&gwt=pay (accessed 30 Jan. 2014).

F. Thompson (2012) *Medicaid Politics: Federalism, Policy Durability, and Health Reform* (Washington, DC: Georgetown University Press).

D. Thorne and E. Warren (2008) 'Get sick, go broke', in J. Hacker (ed.), *Health at Risk: America's Ailing Health System and How to Heal It* (New York, NY: Columbia University Press).

United States Census Bureau (n.d.) *Statistical Abstract of the United States, 1995–2000*, 116th edn. (Washington, DC: U.S. Census Bureau), www.census.gov/prod/www/statistical_abstract.html (accessed 29 Jan. 2014).

— (2012) Health Insurance Historical Tables, Table HIB-1, 'Health insurance coverage status and type of coverage by sex, race and Hispanic origin: 1999 to 2011', https://www.census.gov/hhes/www/hlthins/data/historical/HIB_tables.html (accessed 29 Jan. 2014).

— (2012) Health Insurance Historical Tables, Table HIB-4, 'Health insurance coverage status and type of coverage by state – all persons: 1999 to 2012', https://www.census.gov/hhes/www/hlthins/data/historical/HIB_tables.html (accessed 29 Jan. 2014).

A. Waddan (2013) 'Health care reform after the Supreme Court: even more known unknowns', *Social Policy & Society*, vol. 8, no. 1, pp. 139–43.

6. The politics of food: sense and sustainability

Clodagh Harrington

The challenges facing the Obama presidency have been so numerous and relentless, and some so intense, that a propensity for the administration to focus on high-profile issues such as foreign policy and the economic crisis, soon became the norm. With attention turned to headline-grabbing developments, other more insidious problems were easily overlooked. The early 21st-century crisis in the American food chain did not start, and will not end, with the Obama administration. The impact of this crisis has been multifaceted, with a specific and urgent aspect related to the wellbeing of individuals.

The dietary health of a majority of citizens in contemporary America is deteriorating, starkly demonstrated by the highest (male) obesity rate in the world.[1] An additional and associated problem stemmed from the fact that in 2013, 15 per cent of the population was unable to feed itself without government assistance in the form of food stamps. In contrast, those on the more comfortable end of the nation's socioeconomic spectrum remained largely immune from such ills as the pursuit of high-quality, locally-sourced produce became little short of a fetish for many well-heeled Americans. Meanwhile, the dietary problems and disease burden of the poor continued to grow, even as the Obama administration tried to get a grip on the issues involved in the need to promote a healthier America.

A starting point for any public policy challenge is Deborah Stone's basic question: is there a problem in the first place?[2] Even the term 'problem' is value-laden and open to vastly differing interpretations and solutions. All politics involves a range of perspectives and perceptions, and locating anything resembling a universal truth or collective agreement on action, is little short of mythical. Policymaking inevitably involves a struggle between and amongst institutions, interests and individuals and the realm of food politics and policy is no exception.

Few would deny that serious problems existed concerning the nutritional status of poorer Americans, particularly as poverty and inequality were

---

1 *Organisation for Economic Cooperation and Development Factbook 2013.*
2 Stone, *Policy Paradox: The Art of Political Decision Making.*

exacerbated in the post-2008 era. In 2013 one in six Americans received governmental food assistance and one in three adults were classed as obese.[3] At Michelle Obama's 'Let's Move' campaign launch in 2010, the first lady did not mince her words, declaring that 'the physical and emotional health of an entire generation and the economic health and security of our nation is at stake.'[4] The initiative came at a time when the US Centers for Disease Control (CDC) classed 18 per cent of American children aged 6–18 as obese. Clearly this was problematic, and not just for the individuals involved. Hence, if the answer to Stone's preliminary question was a resounding 'Yes', then progress could be made towards solving the potentially unifying conundrum of 'what is to be done?' Firstly however, a more immediate and complex question arose: 'Whose problem is it?'

Responses ranged from apportioning blame on the individual, since they ought to take responsibility for their own food choices, to lambasting the government for not taxing unhealthy foodstuffs sufficiently and forcing the overweight public to step up to the (healthy) plate. Both extremes were clearly unrealistic, and in addition, the influential role of the industrial food complex has to be considered. It is the purpose of this chapter to outline what the problem is, why it matters and to what extent it is relevant to consider whether government may have a hand in fixing it. The Obama administration has at least opened a dialogue on the topic, albeit an increasingly fractious and partisan one, as the controversy involved in efforts to pass the 2012 Farm Bill clearly illustrated.[5]

Food stamps

When Barack Obama won the 2008 presidential election, there were 28.2 million Americans receiving food stamps. By the time he secured his second term, 47.8 million were Supplemental Nutritional Assistance Program (SNAP) recipients. During this period, spending on the programme rose from $36.4 billion to $74.6 billion. Throughout the 2012 election campaign, presidential candidate Newt Gingrich repeatedly gave Barack Obama the pejorative label, 'the food stamp president'.[6] However, the rise in the availability of food stamps was not necessarily due to the president's unqualified desire for increased government expenditure. It may have been more to do with the direct

---

3   Global Research, 'Poverty in the USA: nearly 50 million Americans on food stamps'; Centers for Disease Control, 'Obesity is common, serious and costly' and 'Prevalence of obesity in the United States, 2009–2010'.

4   Let's Move launch, 9 Feb. 2010, www.letsmove.gov/learn-facts/epidemic-childhood-obesity (accessed 4 Feb. 2014).

5   Rogers, 'Farm Bill talks intensify'.

6   *Washington Post*, 'Gingrich says Obama is the "food stamps president". Is he?'

correlation between the poverty rate and the number of individuals requiring food stamps. The 2012 election campaign focused heavily on the nation's struggling middle classes, with little mention of 47 million Americans living in poverty. Candidates Mitt Romney and Barack Obama criticised each other's approach to those on the lower end of the socioeconomic scale – the former framed as uncaring and disconnected, and the incumbent vilified for handing out food stamps like confetti.

Although poorer citizens requiring extra government assistance at a time of crisis had strong historical precedent, the scale and cost of the food stamp programme had reached epic levels by Obama's second term. The issue went far deeper than the need for a temporary handout. When the first Food Stamps Programme was introduced in 1939, hunger, health and nutrition were key policy challenges for the Roosevelt administration. At its height in the early 1940s, 20 million Americans were recipients of a programme costing $262 million. In 1964, President Johnson introduced the Food Stamps Act and advocated establishing a permanent programme. By the 1970s, one in 50 Americans was receiving food stamps. In 2012, the figure was one in seven. This was a staggering increase, and one that was not fully explained by the 2008 financial collapse as half of all recipients in 2012 had been on the programme for eight years or more.[7]

In 2013, 15 per cent of the US public received food stamps, with the highest uptake rate in Mississippi (22 per cent) and Washington, DC (23 per cent). Usage had increased since the previous year, despite the apparent economic improvement. This raises the question of why there was such a heavy reliance on subsidised food? Perhaps it was because 47 million Americans were in such dire financial circumstances that they could not put food on the table, or maybe it was a result of the administration relaxing the requirements for social welfare programmes as part of its 2009 economic stimulus legislation. Or, conceivably the latter was a response to the former. In any case, the welfare relaxing was a state, rather than a federal initiative.[8]

The US Department of Agriculture's Undersecretary for Food, Nutrition and Consumer Services Kevin Concannon explained that SNAP was designed to extend benefits as poverty levels increase and would contract once the economy showed signs of improvement. Eligibility for SNAP was loosened in the light of the 2008 financial crisis, and for the first time, those entitled could have savings or a low-wage job. For supporters, this appeared a logical response to the severity of the post-2008 situation. The government explained that expanding eligibility would mean that, for example, those searching for work could afford

7   United States Department of Agriculture (USDA), Food and Nutrition Service, 'A short history of SNAP' (n.d.), www.fns.usda.gov/snap/short-history-snap (accessed 4 Feb. 2014); Hoffman, 'Who receives food stamps and why is it critical to continue their support?'

8   Ganong and Liebman, 'Explaining trends in SNAP enrolment'.

to put gas in their car and pay their phone bill – two essential components of jobhunting. For detractors in Washington and elsewhere, it demonstrated the government's determination to reinforce a negative situation and expand welfare dependency. Philosophically, Republicans were not comfortable with the idea of food stamps, perceiving them to be counter to that cornerstone of American civic culture, self-reliance. House Budget Committee Chairman, Republican Paul Ryan suggested that SNAP become a block-grant programme allowing individual states to control spending, and in all likelihood impose cuts to a system that many believed urgently needed scaling back, having gone far beyond its original remit.[9] When President Clinton signed the Personal Responsibility and Work Opportunity Act in 1996, it stipulated that there would be a finite period during which an able-bodied American could be eligible for food assistance. This seemed a reasonable condition. So who were these people who required such long-term help? In a nation where two-thirds of adults were considered to be overweight (and one-third obese) what was the relationship between obesity, nutrition and poverty?

Food insecurity

A 2010 US Department of Agriculture (USDA) report stated that almost 50 million Americans (17 per cent) lived in homes that were 'food insecure'.[10] This term was used to describe a household that sometimes runs out of food, or out of money to buy food, defined as 'limited or uncertain availability of nutritionally adequate and safe foods or limited or uncertain ability to acquire acceptable foods in socially acceptable ways'.[11] Food insecurity was found to be especially high in single-parent households, metropolitan areas and southern states. Unsurprisingly, the biggest surge in food insecurity since measures began in 1995 was over the period 2007–08 when the economic downturn took hold. The USDA estimated that approximately 6 per cent of US households have 'very low food security', that is, 'At times during the year, eating patterns of one or more household members were disrupted and food intake reduced because the household lacked money and other resources for food'.[12]

In addition, the study found that women and children who were recipients of food stamps were the most likely to be obese. Food campaigner Michael Pollan argued that what a person eats for dinner in the early 21st century has become the definitive marker of social status. The 'food movement' has gained momentum as increasing numbers of Americans recognise the significance of the food chain crisis, with its negative impact at a range of levels. Some

9   Paletta and Porter, 'Use of food stamps swells, even as economy improves'.
10   Coleman-Jensen et al, 'Household food security in the United States in 2011'.
11   Andersen (ed.), 'Core indicators of nutritional state for difficult to sample populations'.
12   Coleman-Jensen et al., 'Household food security in the United States in 2011'.

impressive progress has been made to raise awareness and promote locally sourced fresh food, but the challenges to the public and government remain enormous. The freshest, organic food is still a luxury that few can afford. For everyone else, the crucial fact remains that the healthy option is far from the easiest choice and brings with it a raft of health and policy challenges. A study by Drewnowski and Specter, carried out in 2004, demonstrated how food selections related directly to social class – the most nutritious diet was beyond the means of poorer Americans – and provide the example that the cost of nutritious foods, such as asparagus, had risen by between 25 and 29 per cent while the cost of cheap foods, such as white sugar, had risen by only 16 per cent in the same period.[13] A further example, using 2013 prices, compares a one-dollar cheeseburger with a one-dollar portion of broccoli (75 grams) – the former provides 390 calories and the latter 100. This did not result from a common-or-garden green vegetable being astronomically more expensive to cultivate than the contents of a cheeseburger. The answer lies more in the priorities of government subsidies, as a 2011 study by the US Public Interest Research Group (PIRG) entitled 'Apples to Twinkies' highlights. It concludes that had the government given taxpayers the subsidies instead of the farmers, each one would have been given $7.36 to spend on junk food and just 11 cents to spend on apples per year.[14] Hence, food has become the measure of social class, as the affluent public desires high-quality items, created with care by experts. In other words, a system described by Michael Pollan as one 'where wealthy farmers feed the poor crap and poor farmers feed the wealthy high quality food.'[15]

SNAP eligibility and criteria

The SNAP information website outlines the eligibility criteria for its food programme. In 2013, participants were required to be at or below 130 per cent of the federal poverty line. Half of SNAP recipients were under 18 with two-thirds of them living in single-parent households. Three-quarters of SNAP benefits went to houses with children. In terms of ethnic makeup, 43 per cent of SNAP participants were white, 33 per cent African American, 19 per cent Hispanic, 2 per cent Asian and 2 per cent Asian American.[16]

Retailers associated with SNAP were required to meet basic eligibility requirements, such as selling foods that fell into the four major food groups.

13 Drewnowski and Specter, 'Poverty and obesity: the role of energy density and energy costs'.
14 Public Interest Research Group, 'Apples to Twinkies: comparing taxpayer subsidies for fresh produce and junk food'.
15 See www.michaelpollan.com.
16 USDA Food and Nutrition Service, Program Data, SNAP 2013, www.fns.usda.gov/pd/snapmain.htm (accessed 4 Feb. 2014).

This included regular sales of meat, poultry, fish, bread, cereal, dairy, fruit and vegetables. Alternatively, more than half of the dollar amount of all retail sales had to come from the sale of staples. Critics claimed that SNAP did not do enough to encourage users to make healthy food choices and in fact could even be blamed for promoting less healthy options since cheaper foods were more readily available and heavily advertised.

Efforts to encourage healthier SNAP choices have been criticised as condescending and unworkable. The Obama administration was not the first to be faced with managing this delicate public health and political balance but the volume of users and the vastly increased levels of obesity meant that the stakes were raised daily. The USDA's position was that the consumption behaviour of SNAP users did not differ greatly from that of non-SNAP users, although the department did not have any significant data to confirm this. In 2013, the NPD market research group conducted a Food and Beverage Consumption Survey which found that between 2007 and 2010, SNAP pumped over $70 billion into the retail grocery sector.[17] The reasons for this included more Americans participating in the programme due to their reduced financial circumstances. The programme ensured that struggling citizens had access to food while simultaneously guaranteeing that consumers continued to purchase groceries.

Efforts to marry food stamps with consumer nutritional awareness date back to 1990 when the Food Stamp Act was amended to include optional nutritional educational programmes to be combined with food stamp distribution. This was the first such education programme and in 2008 the name was changed to SNAP as a means of highlighting the nutritional focus. The initial SNAP educational programmes (SNAP-Ed) were rolled out in 1992 over seven states at a cost of $661,000 to the federal government. They remained optional, but states were strongly encouraged to partake. Considering the levels of diet-related illness among Americans at the lower end of the socioeconomic scale, making the educational programme obligatory for states to participate in seems like a logical progression. However, the reality demonstrated that a top-down approach to managing a problem could itself be fraught with difficulty. People did not appreciate the government telling them how to shop or what to consume.

The plan was made attractive to states. Those who were interested were required to submit an outline programme of educational activities along with a corresponding budget. The federal government would reimburse half of the cost of approved plans. States would also receive guidance from the Federal Nutrition Service on how to structure their programme. Since the number of SNAP recipients had increased dramatically from 2008, more states signed

17   Coleman-Jensen et al., 'Household food security in the United States in 2011'.

up for the educational aspect of the programme and in conjunction with the federal and state input, numerous organisations including community health agencies, universities and state health departments also participated.[18] The government made further efforts to ensure maximum nutritional benefit for SNAP recipients. Vouchers could not be used for alcohol, tobacco, medicine, hot or in-store food purchases. The Thrifty Food Plan outlined 15 types of consumer food baskets, tailored to different age and gender requirements and was defined by the USDA as 'a national standard for a nutritious diet at a minimal cost'.[19] The plan received much criticism, however, and over time the USDA's Low Cost Food Plan was considered a far more appropriate use of the allocated foods.[20] Nonetheless, all government efforts to promote healthier choices were Sisyphean in the face of the dominant fast food culture. Some of the nation's favourites included the high-fat, high-salt 800-calorie Tender Sandwich sold by Burger King. Such organisations invariably had their own Political Action Committees (PACs) as well as being part of larger food and beverage industry lobbying groups. Sector expenditure averaged $14 million per year to secure the attention of government and this helped to ensure that the politics of food remained divisive.[21]

The Farmer in Chief

Usually, food politics tends not to feature particularly high on the presidential agenda, despite occasions when it has been a major issue, for example when prices skyrocketed during the Nixon administration. Nonetheless, the president is the Farmer in Chief, and the Farm Bill, renewed regularly since its inception in 1933, has always been the subject of intense debate. The problem is not that there is a food shortage in the US, but that there is limited access to affordable nutritious food which disproportionately affects poorer Americans. The rather misleadingly titled Farm Bill is the primary food policy and agricultural tool of the government, dealing with 'food, feed, fuel and fiber'.[22] Subsidies are set for a five-year period, and criteria are heavily influenced by agrarian states. The bills, particularly the subsidy programmes, can be highly contentious, and the iron triangle of the food-industrial complex has vast influence over

18 USDA, 'A short history of SNAP', www.fns.usda.gov/snap/short-history-snap (accessed 4 Feb. 2014).

19 USDA Center for Nutrition Policy and Promotion, 18 Dec., www.cnpp.usda.gov/ USDAFoodPlansCostofFood.htm (accessed 4 Feb. 2014).

20 Hartline-Grafton and Weill, Food Research and Action Center, 'Replacing the thrifty food plan'.

21 Simon, 'Follow the money: are corporations profiting from hungry Americans?'

22 See Washington Sustainable Food and Farming Network, 'Federal Farm Bill re-authorization process and opportunities' (n.d.), http://wsffn.org/our-work/federal-farm-bill-re-authorization (accessed 4 Feb. 2014).

outcomes. Controversially, the food stamp programme is included in the Farm Bill, making up 80 per cent of the cost. Urban lawmakers are drawn into the bill process because the majority of food stamp recipients are city dwellers. Enormous pressure is brought to reduce the cost of the bill and in particular to reduce SNAP benefits or remove them from the bill altogether. The matter was especially contentious for Republicans prior to the 2012 elections, as many within the party argued for up to $30 billion-worth of cuts. Clearly, the issue was a sensitive one as SNAP recipient numbers were not announced in the election month to avoid a backlash against the administration.

Figures from USDA showed that monthly SNAP allowance averaged $133 per person, or $4.43 per day, through the first Obama term. Non-profit organisations like Feeding America argued that drastic reductions in SNAP allowances would force already-struggling Americans to purchase the cheapest, most calorie-dense, low-nutrition foods, thus contributing to obesity and malnourishment.[23] The Drewnowski study found that poorer shoppers decide which foods to buy based on palatability and cost, rather than nutritional considerations. It noted that $1 spent in a Seattle supermarket purchased 1,200 cookie calories as opposed to 250 carrot calories.[24] Recipients of SNAP were not in a position to make the healthiest choice in such circumstances. It is not impossible to prepare relatively nutritious meals on a SNAP budget with meticulous planning and culinary resourcefulness. For example, Mark Bittman in the *New York Times* argued accurately, that home-prepared meals using ingredients such as rice and beans could be cheaper than using processed foodstuffs.[25] In 2013, a 20-pound bag of rice at Walmart cost under $10, and an eight-pound bag of pinto beans cost $8.50.[26] This amount of food goes a long way, but such conclusions assume that poorer Americans have the time, ability, desire and skill to create something tasty with such basics.

In 2007 and 2008, New York City councilman Eric Gioia tried to live on a SNAP budget for a week. The first time, his $28 budget covered the staples, feeding him for five of the seven days, with some 'treats' such as fruit and vegetables. One year later, some food prices had risen by 25 per cent which precluded Gioia from including many of the healthier, and still basic, items. This time, his budget fed him for four days of the planned seven.[27] His experiment thus demonstrated that, even with desire and knowledge, making

---

23 See 'SNAP participation and costs', 6 Dec. 2013, www.fns.usda.gov/pd/snapsummary.htm (accessed 4 Feb. 2014); Feeding America, 'SNAP: facts, myths and realities' (n.d.), http://feedingamerica.org/how-we-fight-hunger/programs-and-services/public-assistance-programs/supplemental-nutrition-assistance-program/snap-myths-realities.aspx (accessed 4 Feb. 2014).

24 Drewnowski and Specter, 'Poverty and obesity'.

25 Bittman, 'Is junk food really cheaper?'

26 See www.walmart.com/.

27 Chin Jou, 'Cutting food stamps will cost everyone'.

the SNAP budget a healthy one was a serious challenge. William Simon, chief executive of Walmart's US operations, told a Goldman Sachs conference in 2010 that SNAP recipients descended on supermarket floors at midnight on the first of every month.[28] This suggests a certain level of desperation among those who struggled to make a month's food budget purchase a month's-worth of food.

In 2013 the struggling town of Woonsocket, Rhode Island, received mainstream media attention when it became the exemplar of the typical effects of the food stamp cycle on an average town. On the first of every month, there was a shopping frenzy, followed by weeks of low purchasing levels. One corner-shop owner, whose modest establishment usually sold eggs, milk and a few other staples, prepared monthly banners in time for the crucial date on which 3,000 pounds of stock would be delivered and sold within a 24-hour period. On the first of each month, the town, like many others, experienced its monthly windfall. In this case, it was $2 million-worth of SNAP expenditure. Once the SNAP money was injected into the economy via the grocery stores, it then flowed out into the wider community – to food companies, banks and employees. What started out in 2008 as a temporary measure to assist those in dire financial need became over time a lifeline for the town's economy. Of Woonsocket's 13,752 citizens, one third were SNAP recipients in 2013 and unemployment was at 12 per cent. This is not unrepresentative of the wider picture.

Despite supposedly being three years into the economic recovery in 2013, SNAP recipience in Woonsocket had risen steadily for the previous six years. Three-quarters of the purchases at the International Meat Market food store were paid for with welfare payment cards, and the store took on an extra three part-time employees to deal with the extra custom. Some states including Maryland, Washington, DC and Virginia started to roll out the SNAP allowance over a longer period – up to ten days in some cases. Elsewhere, such as Rhode Island, the monthly boom-and-bust cycle was the norm.[29]

Nutrition researchers at Cornell University found that such binge purchasing and resultant eating can lead to long-term negative eating patterns, even when the food-insecure period has ended. Overeating, overpurchasing and comfort or binge eating all result from an uneven food supply and such practices are directly linked to obesity. The study also found that women, in particular, who lived in food-insecure households, were more likely to be obese than their food-secure counterparts. Disparity in obesity across income levels was also noticeable. For example, according to the CDC in 2010, 39.2 per cent of white women, at or below 130 per cent of the poverty line, were obese. This

28 Ibid.
29 Saslow, 'Food stamps put Rhode Island town on monthly boom-and-bust cycle'.

was in comparison to 27.5 per cent of white women at or above 350 per cent of the poverty level. Slashing of SNAP benefits would further affect low-income women, whose likelihood of obesity then becomes even higher.[30]

In June 2013, the Senate approved a $995 billion ten-year Farm Bill with sweeping cuts of $24 billion, including $4.1 billion-worth of SNAP reduction.[31] The same month, the 629-page Farm Bill was defeated in the House of Representatives, due to Democrats being unwilling to support massive cuts in the food stamps programme. Agreement on the issue remained elusive in the House for the remainder of the year as Democrats and Republicans argued over the thorny issue of food stamp reduction. The failure to progress was a particular blow to Oklahoma Republican Frank D. Lucas, the chairman of the House Agricultural Committee. The Obama administration was unhappy with the House Bill as it contained severe cuts to the SNAP programme and did not significantly overhaul controversial farm insurance programmes and a range of farm subsidies. The House Bill proposed $40 billion of cuts over a ten-year period, and Massachusetts Democrat Jim McGovern led his party's opposition to the bill, stating that 'the price of a farm bill should not be making more people hungry in America'.[32]

The House Bill demonstrated the extent to which some Republicans would go in order to deal with SNAP fraud. Amendments included drug-testing for recipients and plans to create a 'food-stamp registry'. The White House threatened to veto the House Bill due to the severity of the SNAP reduction plans. The Farm Bill affects, among many other things, food prices, SNAP benefits and school lunches. Chris Edwards, economist at the libertarian Cato Institute called the Farm Bill 'a bi-partisan pork barrel spending spree', while Dottie Rosenbaum, senior policy analyst at the Center on Budget and Policy Priorities, argued that much of the SNAP expenditure criticism was overblown. The growth of SNAP, she said, 'is about addressing the needs of people in a bad economy.'[33] In this atmosphere of partisan gridlock, and overshadowed by a government shutdown, the 2008 Farm Bill expired for the second time in 2013, as lawmakers were unable to reach an agreement on SNAP funding.

Farm policy in the US has been linked with the obesity epidemic, on the rationale that agricultural policy has evolved from paying farmers not to grow food to paying farmers to grow as much as possible. Disproportionate subsidies are offered for soybean and corn, the two main sources of fats and calories in

30 Olson and Lent, 'Food insecurity in rural New York State'; Chin Jou, 'Cutting food stamps will cost everyone'.

31 *New York Times*, 'US Farm Bill: chronology of coverage'.

32 Nixon, 'House rejects Farm Bill as food stamps cuts prove divisive'.

33 Neuman, 'Why the Farm Bill's provisions will matter to you'.

the American diet.[34] Food became increasingly available, prices went down, portions went up (to currently two to five times what they used to be) and at no point has the government told the public to eat less, as this would displease the hugely influential food lobby. The contemporary battle between public health and the corporate agenda remains one-sided, as agribusiness and the food and beverage industry combined spend in the region of $84 million annually on lobbying government.[35]

Industry and interest groups

Efforts to challenge such well-funded interests, even by such heavyweights as New York Mayor Bloomberg, have failed. For example, New York City attempted to impose a two-year ban on food stamp recipients spending their allowance on sugary beverages. This intensely displeased the food lobby who spent $10 million lobbying against the move. Many viewed the plan as paternalistic and, perhaps surprisingly, even those promoting better consumption habits among poorer Americans were reticent about its merits. Some community organisers opposed the soda ban proposal in the context of the government's food and farm subsidies, and the unhealthy cheap food that remains for sale in supermarkets in abundance. One volunteer highlighted the hypocrisy, stating that 'you can't force junk on people and then criticise it at the same time'.[36] A Columbia University study of 19,000 Americans found that on any given day, 68 per cent of food stamp recipients would consume a sugary beverage, compared to 54 per cent of non-food stamp users. A range of research has continuously shown that the consumption of sugary beverages is directly linked to obesity. In 2012, the Brookings Institute reported that two-thirds of Americans were overweight, 35.7 per cent of whom were obese. The figures varied significantly among individual ethnic groups, with 49.5 per cent of African Americans classed as obese. Calorific intake in the US has increased dramatically in the decades since the 1970s with sweetened beverages and high carbohydrate foods the main contributor to this.[37] So, considering how difficult it is for the government to encourage citizens to change their habits for the better, what effort did the Obama administration make to encourage progress?

---

34 Franck et al., 'Agricultural subsidies and the American obesity epidemic'.

35 See www.opensecrets.org.

36 Miller, 'What food says about class in America'.

37 Hammond and Levine, 'The economic impact of obesity in the United States'; Wright et al., 'Trends in intake of energy and macronutrients – United States: 1971–2000', pp. 80–2.

Let's Move

In 21st-century America, obesity rather than hunger was the nation's chief nutritional concern. Since 2008, a paradigm shift occurred with respect to dealing with the problem. Traditionally, the focus was on the individual. 'Eat less, move more' seemed a reasonable mantra until there was a growing realisation, from the White House to the doctor's surgery, that this was an inadequate and clearly unworkable strategy. The focus needed to include every aspect of government policy from public health to education, involving schools, churches, businesses and food and beverage establishments, in addition to households and individuals.

Enter Michelle Obama. In February 2009, the first lady's 'Let's Move' initiative was launched, with the aim of eliminating childhood obesity in a generation. This was an ambitious goal to achieve, even within an extended timeframe. Michelle Obama has been an excellent role model for a healthier America, personally spearheading a campaign which, thanks to her involvement, eight out of ten Americans had heard of.[38] Presenting herself (as far as a first lady can) as credibly down-to-earth, she drew on her own experience as a busy 'working mom' on the south side of Chicago, who allowed her kids to watch too much television and eat unhealthy food. However unlikely this tale was, considering her own high-end socioeconomic status, it gave her political capital to spend. Her 1,100-foot organic vegetable garden at the White House received widespread and supportive media coverage, and the campaign message was clear. Children born in 2010 and beyond would enter a very different food and play environment when they started kindergarten aged five than their older siblings had done. Obama's four-point plan was a positive one. The cornerstones of Let's Move were: making parents more informed with regard to the benefits of nutrition and exercise; improving the quality of food in schools; making healthy food more affordable and accessible for families; and increasing the focus on physical education.[39]

So far, so good. In addition, the first lady recognised the role of the federal government in the programme, but also acknowledged the challenges that accompany the government telling people what to do. In particular, a 'very liberal' president Obama or his wife telling the public what to eat would stick in many throats. Therefore, for Let's Move to have real meaning, a multifaceted public health approach would be required, needing substantial funding and the will of government and business. To demonstrate federal support for the initiative, the president signed a memorandum in February 2010 which created the first-ever task force to provide optimal coordination

38 Thompson, 'Michelle Obama keeps moving with "Let's Move"'.
39 See www.letsmove.org.

between businesses, not-for-profits, government agencies and other relevant organisations to focus collectively on the issue of childhood obesity. Billing it as one of her 'top priorities', Michelle Obama lobbied for the re-introduction of the Child Nutrition Act, originally signed by President Johnson in 1966 at a time when there were many underweight children due to poor nutrition. In the 21st century, undernourishment and obesity are, counterintuitively, two sides of the same healthcare coin. The 2010 $4.5 billion Healthy Hunger-Free Kids Act provided funding for subsidising free school meals and required schools to adhere to health guidelines as outlined by the USDA.[40] This was considered a major step forward, as school was where many children obtained most of their calories.

Michelle Obama's campaign involved working with the major food manufacturers, the US Food and Drug Administration and retailers to move towards ensuring that foodstuffs had clear nutritional labelling on the packaging. In addition, she acknowledged that a 'tailored approach' for the needs of a range of communities was necessary and vowed to work with local mayors and governors to facilitate this. The American Association of Pediatrics also agreed to partner with the government in order to educate the paediatricians involved to work constructively with families and individuals to tackle the problem.

Industry changes

No statistical analysis of childhood obesity reduction was available in early 2014, but other progress could be measured. The legislation was a great leap forward. The private sector also took some steps as a result of Let's Move, including WalMart's 2011 Nutrition Charter, which vowed to include healthier choices in its stores, lower the cost of more nutritious food and label their products more clearly. Other pledges, such as lowering the salt content of its processed food by 25 per cent, were significant. Sodexo and other food giants also agreed to meet recommended requirements for the use of salt, sugar and wholegrain ingredients in their products.[41] The campaign also worked with the California Fresh Works Fund – a public private partnership promoting the creation of retail outlets selling more wholesome food in areas categorised as 'food deserts'. By 2012, over $200 million had been spent on facilitating the provision of healthier grocery outlets to Californians who did not previously have this option.[42] Walmart also committed to opening more stores in areas considered 'food deserts'.

40 White House press statement, 13 Dec. 2010, www.whitehouse.gov/the-press-office/2010/12/13/president-obama-signs-healthy-hunger-free-kids-act-2010-law (accessed 4 Feb. 2014); CNN report, 'Obama signs child nutrition Bill'.

41 Emanuel, 'Let's Move she said – and we have'; also see http://corporate.walmart.com/global-responsibility/hunger-nutrition/healthier-food (accessed 4 Feb. 2014).

42 California Fresh Works Fund, www.cafresh.com (accessed 4 Feb. 2014).

Criticism of Let's Move

Such developments were not met with universal support. The campaign's partnership in particular caused suspicion and derision. For many, Walmart and its wares were part of the problem, so cosying up in such a way undermined, even contaminated, the Let's Move message. This was not unreasonable. Walmart's priority of good publicity and more outlets may have aligned with its corporate social responsibility agenda. However, when Walmart comes to town, local businesses tend to go under. Plus, labour unions did not like the corporate behemoth as its two million employees worldwide had little or no union representation. Critics said the first lady was duped by the corporation. When Let's Move celebrated its third birthday at WalMart in Springfield, Missouri, the store's press release was telling: 'Mrs. Obama will deliver remarks about how supporting the health of American families is also good for business, and remind consumers that it's up to them to continue demanding healthier options.'[43] Clearly, the onus was placed neatly back on the consumer. It is reasonable to assume that those who are nutritionally savvy and know what foods are good for them are the least likely to be shopping at Walmart. However distasteful the partnership between Obama and the corporate giant was, the fact remained that 100 million people shop at Walmart every week in any one of the 3,400 US branches. Hence, it is a force to be reckoned with, and Let's Move recognises this. In addition, the first lady's role is a delicate one. She cannot be perceived to be overtly political.

The campaign received other criticism. *New York Times* columnist Charles Blow argued that anything with the Obama name attached to it would receive a negative response from some quarters.[44] The response from conservatives was, predictably, that Washington should not try to control what people eat. They claimed it smacked of Ronald Reagan's 'nine most terrifying words in the English language', also known as 'I'm from the government and I'm here to help.' As with cigarette smoking, they argued, the choice should be left to the individual. This argument dated back further than the Obama campaign, but the issue remained constant. In 2004 the Center for Consumer Freedom (CCF), set up with funding from the Philip Morris Foundation to confront the restaurant smoking ban, said that the CDC had exaggerated the scale of the obesity epidemic by linking 400,000 deaths to being severely overweight. As a result of interest group pressure, the CDC then revised its claim down to 112,000.[45] The issue was seen as a clear victory for the CCF.

---

43 Nestle, 'Let's Move celebrates its 3rd birthday – at Walmarts'.
44 Blow, 'The biggest losers'.
45 Mayer and Joyce, 'The escalating obesity wars: non-profit's tactics, funding sparks controversy'.

This, and other lobbying by the food and beverage industry, has been highly effective. The Grocery Manufacturers Association (GMA), for example, representing Kraft, Pepsi and other major players in the food and beverage industry with annual sales north of $680 billion, can fight its members' corner and allow specific corporations that wish to avoid their brand being tarnished to oppose limits on advertising junk foods to children. The group is on record as opposing virtually every state bill to restrict the sale of junk food and sodas in schools. It writes letters and sends lobbyists to every state capital to defeat or weaken legislation and has huge lobbying resources and capacity for significant campaign donations.[46] The cost of allowing vested interests to shout loudest in this debate, continues to rise. The individual, society and government all pay a high price.

The costs of obesity

These costs are calculated as direct and indirect. For the most part, the former are medical. Conditions associated with obesity include hypertension, type-2 diabetes, high cholesterol, high blood pressure, heart disease, stroke, bone and joint problems, asthma and arthritis. And there is a reduction in life expectancy. Hence, the more obese people there are, the more money – private and public – has to be spent on diagnosis and treatment. Obese children tend to become obese adults. Research shows that severely overweight teenagers have the arteries of 45 year-olds and will have triple the current rate of heart disease by the time they reach 35.[47] Most of the cost of obesity diagnosis and treatment in the US comes from private money. However, Medicare spending would be 8.5 per cent lower and Medicaid spending would be 11.8 per cent lower in the absence of obesity. Brookings Institute research shows that medical costs for a severely overweight person are 41.5 per cent higher than for a non-obese person. Medical obesity costs in 2011 were estimated at $160 billion, which works out at upwards of $700 per American. That is, all Americans, not just those who are greatly overweight.

Most of the (practical) indirect costs of obesity are employment related. To describe these USDA uses the term 'resources foregone as a result of a health condition'.[48] In terms of productivity, absenteeism is the obvious cost. In addition, presenteeism (obese workers who come to work but are less productive) is another source of loss. Employers pay higher life insurance premiums and increased worker compensation than for their counterparts who are not overweight. Higher disability payments mean increased cost to federal

---

46 Simon, *Appetite for Profit*, pp. 223–4.

47 Pretlow, *Overweight: What Kids Say*, p. iii.

48 Harvard School of Public Health, 'Paying the price for those extra pounds'.

government and welfare loss in the health insurance market. Clearly, these indirect costs are harder to measure and there is more scope for disagreement than when measuring the direct cost of obesity.

In addition, there are other more abstract costs. Society pays, as do families and individuals for whom obesity management is a part of daily life. The change in lifestyle that has accompanied contemporary living doubtless contributes to the epidemic. In the early 21st century, everything is available all of the time. The traditional meal served by a stay-at-home mother three times a day to all family members seated around the table no longer happens in most households. An increase in processed food, snacking, non-homecooked meals, reduced exercise, more driving and more screen time all make for an increasingly unhealthy existence.

Less visible challenges to progress also exist. For example, the Academy of Nutrition and Dietetics (AND) describes itself as the world's largest organisation for food and nutrition professionals. However, AND's sponsors include Coca Cola, Kellogg's, McDonald's, Hershey, Unilever, Mars, the Sugar Association and the National Dairy Council (NDC). Even the NDC counts as a suspect sponsor due to the content of contemporary dairy products. The Academy defends its position by stating that it needs to 'sit at the same table' as the food companies in order to have their ear.[49] Whatever the truth here, the objectivity of any of AND's research findings are undermined by its close relationship with vested interests.

'Put the cupcake down'[50]

The solution to the problem, on paper at least, can be summed up in a few words. The heavenly chorus of food activist Michael Pollan's 'Eat food, not too much, mostly plants' harmonised with the first lady's 'Let's Move' mantra, would solve all ills, if acted upon. In reality, such voices personify Schattschneider's warning about upper class accents,[51] as those reading Pollan's books doubtless have a gym membership and a WholeFoods store account already. Meanwhile, the $1 trillion food and beverage industry speaks directly to the masses and is not keen to embrace or promote such messages, for obvious reasons. These businesses do not want to see their products go the way of alcohol and tobacco, that is, vilified, heavily taxed and regulated. Of course, the regulation of food intake is far more complex than that of other substances,

49 Deardorff, 'Should nutrition groups take corporate money?'; Academy of Nutrition and Dietetics, www.eatright.org (accessed 4 Feb. 2014); www.zoeharcombe.com (accessed 4 Feb. 2014).

50 *Veep*, Series 1, Episode 5 (obesity management episode), HBO, May 2012.

51 'The flaw in the pluralist heaven is that the heavenly chorus sings with a strong upper-class accent', from Elmer Eric Schattschneider's *Semi-Sovereign People*, published in 1960.

as people cannot 'just say no' to food. However, there is finally an increasing realisation among elements within the government, media and public, that the relentless availability of low-cost, low-nutrition, high-calorie, pleasure-inducing foods is a major $160 billion per year public health problem. The US government remains 'up to its ears' in obesity-promoting policies, including the classification of the tomato sauce on pizza as a vegetable, allowing food stamps to be used on any food (including soft drinks) and permitting food and beverage companies to deduct marketing expenses from taxes.[52]

Healthy doesn't sell

Public health attorney Michele Simon has outlined the problems associated with allowing 'the best science money can buy'. For example, if research funded by Coca Cola finds that marketing soft drinks to young children is nothing to be concerned about, then this makes a mockery of science and the process of accountability.[53] There are endless examples of corporations ensuring that the 'research' reaches the correct conclusions. Other credible sources provide worrying details. The *European Journal of Epidemiology* published a study in 2012 with findings based on 7,000 children, which found infants who ate healthier foods had higher IQ scores by age eight than those who did not. Unsurprisingly, the unhealthiest foods led to a lowering of IQ points. Sweets, biscuits, candy, soda and crisps were among the main culprits. Such foods are cheap, relentlessly available and tasty.[54] Some have argued that they are addictive, and should be recognised as such. Findings in a range of studies have shown that better nutrition is continuously linked to brain size, vision development, healthy body and weight, and improved concentration and performance in school.[55] There is little doubt that President Obama, the first lady and many within the administration remain acutely aware of these facts. The challenge, however, is to steer that narrow course of promoting the public good, in the least paternalistic way. This is a profound dilemma for the administration.

Conclusion

French sociologist Claude Fischler concludes that the American attitude to food is unique.[56] In France, when a person is asked what term they associate

52 Nestle, 'What role should government play in combating obesity?

53 Simon, *Appetite for Profit*, p. 169.

54 Smithers et al., 'Dietary patterns at 6, 15 and 24 months of age are associated with IQ at 8 years of age', pp. 525–35.

55 Glewwe and King, 'The impact of early childhood nutritional status on cognitive development: does the timing of malnutrition matter?', pp. 81–113.

56 C. Fischler et al., 'Attitudes to food and the role of food in life in the U.S.A., Japan, Flemish Belgium and France', pp. 163–80.

with the word 'egg', they say 'breakfast'. In the US, the response is 'cholestorol'. Food in America is considered in terms of the sum of its parts, carbohydrates and calories, rather than conviviality and a shared experience. While businesses outside of the metropolitan areas in Mediterranean countries still close for two to three hours for the lunch period, at any given mealtime, 20 per cent of Americans are eating in their car.[57] As well as how they eat, and what they eat, Americans perceive food in a very different way to many other cultures. They are food libertarians, who want to eat what they want, when, where and how they want. Fischler's surveys found no specific times that American families regularly eat together. In France, meal times are highly predictable and regular. Less than 9 per cent of the French population is considered to be overweight. Joel Berg of the New York Coalition Against Hunger (NYCAH) says that Americans are taking steps in the right direction, but there is still much to be done.[58] A move towards viewing food as a cherished and finite resource rather than simply a consumer product would be a step in the right direction.

The time has come for a broad food policy dialogue in Washington. The conversation is still too fragmented, and the food movement is still in its infancy. There is a need for social justice in the agricultural sphere, from a range of perspectives. Public health, childhood nutrition, workers' rights, animal welfare and environmental concerns should not be hostages to the fortunes of vested interests and agribusiness. Locavore efforts to promote healthy eating habits to poorer Americans are on the rise. SNAP vouchers are accepted at farmer's markets, and community gardens are increasingly doing outreach work. Municipalities are establishing bus routes between poorer neighbourhoods and well-stocked supermarkets. It's a start.

The food chain crisis in the US began decades before the Obama administration and will not be solved by a single liberal president or his well-meaning first lady. However, despite the enormous rise in food stamp recipients and the staggering growth of obesity and related illnesses, there are slim signs of change and progress. Michelle Obama has done as much as a first lady can within the choking confines of her supposedly apolitical role to highlight the importance of healthy life choices. Her husband's administration has also taken some significant steps forward. However, changes in culture do not come about overnight or via a single initiative. America is, and will remain, a fast-food nation. There is a pressing need to be more than this.

History demonstrates that meaningful change is possible. Sustained campaigns work, and the grassroots food movement has gained considerable momentum within a few short years. Access to clean, real and fair food for all Americans is not impossible. The current moves, both within and without

57 Pollan, 'Cooking as a political act'.
58 NYCAH blog, 'Food stamps soda ban: the wrong way to fight obesity', 6 Dec. 2010, https://nyccah.org/node/1182 (accessed 29 April 2014).

government, towards fixing the broken food chain, and in turn reducing obesity and food stamp dependency, are brave and bold. The healthiest food choice simply *must* become the most available choice, and making this more of a reality is in part at least the responsibility of the administration. Politically, socially, economically and emotionally, food is a crucial issue that President Obama, and his successors, cannot ignore.

References

S.A. Andersen (ed.) (Life Sciences Research Office) (1990), 'Core indicators of nutritional state for difficult to sample populations', *The Journal of Nutrition*, vol. 120, pp. 1557S–1600S, http://jn.nutrition.org/content/120/11_Suppl/1555.full.pdf (accessed 4 Feb. 2014).

M. Bittman (2011) 'Is junk food really cheaper?', *New York Times*, 24 Sep., www.nytimes.com/2011/09/25/opinion/sunday/is-junk-food-really-cheaper.html?pagewanted=all (accessed 4 Feb. 2014).

C. Blow (2011) 'The biggest losers', *New York Times*, 11 March, www.nytimes.com/2011/03/12/opinion/12blow.html?scp=3&sq=charles%20blow%20obesity&st=cse&_r=0 (accessed 4 Feb. 2014).

CNN (2010) 'Obama signs child nutrition Bill', 13 Dec., www.cnn.co.uk/2010/POLITICS/12/13/child.nutrition/index.html (accessed 4 Feb. 2014).

Centers for Disease Control (2012) 'Obesity is common, serious and costly', www.cdc.gov/media/matte/2012/05_weight_of_nation.pdf (accessed 4 Feb. 2014); 'Prevalence of obesity in the United States, 2009–2010', NCHS Data Brief no. 82 (National Center for Health Statistics), Jan., www.cdc.gov/nchs/data/databriefs/db82.pdf (accessed 4 Feb. 2014).

Chin Jou (2013) 'Cutting food stamps will cost everyone', *The Atlantic*, 17 June, www.theatlantic.com/health/archive/2013/06/cutting-food-stamps-will-cost-everyone/276905/ (accessed 4 Feb. 2014).

A. Coleman-Jensen, M. Nord, M. Andrews and S. Carlson (2012) 'Household food security in the United States in 2011', USDA Economic Research Service, Sep., www.ers.usda.gov/publications/err-economic-research-report/err141.aspx (accessed 4 Feb. 2014).

J. Deardorff (2012) 'Should nutrition groups take corporate money?', *Chicago Tribune*, 10 Feb., http://articles.chicagotribune.com/2012-02-10/features/chi-should-nutrition-groups-take-corporate-money-20120210_1_nutrition-groups-nutrition-professionals-public-health (accessed 4 Feb. 2014).

A. Drewnowski and S.E. Specter (2004) 'Poverty and obesity: the role of energy density and energy costs', *The American Journal of Clinical*

Nutrition, vol. 79, no. 1, pp. 6–16, http://ajcn.nutrition.org/content/79/1/6.full (accessed 4 Feb. 2014).

E.J. Emanuel (2012) 'Let's Move she said – and we have', *New York Times* opinionator blog, 13 Feb., http://opinionator.blogs.nytimes.com/2012/02/13/lets-move-she-said-and-we-have/ (accessed 4 Feb. 2014).

C. Fischler et al. (1999) 'Attitudes to food and the role of food in life in the U.S.A., Japan, Flemish Belgium and France: possible implications for the diet–health debate', *Appetite*, vol. 33, pp. 163–180, article no. appe.1999.0244, http://faculty.som.yale.edu/amywrzesniewski/documents/Attitudestofoodandtheroleoffood.pdf.

C. Franck et al. (2013) 'Agricultural subsidies and the American obesity epidemic', *American Journal of Preventative Medicine*, 9 July, www.ajpmonline.org (accessed 4 Feb. 2014).

P. Ganong and J.B. Liebman (2013) 'Explaining trends in SNAP enrolment', Harvard Kennedy School, www.hks.harvard.edu/jeffreyliebman/ExplainingTrendsInSNAPEnrollment.pdf (accessed 4 Feb. 2014).

P. Glewwe and E.M. King (2001) 'The impact of early childhood nutritional status on cognitive development: does the timing of malnutrition matter?', *World Bank Economic Review*, vol. 15, no. 1, pp. 81–113.

Global Research (2013) 'Poverty in the USA: nearly 50 million Americans on food stamps', March, www.globalresearch.ca/poverty-in-the-u-s-a-nearly-50-million-americans-on-food-stamps/5328986 (accessed 4 Feb. 2014).

R.A. Hammond and R. Levine (Brookings Institute) (2010) 'The economic impact of obesity in the United States', in *Diabetes, Metabolic Syndrome and Obesity: Targets and Therapy* (DovePress), pp. 285–95, www.brookings.edu/~/media/research/files/articles/2010/9/14%20obesity%20cost%20hammond%20levine/0914_obesity_cost_hammond_levine.pdf (accessed 4 Feb. 2014).

H. Hartline-Grafton and J. Weill (2012) 'Replacing the thrifty food plan in order to provide adequate allotments for SNAP beneficiaries', Food Research and Action Center, Dec., http://frac.org/pdf/replacing_tfp_to_provide_adequate_snap.pdf (accessed 4 Feb. 2014).

Harvard School of Public Health (n.d.) 'Paying the price for those extra pounds', www.hsph.harvard.edu/obesity-prevention-source/obesity-consequences/economic/ (accessed 4 Feb. 2014).

B. Hoffman (2013) 'Who receives food stamps and why is it critical to continue their support?', *Forbes*, 23 Sep., www.forbes.com/sites/

bethhoffman/2013/09/23/who-receives-food-stamps-and-why-it-is-critical-to-continue-their-support/ (accessed 4 Feb. 2014).

C. Mayer and A. Joyce (2005) 'The escalating obesity wars: non-profit's tactics, funding sparks controversy', *Washington Post*, 27 April, www.washingtonpost.com/wp-dyn/articles/A18758-2005Apr27.html?nav=E8 (accessed 4 Feb. 2014).

L. Miller (2010) 'What food says about class in America', *Newsweek*, 22 Nov., www.newsweek.com/what-food-says-about-class-america-69951 (accessed 4 Feb. 2014).

M. Nestle (2012) 'What role should government play in combating obesity?' *Wall Street Journal*, 18 Sep., http://online.wsj.com/news/articles/SB10000 872396390444812704577609482961870876 (accessed 4 Feb. 2014).

— (2013) 'Let's Move celebrates its 3rd birthday – at Walmarts', 5 March, www.foodpolitics.com/2013/03/lets-move-celebrates-its-3rd-birthday-at-walmarts/ (accessed 4 Feb. 2014).

S. Neuman (2012) 'Why the Farm Bill's provisions will matter to you', National Public Radio, 13 June, www.npr.org/2012/06/13/154862017/why-the-farm-bills-provisions-will-matter-to-you (accessed 4 Feb. 2014).

New York Times (2013) 'US Farm Bill: chronology of coverage', 13 Dec., http://topics.nytimes.com/top/reference/timestopics/subjects/f/farm_bill_us/ (accessed 4 Feb. 2014).

R. Nixon (2013) 'House rejects Farm Bill as food stamps cuts prove divisive', *New York Times*, 20 June, www.nytimes.com/2013/06/21/us/politics/house-defeats-a-farm-bill-with-big-food-stamp-cuts.html?_r=0 (accessed 4 Feb. 2014).

C. Olson and M. Lent (2008) 'Food insecurity in rural New York State', *Research and Policy Brief Series*, 17 May, http://cardi.cornell.edu/cals/devsoc/outreach/cardi/publications/loader.cfm?csModule=security/getfile&PageID=244569 (accessed 4 Feb. 2014).

Organisation for Economic Cooperation and Development (2013) *Organisation for Economic Cooperation and Development Factbook 2013*, www.oecd-ilibrary.org/sites/factbook-2013-en/12/02/03/index.html?itemId=/content/chapter/factbook-2013-100-en (accessed 4 Feb. 2014).

D. Paletta and C. Porter (2013) 'Use of food stamps swells, even as economy improves', *Wall Street Journal*, 27 March, http://online.wsj.com/news/articles/SB10001424127887323699704578328601204933288 (accessed 4 Feb. 2014).

M. Pollan (2013) 'Cooking as a political act', London School
of Economics lecture, 30 May, www.lse.ac.uk/publicEvents/
events/2013/05/20130530t1830vNT.aspx (accessed 4 Feb. 2014).

R.A. Pretlow (2009) *Overweight: What Kids Say* (North Charleston, SC:
CreateSpace).

D. Rogers (2013), 'Farm Bill talks intensify', Politico.com, 20 Nov., www.
politico.com/story/2013/11/food-stamp-costs-farm-bill-100158.html
(accessed 4 Feb. 2014).

M. Russo and D. Smith (2013) 'Apples to Twinkies: comparing taxpayer
subsidies for fresh produce and junk food' (for the PIRG), July, www.
uspirg.org/sites/pirg/files/reports/Apples_to_Twinkies_2013_USPIRG.
pdf (accessed 4 Feb. 2014).

E. Saslow (2013) 'Food stamps put Rhode Island town on monthly
boom-and-bust cycle', *Washington Post*, 16 March, http://articles.
washingtonpost.com/2013-03-16/national/37768635_1_food-stamps-
woonsocket-mother-s-day (accessed 4 Feb. 2014).

M. Simon (2006) *Appetite for Profit: How the Food Industry Undermines our
Health and How to Fight Back* (New York, NY: Nation Books).

— (2012) 'Follow the money: are corporations profiting from hungry
Americans?', June, www.eatdrinkpolitics.com/wp-content/uploads/
FoodStampsFollowtheMoneySimon.pdf (accessed 4 Feb. 2014).

L. Smithers et al. (2012) 'Dietary patterns at 6, 15 and 24 months of age are
associated with IQ at 8 years of age', *European Journal of Epidemiology*,
July, vol. 27, issue 7, pp. 525–35.

D. Stone (2001) *Policy Paradox: The Art of Political Decision Making* (London:
W.W. Norton & Co).

K. Thompson (2012) 'Michelle Obama keeps moving with "Let's Move"',
Washington Post, 9 Feb., www.washingtonpost.com/politics/michelle-
obama-keeps-moving-with-lets-move/2012/02/09/gIQAAAQc1Q_story.
html (accessed 4 Feb. 2014).

Washington Post (2012) 'Gingrich says Obama is the "food stamps president".
Is he?', 18 Jan., www.washingtonpost.com/blogs/wonkblog/post/gingrich-
says-obama-is-the-food-stamp-president-is-he/2012/01/18/gIQA1Ino8P_
blog.html (accessed 4 Feb. 2014).

F. Wright, M.D. Carroll, C.L. Johnson (2004) 'Trends in intake of energy
and macronutrients – United States: 1971–2000', *Morbidity and Mortality
Weekly Report* (for the CDC), vol. 53, no. 4, 6 Feb., pp. 80–2, www.cdc.
gov/mmwr/PDF/wk/mm5304.pdf (accessed 4 Feb. 2014).

7. Obama and the environment

John Berg

D uring Barack Obama's years in office public awareness has grown of the need for action to deal with the crisis of the environment, or at least the crisis of climate change. There has not been a corresponding growth of awareness within the US Congress, however. In consequence, Obama has turned increasingly, in this as in other areas, to the possibility of executive action to protect the environment. This chapter will first survey and evaluate Obama's attempts to deal with the challenges of climate change, then review some of the other important environmental issues faced by his administration.

Confronting climate change

As I have stated in earlier work, President Obama took office with three institutional channels for action on climate change available to him. He could pursue a binding international agreement under the United Nations Framework Convention on Climate Change (UNFCCC), a treaty to which the US remained a party even after its withdrawal from the Kyoto Protocol; he could work with Congress to pass a federal law restricting greenhouse gas emissions; or he could ask the US Environmental Protection Agency (EPA) to use its newly-confirmed statutory power to regulate carbon emissions as a pollutant. By the middle of his first term, it appeared that the first two channels had failed, and the EPA was beginning to develop a plan to use the third.[1] There have since been a few hopeful stirrings in the international arena, continued blockage in Congress, and more steps towards regulatory action by the EPA. In addition, growing support for the demand that the President act to block a pipeline (called 'Keystone XL' or 'KXL') to carry tar sands oil from where it is extracted in Alberta to refineries in Texas may force him to a decision he seems to prefer to avoid. The remainder of this section will examine each of these areas.

Copenhagen and the future: international negotiation at a snail's pace

Barack Obama assumed the US presidency with the Kyoto Protocol battered but intact. Although President George W. Bush had withdrawn the US from

---

1 Berg, 'Environmental policy: the success and failure of Obama'.

the agreement, enough other countries had signed on for it to go into effect in 2005, and some had reduced their greenhouse gas emissions. However, the initial treaty commitments were set to expire in 2012, and several issues remained to be resolved in moving forward: the US had withdrawn; countries that were less developed but industrialising rapidly, such as China and India, had not been required to make reductions; and the pledged rate of greenhouse gas reduction was far lower than what was needed to prevent an average global temperature rise of 4º Celsius, let alone 2º Celsius, the maximum increase many scientists considered to be permissible without severe ecological and social disruption.[2] These problems were scheduled to be tackled, and a new agreement arrived at, during the 15th Conference of the Parties (COP) to the UNFCCC that was due to be held in Copenhagen in December 2009. Since the new president had expressed his support for climate action during the campaign, there was hope that a strong agreement would be forthcoming in Copenhagen.

Those hopes were dashed. Preliminary meetings over the summer of 2009 made little progress, and it became clear by December that any forward motion would require dramatic and substantive leadership from Obama. Instead of offering such leadership, Obama initially decided not to attend; when he did eventually appear on the last day he chose to abandon the UNFCCC process and instead to negotiate a side agreement – the 'Copenhagen Accord' – with only four other countries, Russia, China, Brazil and South Africa. This allowed him to claim that he had brought China to the table, but he had done so only by taking both quantitative targets for greenhouse gas reductions and any means of enforcement of those targets off that table. The Accord was merely a mutual pledge to reduce emissions as each signatory thought appropriate.[3] Although the UNFCCC has limped on, with subsequent meetings in Cancún, Durban and Doha, it no longer seems capable of bringing about the reductions that are needed. Alden Meyer of the Union of Concerned Scientists summed up the outcome of the 2010 Cancún meeting (the 16th COP) with the statement that 'The outcome wasn't enough to save the planet, but it did restore the credibility of the United Nations as a forum where progress can be made.'[4] The agreement affirmed that developed countries should cut greenhouse gas emissions and that less-developed countries should receive billions of dollars in aid to help them reduce their own emissions, but it neither specified where those billions would come from nor established a mechanism for enforcing the cuts. Little progress was made in Durban, and by the time of the Doha conference in

2   Hansen et al., 'Target atmospheric CO2: where should humanity aim?', pp. 217–31.
3   Berg, 'Environmental policy: the success and failure of Obama'; Karaim, 'Climate change', pp. 3–26.
4   Quoted in Goldenberg, 'Cancún agreement rescues UN credibility but falls short of saving planet'.

2012, one observer declared that it was a 'success' because it made procedural changes that represented 'progress' towards a more substantive agreement in 2015.[5] However, few of the substantive disagreements required for a new agreement had been resolved.

The basic obstacle to progress has been the US Senate, in which there simply are not enough votes to ratify an effective climate treaty. As Karaim points out, the less-developed countries have little reason to offer concessions when they know that the United States does not have the ability to win ratification of an effective treaty.[6] Congressional intransigence extended as well to the second possible channel for action, the passage of a climate bill through the US Congress.

The Waxman-Markey Act: unsurprising congressional stalemate

The second possible tool for change was the passage of a new climate law. To this end, the Waxman-Markey Act was introduced early in 2009. The bill was criticised by environmentalists for its inclusion of what had come to be called 'clean coal', and for its reliance on a carbon-trading provision that many considered to be riddled with loopholes.

The phrase 'clean coal' requires explanation. It referred originally to coal that had a low sulphur content, and therefore made a smaller contribution than other kinds of coal to acid rain. However the coal industry, along with President Obama, has appropriated the term to refer to carbon capture and storage, a proposed regime in which all the carbon dioxide produced by burning coal would be captured and stored permanently. The storage must be more permanent than anything now known, since carbon dioxide that leaks out in a century or two makes the same contribution to climate change as carbon dioxide released today; hence, many consider such a technology inherently impossible. However, coal is a major product of Ohio, a key state in presidential elections, so both Obama and his 2012 opponent, Mitt Romney, consistently referred to 'clean coal' or 'clean coal technology' as a vital step towards combatting climate change.[7]

Environmentalists also criticised the cap-and-trade provisions of the bill, although this criticism was more contingent than that of clean coal. Cap-and-trade is a system whereby the government issues permits to emit a fixed amount of greenhouse gases, and decreases this amount periodically until the target reduction is achieved. Those who receive these permits may either use them to allow emissions, or sell them to someone else. Since such sales are a source of profits, polluters are thereby given an incentive to achieve greater

5   Hedegaard, 'Why the Doha climate conference was a success'.

6   Karaim, 'Climate change'.

7   Berg, 'Environmental policy: the success and failure of Obama'.

efficiency, and the market in permits allows a certain amount of flexibility. Environmentalists had no objection at all to a cap on emissions, and objected to emissions trading primarily because of two details. First, the permits were to be given out free, rather than sold at auction, thereby rewarding the polluters and depriving the government of a revenue source; and second, the bill allowed for carbon offsets, a variety of activities that could be treated as equivalent to reducing emissions. Many offsets, such as agreeing not to cut down a forest, were questionable; in one case, a project in Indonesia was awarded offset credits for creating a plantation of palm oil trees, even though the original forest had been cut down to make way for the plantation. Environmentalists therefore considered offsetting to be a huge loophole.[8]

At the same time, the bill was attacked by the right-wing of the congressional Republican party as a disguised tax that would undermine any possibility of economic recovery because of the burden it would allegedly place upon industry. Michelle Bachmann (Republican-Minnesota) referred to the programme as 'tax and trade',[9] while Senate Minority Leader Mitch McConnell (Republican-Kentucky) called it the 'light switch tax'.[10]

The Waxman-Markey Bill passed the House of Representatives, 219 as against 212, on 26 June 2009. However, it was unable to move through the Senate because of threatened filibusters. A new, weaker bill was offered by Senators McCain (Republican-Arizona) and Lieberman (Independent-Connecticut), but went nowhere. Legislation and treaties were both barred by the institution of the filibuster.

Following the Republican capture of the House of Representatives in the 2010 election, further action on a climate bill joined the rest of the President's initiatives in a state of perpetual blockage. As in other areas, Obama then turned to consideration of what he might be able to do on his own authority. The most promising possibility was for the EPA to begin to regulate greenhouse gases as a form of air pollution.

EPA regulation of greenhouse gases

The basis for EPA action on greenhouse gases had been established in 2007, during the George W. Bush administration, when the Supreme Court ruled that the EPA did have the legal authority to issue such regulations.[11] Although carbon dioxide does not affect human health directly, through inhalation, in

---

8   Fogarty, 'Indonesia forest projects target 13 mln CO2 offsets'; Macalister, 'Britain's big polluters accused of abusing EU's carbon trading scheme'; Viard, 'The cap-and-trade giveaway'.

9   Bachmann, '"Cap and trade?" More like "tax and spend"'; Galbraith, 'Michele Bachmann seeks "armed and dangerous" opposition to cap-and-trade'.

10 Rees, 'McConnell speaks out about cap and trade'.

11 *Massachusetts v. EPA*, 2007.

the same way that particulates, ozone or mercury do, the Court accepted the argument that it does affect human health by changing the climate, and thus fits the criteria for EPA regulation laid down by the Clean Air Act.

Following the Supreme Court decision, the EPA proposed a draft proposal to the Office of Management and Budget (OMB) to issue a finding that increased concentrations of six greenhouse gases[12] in the atmosphere were a danger to human health, and that motor vehicle emissions contributed to these concentrations. The proposed finding would have been the necessary first step in issuing greenhouse gas emission standards for motor vehicles; however, it was blocked by the Bush White House, and the EPA then withdrew the proposal. Nevertheless, in 2008 the agency did issue an Advanced Notice of Proposed Rulemaking summarising the scientific evidence on climate change and enabling the Obama administration to move fairly quickly to issue a proposed finding similar to the withdrawn one, which it did on 17 April 2009. The agency held two public hearings and received some 380,000 public comments, to which it responded in an 11-volume document. The finding was then issued on 7 December 2009.[13]

This finding, and motor vehicle and stationary source regulations based on it, were challenged in a lawsuit brought by 14 states (while 15 others filed briefs in support of the agency). This challenge was rejected by the Court of Appeals for the District of Columbia in a decision issued on 26 June 2012. The three-judge panel declared unanimously that the EPA was 'unambiguously correct' in claiming the authority to regulate greenhouse gases, given the scientific findings, and rejecting challenges to those findings with the statement, 'This is how science works. The E.P.A. is not required to reprove the existence of the atom every time it approaches a scientific question.'[14] Meanwhile, the EPA had issued a proposal for carbon emission standards for power plants on 13 April 2012, and was in the process of collecting public comments on that proposal.[15]

These developments came during President Obama's re-election campaign, at a time when he sought to project an image of single-minded concentration on jobs and economic growth, and when climate issues were strangely absent from the debate.[16] One year later, no longer concerned with a future re-election campaign, he released his Climate Action Plan (CAP) in a speech at

12 The six gases are carbon dioxide, methane, nitrous oxide, hydrofluorocarbons, perfluorocarbons and sulphur hexafluoride.

13 US Environmental Protection Agency, *EPA's Endangerment Finding: Legal Background*, summary.

14 Wald, 'Court backs E.P.A. over emissions limits intended to reduce global warming'.

15 See Barringer, 'For new generation of power plants, a new emission rule from the E.P.A' (report based on a pre-release draft of the proposal).

16 Berg, 'Issue suppression and the crisis of the American party system: the cost of two-party duopoly'.

Georgetown University on 25 June 2013. In the plan he made a strong case for regulating carbon emissions, grouping that element with 'other toxins, like mercury and arsenic', that are already regulated.[17] This grouping is not accurate – while carbon in the atmosphere does harm human health, it is not a 'toxin' in any normal sense – but it does constitute a strong rhetorical stand in favour of controlling carbon emissions.

The EPA cited this plan when it issued a revision of its 2012 proposal on 20 September 2013, describing its action as 'the first milestone' in implementing the President's plan.[18] More importantly, the revision was a response to industry comments; among other things, it allowed emissions for new coal-fired plants to be somewhat higher than those for new plants fired by natural gas. Large new gas plants would be limited to emissions of 1,000 pounds of carbon dioxide per megawatt hour, while small gas and coal plants would be allowed 1,100 pounds.[19]

The regulations themselves are not a significant step towards greenhouse gas reduction. First, they apply only to new plants; most new gas-fired plants meet the standard already, and no new coal plants are scheduled to be built. Ideally, reduction of greenhouse gas emissions would involve closing old fossil-fuel plants and not replacing them with new ones; in contrast, these standards would allow construction of new plants to proceed, and do nothing about old ones. Moreover, since carbon dioxide is necessarily produced in the combustion of coal (which is almost pure carbon) and natural gas (which is carbon combined with hydrogen), carbon emissions can be reduced only by achieving greater efficiency in the conversion of heat to electricity, an area in which there is not much room left for improvement, or by carbon sequestration, a technology which is not available on the scale that would be needed.

In addition, the target in the president's climate plan is to reduce greenhouse gases by 17 per cent below 2005 levels by 2020. Since the Kyoto Protocol would have required a reduction by 7 per cent below 1990 levels by 2012, while emissions actually rose 10 per cent by 2011, this is inadequate.[20] Even the Kyoto target was inadequate; the Earth Policy Institute calculates that the goal of keeping atmospheric concentration of carbon dioxide below 400 parts per million would require an 80 per cent reduction in emissions from 2006 to 2020.[21]

17   Executive Office of the President, 'The President's Climate Action Plan'.

18   US Environmental Protection Agency, *EPA Proposes Carbon Pollution Standards for New Power Plants*.

19   US Environmental Protection Agency, *EPA Proposes Carbon Pollution Standards*.

20   US Environmental Protection Agency, *U.S. Greenhouse Gas Emissions*.

21   Brown et al., 'Time for Plan B: cutting carbon emissions 80 percent by 2020'.

US emissions in 2012 did drop by about 8 per cent over the previous year, due to a mild winter, a reduction in gasoline use, and the abundance of cheap natural gas, which emits less carbon dioxide per megawatt-hour than coal. However, burning natural gas still produces 1,100 pounds of carbon dioxide per megawatt-hour, an amount that must be reduced to 350–400 pounds if the atmospheric concentration of the gas is to be prevented from increasing.[22] Moreover, the abundance of natural gas is due to the spread of a new extraction technology, hydrofracturing, which carries a considerable environmental risk of its own.

To sum up, then, the proposed regulations of emissions from new power plants do not constitute a reduction from what the industry is currently building, and will not come close to what is needed to hold greenhouse gas concentration to a satisfactory level. However, the regulations would constitute a breakthrough in treating carbon dioxide as a pollutant, and their issuance would trigger a requirement under the Clean Air Act that the EPA proceed to develop a carbon-emissions standard for existing plants as well. The Sierra Club and the League of Conservation Voters have launched campaigns to rally public support, while 350.org has seized on the statement that the Keystone XL pipeline should not be approved if it would 'significantly exacerbate' carbon dioxide emissions.[23] On the other hand, Tom Weis of Climate Changes Solutions denounced the plan as a 'cloud shot' instead of a 'moon shot'.

> Unfortunately for all of us, the blueprint he presented is more PR than plan, and has zero chance of stabilizing the climate. To the contrary, it promises even more climate chaos by promoting fracking, mountaintop removal coal mining, offshore and Arctic oil drilling and tar sands exploitation. It also threatens future generations with the specter of more radioactive nuclear power.[24]

The CAP is a first step, but a small one. The real test will be whether it is followed by action that begins to approach what is needed. However, Obama faces a more immediate trial, forced upon him by the environmental movement, in dealing with the proposed Keystone XL pipeline.

The Keystone XL pipeline: a new approach to reducing greenhouse gas emissions

Generally, climate scientists have calculated how much greenhouse gas emissions would have to be reduced to maintain the atmospheric concentration of those gases below a given level, and then looked for ways to achieve those reductions. In practice, this has meant decreasing the *rate* of emissions per kilowatt hour

22 Nuwer, 'A 20-year low in U.S. carbon emissions'.
23 Childers, 'Environmental groups seek to rally support for Obama's Climate Action Plan'.
24 Weis, 'President Obama's Climate Action Plan: not even close'.

generated, mile driven, or ton of freight moved one mile. However, more efficient energy use may simply lead to the use of more of it, rather than to a decrease in emissions, a phenomenon known as the Jevons Paradox.[25] Such an increase is only a possibility, dependent on many other factors; what is true, however, is that unless energy use is regulated directly, it may increase regardless of efficiencies.

A few years ago, James Hansen began to look at the problem from a different direction, asking how much total carbon could be absorbed by the atmosphere without disastrous effect, and what would be the effect of burning the reserves of coal and oil now known to exist. In an article published in 2013 he and his co-authors concluded that burning all known fossil fuels would lead to a rise in average global temperature of 16° Celsius, with a rise at the poles of 30°, an increase that 'would make most of the planet uninhabitable by humans, thus calling into question strategies that emphasize adaptation to climate change.'[26]

Motivated by this analysis, and following a conversation with Hansen, who reportedly told him that it would be 'game over for the planet' if the oil in the Alberta tar sands was burned as fuel, Bill McKibben of 350.org launched a campaign of civil disobedience and political organising to block the proposed Keystone XL pipeline as a way of impeding the production of fuel from the Alberta tar sands.[27]

The tar sands or oil sands of Alberta lie beneath an area of 140,000 square kilometres, and hold an estimated 1.75 trillion barrels of oil. At the prices prevailing in 2013, it is estimated that 10 per cent of this reserve, or 175 billion barrels can be extracted profitably. For comparison, the total proven reserves of Saudi Arabia are slightly over 250 billion barrels.[28] McKibben and 350.org began to argue that the world could not survive if this new source of fossil fuels was brought into production, and that there was a convenient way to stop such a development: by denying permission for construction of a pipeline planned to bring the tar sands oil from Alberta to refineries in the United States. Because the pipeline would cross the border from Canada to the US, it would require a permit from the US State Department, which is responsible to the president; so 350.org launched a campaign directed at Obama, calling on him to stop it. The campaign combined civil disobedience, including a series of arrests of demonstrators who sat down on the street in front of the White House, with calls on the president to keep his promise to protect the climate. During 2011 and 2012 activists presented themselves as people who

25 Jevons argued that more efficiency in the use of a resource would lead to a lower price for that resource, which in turn would lead to greater demand for it. See his *The Coal Question*.

26 Hansen et al., 'Climate sensitivity, sea level and atmospheric carbon dioxide'.

27 Mayer, 'Taking it to the streets'.

28 Government of Alberta, *Alberta's Oil Sands: Opportunity. Balance*.

had supported Obama enthusiastically during the 2008 campaign, and wanted to do so again, but would be unable to if he allowed the pipeline to go ahead.

Opponents of the pipeline launched a civil disobedience campaign in August 2011, with daily waves of protesters being arrested in front of the White House over a two-week period.[29] That autumn, on 7 November, 10,000 people surrounded the White House, some dressed as polar bears and others carrying a mock pipeline.[30] Three days later Obama ordered the State Department to conduct a new review of the proposal, with its contribution to greenhouse gas emissions included in the review. Among other things, this deferred any decision until after the 2012 presidential election.[31]

Although some anti-pipeline activists hailed the president's order as a victory,[32] the issue is still alive. As noted above, Obama said in his 2013 climate speech that the project should not be approved if it would 'significantly exacerbate' greenhouse gas emissions, but that wording is ambiguous enough to allow for him to decide either way. As this is written, House Republicans are threatening to include approval of the pipeline's permit in any bill to raise the ceiling on the amount of the national debt.[33]

The total carbon content of the Alberta tar sands is estimated at 230 gigatonnes, greater than that of all proven crude oil reserves in the world (139 gigatonnes). Even the ten per cent of that recoverable at current prices would make a substantial contribution to global warming, and there is no reason not to expect that a greater percentage will become available in the future as technology improves and prices rise.[34] Obama's decision on the pipeline may prove more important than anything else in his climate plan.

As important as climate is, Obama has faced other environmental issues as well. Some of these will be examined in the following section.

Other environmental issues

Along with action to protect the climate, Obama had promised during the 2008 campaign to stop political interference with scientific findings, as had happened with standards for arsenic in drinking water and for ambient ozone during the George W. Bush administration. He had also developed the idea of 'green jobs' as a campaign theme, and appointed a green jobs coordinator to

29 Goodman, 'Over 160 arrested in ongoing civil disobedience against Keystone XL tar sands pipeline' (radio interview with Bill McKibben of Tar Sands Action).

30 Kollipara, 'Keystone pipeline protesters surround White House'.

31 Revkin, 'Keystone oil pipeline decision moved after election'.

32 McKibben, 'Big news: we won. You won'.

33 Shear, 'Republicans see Keystone pipeline as a card to play in last-minute fiscal talks'.

34 Pierrehumbert, 'Keystone XL: game over?'

his staff when he took office. As this chapter will show, his record on meeting these promises has been mixed.

Respecting science: contrasting examples

During the Clinton administration the EPA had issued a new standard for arsenic in drinking water, lowering the permissible level from 50 to 10 parts per billion. However, this standard was withdrawn soon after George W. Bush took office. Both Bush and his EPA administrator, Christine Todd Whitman, asserted that the stricter standard was not merited by scientific evidence; it was, however, the standard recommended by the World Health Organization and adopted in the European Union.[35]

Many US scientists did not agree with the claim that the looser standard was merited; Stuart Rojstaczer, director of the Duke University Center for Hydrologic Science, accused Bush and Whitman of being 'more concerned with pleasing special interests than with saving lives'[36] and the regulatory action was challenged in court by the Natural Resources Defense Council. The public was not particularly enthusiastic about the idea of drinking water with more arsenic, and Obama's pledge to reverse the action was popular.

Low-level exposure to arsenic, such as that found in drinking water, has been associated with the development of skin cancer and of various internal cancers, such as bladder, kidney, liver and lung cancer. It is also associated with toxicity to the nervous system, heart and blood vessels.[37] Obama directed the EPA to re-open the arsenic standard with a view to tightening it, and the new standard of 10 parts per billion was issued on 22 January 2011. In this case, science had triumphed over politics.

Science did not fare as well in the case of ambient ozone regulation. Although the ozone layer in the stratosphere plays a beneficial role by blocking harmful ultraviolet radiation, ozone in the air around us has several harmful health effects. Protracted exposure to it is associated with a variety of respiratory illnesses, including asthma.[38]

Although some ozone is produced naturally, for example during thunderstorms, most formed at ground-level is the result of human activity. It is created on warm, sunny days by reactions involving nitrogen oxides, volatile organic compounds and carbon monoxide – all products of combustion, particularly in automobiles, trucks, buses and aeroplanes.[39] Because of these

---

35 Information in this section is drawn from Berg, 'Environmental policy: the success and failure of Obama'; see also Jehl, 'E.P.A. to abandon new arsenic limits for water supply'.

36 Rojstaczer, 'Arsenic in water: how much is safe?'

37 Mushak, 'Arsenic and old laws'.

38 Jerrett, et al., 'Long-term ozone exposure and mortality', pp. 1085–95.

39 Richmond, 'Assessing Obama's decision not to support EPA's revised ozone standard', pp. 25–41.

adverse health effects, the EPA maintains a National Ambient Air Quality Standard for ozone, most recently set at 75 parts per billion over an eight-hour period. An area where the concentration exceeds this level for eight hours or longer is in violation, and persistent such infractions require the state government to take correct action.

In 2009, because recent scientific findings indicated that ozone was more dangerous than previously thought, EPA administrator Lisa Jackson proposed that the standard for ambient ozone be reduced from 75 to 60–70 parts per billion over an eight-hour period. An initial scientific review was completed, and public comments solicited. However, the proposed regulation was rejected by Obama in September 2011; in rejecting it he cited 'the importance of reducing regulatory burdens and regulatory uncertainty, particularly as our economy continues to recover.'[40]

A crucial role in the rejection of the proposed new standard was played by the Office of Information and Regulatory Affairs (OIRA), a branch of the OMB. Originally established in the Carter administration under the Paperwork Reduction Act, OIRA was developed further by President Reagan as a tool for subjecting proposed regulations to cost-benefit analysis, and has gradually come to be a focus for industry lobbying.[41] In this case, such lobbying was successful, producing a decision condemned by a long list of environmental and health organisations and leading to a still-pending lawsuit.[42] President Obama seems here to have prioritised other concerns over human health; his commitment to putting science before politics has held only some of the time. On the other hand, his green jobs initiative worked out more positively, as the next section will demonstrate.

Green jobs

The green jobs initiative was not so much a policy as a way of talking about policy, a rhetorical device for undercutting the common notion that environmental protection and economic prosperity were conflicting goals. Soon after taking office Obama appointed Van Jones, a charismatic young African-American man, to the White House staff with the title of green jobs coordinator. Jones had published a book on green jobs, and had promoted the idea actively within Obama's campaign for the presidency.[43] Jones was not to last long in

40 Quoted in Richmond, 'Assessing Obama's decision'.

41 Center for Progressive Reform, 'OIRA 101', www.progressivereform.org/oira101.cfm (accessed 21 March 2014); Heinzerling, 'Who will run the EPA?', pp. 39–43. For a different view from the then-director of OIRA, see Sunstein, 'The Office of Information and Regulatory Affairs: myths and realities', pp. 1838–78.

42 Richmond, 'Assessing Obama's decision'.

43 Jones and Conrad, *The Green-Collar Economy: How One Solution Can Fix Our Two Biggest Problems.* For Jones's campaign activity, see Mufson, 'The green machine: promoting the future, Van Jones has no shortage of energy'.

government; conservative Republicans seized upon activities from earlier in his life, when he had belonged to a black revolutionary organisation with a Marxist orientation called Standing Together to Organize a Revolutionary Movement (STORM). Various radical political statements he had made were unearthed and circulated. As in the cases of Reverend Jeremiah Wright[44] and Shirley Sherrod,[45] Obama chose to duck the controversy rather than risk being perceived as an angry black man himself. Jones resigned, and the position of green jobs coordinator was left vacant.

However, Jones's departure was not the end of the green jobs concept. As Stephen Cohen has pointed out, Obama's 2011 State of the Union address, criticised by many environmentalists for failing to say anything about climate, actually presented a strong climate programme partially disguised as job creation: one million electric cars on the road by 2015, and 80 per cent of electricity from 'clean energy' sources by 2035.[46] Cohen argues that 'These energy goals, when coupled with EPA's regulation of greenhouse gasses under the Clean Air Act, are the Obama climate policy. While it is less comprehensive than cap and trade or a carbon tax, it is a real, operational policy.'[47]

This emphasis on jobs continues. Obama's climate plan is full of such statements as 'Since 2009, the Department of Interior has approved 25 utility-scale solar facilities, nine wind farms, and 11 geothermal plants, which will provide enough electricity to power 4.4 million homes and support an estimated 17,000 jobs.'[48] The president is clearly eager to have his climate programme perceived as one that creates prosperity, rather than sacrifice.

Emphasising the positive benefits of environmental protection, rather than calling on everyone to sacrifice, is a good idea.[49] Unfortunately, Obama tends to lose sight of the environment while he promotes the economic benefits. For example, in the 2011 State of the Union address mentioned above, he defined 'clean energy' as follows: 'Some folks want wind and solar. Others want nuclear, clean coal and natural gas. To meet this goal, we will need them all – and I urge Democrats and Republicans to work together to make it happen.'[50]

There is nothing clean about any of these energy sources. Coal and natural gas both produce greenhouse gases when they are burned; and while it is true

44 For an excellent account of the Wright controversy from the viewpoint of his former congregation, see Grant and Grant, *The Moment: Barack Obama, Jeremiah Wright, and the Firestorm at Trinity United Church of Christ*.

45 See Sherrod, *The Courage to Hope: How I Stood up to the Politics of Fear*.

46 The White House, Office of the Press Secretary, 'Remarks of President Obama in the State of the Union Address – as prepared for delivery'.

47 Cohen, 'The transition from environmental politics to sustainability politics'.

48 'The President's Climate Action Plan', p. 6.

49 Lappé, *EcoMind: Changing the Way We Think, to Create the World We Want*.

50 'The President's Climate Action Plan'.

that some experts believe that nuclear power is better for the planet than fossil fuels, both sides of that debate agree that it generates highly toxic waste that must be controlled for hundreds of thousands of years. Here, as in other areas, President Obama has chosen to promote his policies by confusing the public.

Conclusion

At the time of writing the federal government was mostly closed because of the refusal of the House of Representatives to pass a resolution to allow it to continue to spend money; there was a real possibility that the government would default on its debt because of the political impasse. Given this level of conflict, Obama must be commended for accomplishing anything at all in the environmental area. He has made real steps towards reducing the rate of greenhouse gas emissions and moving the country towards renewable energy.

Unfortunately, a different standard has to be applied in environmental matters. Along with asking whether the president has done as much as could be expected, the question must be asked 'has he has done enough to save the planet?', and here the answer is that he has not. Moreover, it is the very approach by stealth that has allowed him to make progress – for example, by relabelling environmental preservation as green jobs – that has also meant he has failed to raise public understanding of the threat to the planet and the need for stronger action to protect the climate. Ultimately, congressional denial of climate change and resistance to cutting emissions will only be overcome if the public comes to understand how dangerously wrong such resistance is. Changing public consciousness may be the most important thing the president can do, and he has not done much of it. His Climate Action Plan and his strong speech in its favour showed signs of such change in his second term. We should all hope that this is the case, as there is not much time left.

References

M. Bachmann (2008) '"Cap and trade?" More like '"tax and spend"', *StarTribune.Com*, 9 June, www.startribune.com/opinion/commentary/19678679.html?page=1&c=y (accessed 6 Feb. 2014).

F. Barringer (2012) 'For new generation of power plants, a new emission rule from the E.P.A', *New York Times*, 27 March, www.nytimes.com/2012/03/28/science/earth/epa-sets-greenhouse-emission-limits-on-new-power-plants.html?_r=0 (accessed 6 Feb. 2014).

J.C. Berg (2012) 'Environmental policy: the success and failure of Obama', in W. Crotty (ed.), *The Obama Administration: Promise and Performance* (Lanham MD: Lexington).

— (2013) 'Issue suppression and the crisis of the American party system: the cost of two-party duopoly', paper presented at the American Politics Group, Leicester, Social Science Research Network, http://papers.ssrn.com/sol3/papers.cfm?abstract_id=2198572 (accessed 6 Feb. 2014).

L.R. Brown, J. Larsen, J.G. Dorn and F.C. Moore (2008) 'Time for Plan B: cutting carbon emissions 80 percent by 2020' (Environmental Policy Institute), www.earth-policy.org/press_room/C68/80by2020 (accessed 6 Feb. 2014).

A. Childers (2013) 'Environmental groups seek to rally support for Obama's Climate Action Plan', *Bloomberg BNA*, 16 Aug., www.bna.com/environmental-groups-seek-n17179875873/ (accessed 6 Feb. 2014).

S. Cohen (2011) 'The transition from environmental politics to sustainability politics', *Huffington Post* ('Green' section), 31 Jan., www.huffingtonpost.com/steven-cohen/the-transition-from-envir_b_816198.html (accessed 6 Feb. 2014).

Executive Office of the President (2013) 'The President's Climate Action Plan', www.whitehouse.gov/sites/default/files/image/president27sclimateactionplan.pdf (accessed 6 Feb. 2014).

D. Fogarty (2009) 'Indonesia forest projects target 13 mln CO2 offsets' (for Reuters), www.reuters.com/article/latestCrisis/idUSSP436960 (accessed 6 Feb. 2014).

K. Galbraith (2009) 'Michele Bachmann seeks "armed and dangerous" opposition to cap-and-trade', 'Green' (a *New York Times* blog about energy and the environment), 25 March, http://green.blogs.nytimes.com/2009/03/25/michele-bachmann-seeks-armed-and-dangerous-opposition-to-cap-and-trade/ (accessed 6 Feb. 2014).

C. A. Grant and S.J. Grant (2013) *The Moment: Barack Obama, Jeremiah Wright, and the Firestorm at Trinity United Church of Christ* (Lanham, MD: Rowman & Littlefield).

S. Goldenberg (2010) 'Cancún agreement rescues UN credibility but falls short of saving planet', *The Guardian*, 12 Dec., www.theguardian.com/environment/2010/dec/12/cancun-agreement-rescues-un-credibility (accessed 6 Feb. 2014).

A. Goodman (2011) 'Over 160 arrested in ongoing civil disobedience against Keystone XL tar sands oil pipeline', radio interview with Bill McKibben from Tar Sands Action, *Democracy NOW*, www.democracynow.org/2011/8/23/over_160_arrested_in_ongoing_civil (accessed 6 Feb. 2014).

Government of Alberta (2008) *Alberta's Oil Sands: Opportunity. Balance* (Edmonton: Government of Alberta), www.environment.alberta.ca/documents/Oil_Sands_Opportunity_Balance.pdf (accessed 6 Feb. 2014).

J. Hansen et al. (2008) 'Target atmospheric CO2: where should humanity aim?', *The Open Atmospheric Science Journal*, vol. 2, no. 1, pp. 217–31, www.columbia.edu/~jeh1/2008/TargetCO2_20080407.pdf (accessed 6 Feb. 2014).

J. Hansen, M. Sako, G. Russell and P. Kharecha (2013) 'Climate sensitivity, sea level and atmospheric carbon dioxide', *Philosophical Transactions of the Royal Society*, vol. 371, no. 2001, http://rsta.royalsocietypublishing.org/content/371/2001/20120294.abstract?sid=9cf2cd48–5f7f-4bb8–8721-c40d19a13064 (accessed 6 Feb. 2014).

C. Hedegaard (2012) 'Why the Doha climate conference was a success', *The Guardian*, 14 Dec., www.theguardian.com/environment/2012/dec/14/doha-climate-conference-success (accessed 6 Feb. 2014).

L. Heinzerling (2013), 'Who will run the EPA?', *Yale Journal on Regulation*, vol. 30, pp. 39–43, http://jreg.commons.yale.edu/who-will-run-the-epa/ (accessed 31 March 2014).

D. Jehl (2001) 'E.P.A. to abandon new arsenic limits for water supply', *New York Times*, 21 March, www.nytimes.com/2001/03/21/us/epa-to-abandon-new-arsenic-limits-for-water-supply.html (accessed 6 Feb. 2014).

M. Jerrett, et al. (2009) 'Long-term ozone exposure and mortality', *New England Journal of Medicine*, vol. 360, no. 11, pp. 1085–95, www.nejm.org/doi/full/10.1056/NEJMoa0803894 (accessed 6 Feb. 2014).

W.S. Jevons (1866) *The Coal Question; an Enquiry Concerning the Progress of the Nation, and the Probable Exhaustion of Our Coal-Mines* (London: Macmillan).

V. Jones and A. Conrad (2008) *The Green-Collar Economy: How One Solution Can Fix Our Two Biggest Problems* (New York, NY: HarperOne).

R. Karaim (2011) 'Climate change', in *Global Environmental Issues: Selections from The CQ Researcher* (Washington, DC: CQ Press), pp. 3–26.

P. Kollipara (2011) 'Keystone pipeline protesters surround White House', *San Francisco Chronicle*, 7 Nov., www.sfgate.com/news/article/Keystone-pipeline-protesters-surround-White-House-2324253.php (accessed 6 Feb. 2014).

F. M. Lappé (2011) *EcoMind: Changing the Way We Think, to Create the World We Want* (New York, NY: Nation Books).

T. Macalister (2009) 'Britain's big polluters accused of abusing EU's carbon trading scheme', *The Guardian*, 27 Jan., www.theguardian.com/

business/2009/jan/27/industry-abusing-ets-carbon-trading (accessed 6 Feb. 2014).

B. McKibben (2011) 'Big news: we won. You won', www.tarsandsaction.org/ big-news-won-won/ (accessed 6 Feb. 2014).

J. Mayer (2011) 'Taking it to the streets', New Yorker, 28 Nov., www. newyorker.com/talk/comment/2011/11/28/111128taco_talk_mayer (accessed 6 Feb. 2014).

S. Mufson (2008) 'The green machine: promoting the future, Van Jones has no shortage of energy', Washington Post, 9 Dec., www.washingtonpost. com/wp-dyn/content/article/2008/12/08/AR2008120803569.html (accessed 6 Feb. 2014).

P. Mushak (2000) 'Arsenic and old laws: a scientific and public health analysis of arsenic occurrence in drinking water, its health effects, and EPA's outdated arsenic tap water standard', www.nrdc.org/water/drinking/ arsenic/aolinx.asp (accessed 6 Feb. 2014).

R. Nuwer (2012) 'A 20-year low in U.S. carbon emissions', New York Times ('Green' section), 17 Aug., http://green.blogs.nytimes.com/2012/08/17/a-20-year-low-in-u-s-carbon-emissions/?_r=0 (accessed 6 Feb. 2014).

R.T. Pierrehumbert (2011) 'Keystone XL: game over?', Real Climate: Climate Science from Climate Scientists, 2 Nov., www.realclimate.org/index.php/ archives/2011/11/keystone-xl-game-over/ (accessed 6 Feb. 2014).

D. Rees (2009), 'McConnell speaks out about cap and trade', WYMT News, 12 Aug., www.wkyt.com/wymt/home/headlines/53085962.html (accessed 6 Feb. 2014).

A.C. Revkin (2011) 'Keystone oil pipeline decision moved after election', New York Times, 10 Nov., http://dotearth.blogs.nytimes.com/2011/11/10/ keystone-oil-pipeline-decision-moved-after-election/?ref=keystonepipeline (accessed 6 Feb. 2014).

M.E. Richmond (2012) 'Assessing Obama's decision not to support EPA's revised ozone standard: a further retreat from a progressive agenda?', Race, Gender and Class Journal, vol. 20, no. 1–2 (University of New Orleans), pp. 25–41, http://rgc.uno.edu/journal/journal10-16.cfm (accessed 6 Feb. 2014).

S. Rojstaczer (2001) 'Arsenic in water: how much is safe?', New York Times, 21 March, www.nytimes.com/2001/03/23/opinion/l-arsenic-in-water-how-much-is-safe-528323.html (accessed 6 Feb. 2014).

M.D. Shear (2013) 'Republicans see Keystone pipeline as a card to play in last-minute fiscal talks', New York Times, 24 Sep., www.nytimes.

com/2013/09/25/us/republicans-see-keystone-pipeline-as-a-card-to-play-in-last-minute-fiscal-talks.html (accessed 6 Feb. 2014).

S. Sherrod (2012) *The Courage to Hope: How I Stood up to the Politics of Fear* (New York, NY: Atria).

C.R. Sunstein (2013) 'The Office of Information and Regulatory Affairs: myths and realities', *Harvard Law Review*, vol. 126, no. 7 (May), pp. 1838–78.

The White House Office of the Press Secretary (2011) 'Remarks of President Obama in the State of the Union Address – as prepared for delivery' (Washington, DC: White House), www.whitehouse.gov/the-press-office/2011/01/25/remarks-president-barack-obama-state-union-address-prepared-delivery (accessed 6 Feb. 2014).

United States Environmental Protection Agency (2007) *EPA's Endangerment Finding: Legal Background*, summary (Washington, DC: Environmental Protection Agency), 1, www.epa.gov/climatechange/Downloads/endangerment/EndangermentFinding_LegalBasis.pdf (accessed 31 March 2014).

— (2013) 'EPA proposes carbon pollution standards for new power plants: Agency takes important step to reduce carbon pollution from power plants as part of President Obama's Climate Action Plan', http://yosemite.epa.gov/opa/admpress.nsf/0/da9640577ceacd9f85257beb006cb2b6!Open Document (accessed 31 March 2014).

— (2013) '*U.S. greenhouse gas emissions*', online indicator, www.epa.gov/climatechange/science/indicators/ghg/us-ghg-emissions.html (accessed 31 March 2014).

A. Viard (2009) 'The cap-and-trade giveaway', *The American: The Journal of the American Enterprise Institute*, 26 June, www.american.com/archive/2009/june/the-cap-and-trade-giveaway (accessed 6 Feb. 2014).

M.L. Wald (2012) 'Court backs E.P.A. over emissions limits intended to reduce global warming', *New York Times*, 26 June, www.nytimes.com/2012/06/27/science/earth/epa-emissions-rules-backed-by-court.html (accessed 6 Feb. 2014).

T. Weis (2013) 'President Obama's Climate Action Plan: not even close', *Huffington Post*, 13 Aug., www.huffingtonpost.com/tom-weis/obama-climate-plan_b_3744885.html (accessed 6 Feb. 2014).

8. 'Heart and hand'? US–UK relations under President Obama

Ashlee Godwin

The last meeting between the leaders of the United States and United Kingdom prior to the November 2012 election hinted at a bilateral relationship in good health.[1] Of course, by this point, Barack Obama and David Cameron had dropped Winston Churchill's term, the 'special relationship',[2] in favour of their own descriptor, the 'essential relationship', which it was felt better reflected the reality of changing times. Nevertheless, their coauthored op-ed, published at the outset of Cameron's visit, applied the description 'heart and hand', another Churchillian phrase (used by him to hail the possibilities when the two countries work together), to bilateral relations in the 21st century:

> The alliance between the United States and Great Britain is a partnership
> of the heart, bound by history, traditions and values we share. But what
> makes our relationship special – a unique and essential asset – is that we
> join hands across so many endeavours.[3]

The Obama administration's first term witnessed the continuation and initiation of many such joint endeavours, especially in the realms of security and diplomacy, as might be expected. Yet the administration's apparent disregard for the UK in its early months in office suggested that such references to the 'heart' were merely politically-expedient rhetoric, confirming for some (especially in the UK) a persistent trend in this regard. Furthermore, policies such as the Asia 'rebalancing', first formally outlined in 2011, served only to underscore the significance of broad geopolitical changes and their likely impact on the US–UK relationship in the longer term. Indeed, with the United States increasingly looking to the Asia-Pacific for the economic and political prosperity that underpins its leadership in the global arena, and with the UK – like other former 'Great Powers' of Europe – experiencing perceptible decline in terms of resources if not ambition, at least in relative terms, it is not difficult

---

1 Obama and Cameron, 'United States and Great Britain: an essential relationship'.
2 Coined as the Iron Curtain descended across Europe.
3 Obama and Cameron, 'United States and Great Britain: an essential relationship'.

to see why some observers concluded that the UK 'faces a growing struggle to remain relevant in U.S. eyes.'[4]

However, those who ask how the UK can best remain relevant or useful to the US are asking the wrong question: instead, it is necessary to assess where their interests continue to converge. In fact, so long as the US and the UK both retain an interest in maintaining the liberal-democratic world they built between them,[5] there will remain areas of global governance and matters of stability on which they can fruitfully collaborate. It is in these areas, therefore, that the two countries – in Cameron's words, 'the united states of liberty and enterprise'[6] – will more naturally remain important to each other.

The changing geopolitical landscape

Upon his election at the end of 2008, President Obama inherited three major significant strategic challenges, shared to a lesser or greater extent by the UK.

First, the previous seven years had severely tarnished the reputations of the US and the UK, as they became bogged down in costly and unpopular wars in Afghanistan and Iraq[7] – the latter explicitly declared illegal by Kofi Annan, the then UN Secretary-General.[8] The United States' credibility was particularly damaged by the controversial practices allegedly used in the prosecution of the War on Terror, while in the UK the centrality of the relationship with the US to British foreign policy came under intense and prolonged scrutiny.

The two countries were also experiencing similar and considerable fiscal difficulties due to the global crisis that took hold in 2007–08, sending their economies into deep recession. For both the US and the UK, this reduced the time, energy, money and political capital that could be expended on serious foreign policy issues – of particular concern to Obama given his ambitious domestic agenda. Furthermore, it undermined the credibility of the US as a global leader and of the international financial system its leadership underpinned, while making it significantly more difficult for the UK to meet its long-standing aim of maintaining its status as 'a country whose political, economic and cultural authority far exceeds [its] size'.[9]

4   Mix, 'The United Kingdom and U.S.-UK relations', p. 8.

5   Russell Mead, *God and Gold: Britain, American and the Making of the Modern World*, pp. xii–xiii.

6   'PM and President Obama remarks at White House arrival ceremony', 14 March 2013. See transcript at: https://www.gov.uk/government/speeches/pm-and-president-obama-remarks-at-white-house-arrival-ceremony (accessed 13 Feb. 2014).

7   Haass, 'The irony of American strategy: putting the Middle East in proper perspective'.

8   MacAskill and Borger, 'Iraq war was illegal and breached UN charter'.

9   HM Government, *A Strong Britain in an Age of Uncertainty: The National Security Strategy*, p. 4.

Most importantly, the economic crisis hastened the relative decline of the US and the UK, thereby augmenting the effects of the third strategic challenge: 'the rise of the rest' as power shifted away from the west.[10] By 2009, it was clear that a whole range of powers that were rising economically and politically – primarily the BRIC countries of Brazil, Russia, India and China – might soon be in a position to challenge US leadership on the world stage. The tangible result of this diffusion of power was that resources were stretched even further as the two countries sought to navigate a much more complex geopolitical system, a constraint more keenly felt by the UK which, lacking the superpower's advantage in terms of resources and stature, found it increasingly difficult to project its already diminished influence abroad.

Thus although the US and the UK were faced with the same changes to the geopolitical landscape that had unfolded while they were preoccupied in the Middle East, their dissimilar standing on the global stage meant that they felt the impact of this shift in the global balance of power differently. As a result, their responses to these challenges were necessarily shaped by their divergent experiences, long-term goals and the options available to them.

The Obama administration's response was threefold: first, to disentangle the US from ongoing combat operations in Iraq and Afghanistan; second, to restore American leadership through 'smart power' activities such as the Global Health and Feed the Future initiatives; and third, to rebalance its focus towards the Asia-Pacific, given the region's centrality to American economic and strategic interests. Indeed, although not official policy until October 2011, the administration's intention to harness Asia's 'growth and dynamism' was clear from the start, as was the attendant need to ensure security there.[11]

The hallmark of the pursuit of these goals has been an increased emphasis on multilateralism, diplomacy and development. This speaks to the administration's desire to rehabilitate the US within the international community as well as for increased burden-sharing on the part of its allies, with the US acting as the catalyst that creates the conditions for success without becoming entangled itself.[12] Crucially, this also betrays an attempt to tie emerging powers, including China, into the world order that the US and its western allies built as World War Two drew to a close; to shape a potentially hostile world order as it emerges by giving these countries a voice in the system and therefore, consequently, a vested interest in its upkeep.

This approach, however, raises significant questions for the UK, whose desire to continue punching above its weight in global affairs is being undermined not only by its own relative decline, but also by a lack of resources with which to

---

10   Zakaria, 'The future of American power: how America can survive the rise of the rest'.

11   H. Clinton, 'America's Pacific century'.

12   The Economist, 'Time to engage'.

shoulder a greater share of the burden, as desired by its foremost ally. As such, despite the assertion in the United States' 2010 National Security Strategy that the 'relationship with [its] European allies remains the cornerstone for U.S. engagement with the world',[13] in an increasingly 'G20 world'[14] in which the centre of gravity has shifted towards the Asia-Pacific, these 'traditional' alliances may become less relevant to the US. Therefore, a long-standing and intimate ally such as the UK can reasonably expect its relationship with the US to evolve in the coming years and its influence to be diluted, thereby heightening the impact of the changing geopolitical conditions on its own international status.[15]

A four-tiered relationship

The term 'special relationship' was once assumed to encompass both the emotional facets of the US–UK relationship – born of shared heritage, culture, values and language, melded in the 'crucible' of World War Two[16] – and the practical elements: that is, the infrastructure established after 1945 that enabled long-term and unusually close cooperation in matters of vital importance to national security, signifying their common interests during the Cold War as it unfolded.

The strength, historically, of the emotional ties is debatable. Today, however, undue emphasis on this aspect of the relationship, weakened by demographic changes in both countries, undoubtedly engenders false expectations of what it can deliver – manifested in the recommendation by the UK House of Commons Foreign Affairs Committee (FAC) in 2010 that the term 'special relationship' no longer be used because of its misleading connotations of 'totality'.[17]

By contrast, the infrastructure established after World War Two remains strong, underpinned now by 'the habits of cooperation' and 'high degree of mutual trust' that encapsulate the maturity of the relationship.[18] This durability is also born of the fact that the two countries continue to share a broad interest in maintaining global stability, especially given their mutual economic emphasis on trade. It is this consideration that has been the driving factor behind many of the collaborative efforts witnessed during the Obama administration's first term, including diplomacy in relation to Iran and Syria,

13 The White House, 'U.S. National Security Strategy', p. 41.

14 The Group of Twenty – finance ministers and central bank governors from 19 countries and the European Union, together representing 20 of the world's major economies – which meets to discuss global economic issues.

15 HM Government, *A Strong Britain in an Age of Uncertainty: The National Security Strategy*, p. 15.

16 Edelman, 'A special relationship in jeopardy'.

17 FAC, House of Commons, *Global Security: UK–US Relations*, p. 22.

18 Mix, 'The United Kingdom and U.S.–UK Relations', p. 1.

military operations in Libya and the Gulf of Aden, and the implementation of soft power initiatives aimed at ensuring stability before a crisis emerges, rather than seeking to restore it after the fact.

Nevertheless, as a 'living' relationship, it cannot be expected that the two countries' interests will always converge or that domestic imperatives will not frequently prevail. Secretary Hillary Clinton's assertion in March 2010 that the UK and Argentina should discuss the sovereignty of the Falkland Islands neatly demonstrates the former, given the American emphasis on cultivating relations with Latin America;[19] while Cameron's initiation in July 2010 of an investigation into possible UK complicity in extraordinary rendition is an apposite example of the latter. Such divergence in individual areas of policy does not, however, preclude extensive cooperation in others.

It is also true that the UK is not alone in its close cooperation with the United States, especially on defence matters, being one of several countries 'plugged into' the American-led global security architecture.[20] The US has many similarly 'special' relationships with countries in different regions; for example, with Canada for purposes of domestic security, and Japan, which plays an equivalent role in Asia to that performed by the UK in Europe. Thus the UK's relationship with the US is not '*the* special relationship' but '*a* special relationship'.[21]

Where the relationship does differ, however, is in the UK's unmatched access to US policy deliberations, thereby endowing it with the opportunity to air its views and concerns as well as to shape the way the administration thinks about an issue before policy is finalised. The constructive criticism which it provides in confidence can be valued by the US,[22] which benefits from the views of a trusted friend and ally with interests, language and values in common, but with a different background and, often, an alternative perspective.[23] However, this access rarely translates into influence over final policy, not least because 'This is an unequal relationship in the sense that the United States is a global power.'[24]

Thus, as Sir Jeremy Greenstock, former UK Ambassador to the United Nations (UN), notes, the relationship is not special 'unless we are introducing substance to make it special.'[25] This is especially so under the Obama administration, which takes a much more 'transactional' approach to the

19   Thompson, 'Clinton urges talks on the Falkland Islands'.

20   Interview with John Bassett, associate fellow in cyber security, Royal United Services Institute for Defence and Security Studies (RUSI), Sep. 2013.

21   Ibid.

22   Interview with James de Waal, visiting fellow, Chatham House, Sep. 2013.

23   Interview with Air Vice-Marshal Michael Harwood, former UK defence attaché to the US (2010–13), London, Sep. 2013.

24   FAC, *Global Security*, p. 56.

25   Ibid., p. 21.

United States' external relationships, including with the UK,[26] not least because of its emphasis on burden-sharing. As such, it is important to assess the substance of the relationship since the change in administration in 2009 across the four broad tiers: political; economic and cultural; diplomatic; and defence and security.

Tier I: Political relations

The 'stronger than usual outbreak' of anxiety among British media and political commentators about the future of US–UK relations under Obama – focused primarily on his lack of natural affinity with the UK (and Europe) – peaked shortly after the president's inauguration in January 2009, prompting frustrated US Embassy officials to observe that: 'This over-reading would often be humorous, if it were not so corrosive.'[27]

Nevertheless, there proved to be a seed of truth in these concerns. With Prime Minister Tony Blair previously accused of being Bush's 'poodle' and his successor Gordon Brown having subsequently distanced himself from the Bush administration, it was hoped that the rock-star candidate, once elected, would sweep away the hangover of the Iraq years. Instead, the Obama administration initially adopted an attitude of 'benign neglect', the like of which had not been seen for decades.[28] This can be attributed partly to disadvantageous timing, with Brown in the twilight of his premiership, but also to the UK's lack of familiarity with Obama's 'kitchen cabinet' advisers, such as Susan Rice and Samantha Power.[29] This perceptible aloofness left some declaring the relationship to be in trouble, 'suffering from neglect on both sides'.[30]

However, there does seem to have been a step-change in top-level relations with the change in government in the UK in May 2010, possibly because Obama had found working with China, India and Turkey to be 'tougher than initially expected'.[31] Robert Singh, by contrast, suggests that political officials in the State Department had by this point begun to appreciate the 'diplomatic heft' of the UK and that the British and French success in corralling allies, including the United States, into contributing to the 2011 military operation in Libya was a 'watershed' in political, if not military, terms.[32] While the administration felt boxed in by the manoeuvring of its European allies, the

---

26 Interview with Robert Singh, professor of politics, Birkbeck, University of London, Sep. 2013.

27 US Embassy Cable, 'Subject: the British ask, is our relationship still special in Washington?', 9 Feb. 2009.

28 Interview with Robert Singh.

29 Ibid.

30 Inboden, 'Is there still time to save the special relationship?'.

31 Kupchan, 'No dilemma between Europe and Asia for Washington strategists'.

32 Interview with Robert Singh.

operation did at least fit with Obama's view of the US as a facilitator. It also demonstrated that the coalition government could 'get things done', unlike its predecessor, whose waning political will regarding the Middle East campaigns had sown disenchantment within the Bush administration.[33]

Since then, it appears that Obama and Cameron have developed a working relationship that is business-like, if not particularly close. In crude terms, it means that the British Prime Minister can still gain direct access relatively quickly to his American counterpart, although this unrivalled connection is not institutionalised at other levels of the body politic.[34] The complexity of the US governance structure means that, without stronger linkages with members of Congress responsible for the nuts and bolts of policy, it will remain challenging to translate this access into actual influence over policy choice.

Tier II: Economic and cultural interaction

The strength of the relationship at this tier is most easily illustrated through numbers. Put simply, at $900 billion, the bilateral investment relationship is the largest in the world.[35] The US remains the number one destination of UK exports, valued in 2011 at $45.9 billion, while UK imports from the US that year were worth $44.7 billion.[36] However, this deep economic connection increased the two countries' vulnerability at the height of the global crisis,[37] impacting on their respective foreign policy options and exposing differences at the political level: having initially collaborated in steering the G20 away from fiscal protectionism, and despite the meticulous coordination between the Bank of England and Federal Reserve at the outset of the crisis, the US and the UK diverged in their domestic responses thereafter, with the latter pursuing stringent austerity measures.

Culturally, tourism remains an important element: indeed, in 2010, 3.85 million Britons visited the US and 2.71 million Americans made the return journey.[38] The two countries are also each other's most important scientific research partners, together producing eight of the nine Nobel prizes in science in 2010;[39] and the media is becoming an increasingly strong link: while US television programmes and films have long had a firm foothold in the UK, their British counterparts are becoming ever more popular across the Atlantic.[40]

33   Interview with John Bassett.
34   Interview with Robert Singh.
35   'PM and President Obama remarks at White House arrival ceremony'.
36   Mix, 'The United Kingdom and U.S.–UK relations', p. 13.
37   Ibid.
38   US Department of State, United Kingdom 'Fact Sheet'.
39   'PM and President Obama remarks at White House arrival ceremony'.
40   FAC, *Global Security*, p. 12.

Although such observations are difficult to demonstrate in quantitative and qualitative terms, they do suggest that fears concerning the effect of the significant demographic changes in both countries are, for the time being at least, overstated.[41]

Tier III: Joint diplomatic endeavours

The shared membership by the US and the UK of many major multilateral fora is amplified by their respective access to other frameworks on the basis of regional and historical links. It is not surprising, therefore, that the two frequently coordinate their diplomatic efforts in areas of mutual interest, with recent high-profile examples including: imposing sanctions on the Iranian regime through the UN and 'coordinating [their] diplomatic approach with China, France, Germany and Russia';[42] obtaining UN Security Council resolutions authorising counter-piracy operations in the Gulf of Aden and the establishment of a no-fly zone over Libya (having gained the explicit backing of regional partners such as the Arab League); and, in relation to the early months of the Syrian crisis, working with international partners to 'tighten the noose around Bashar al-Assad'.[43]

Recent events have confirmed the particular value to the US of the UK's diplomatic expertise and its alternative approach as a global power without superpower status. As explained by Sir Jeremy Greenstock: 'The UK is a lot better at the tactical handling of other [UN] delegations and of language in drafting texts and tactical manoeuvring. ... The Americans appreciate that, because it brings them something they don't normally have.'[44] The UK also remains a key ally in the North Atlantic Treaty Organization (NATO) – supporting the US at the 2012 Chicago Summit, for instance, in making the case for withdrawal from Afghanistan by the end of 2014 – and especially in the EU, where it has been instrumental in the imposition of sanctions on Iran and Syria. Finally, the UK's willingness to lead on diplomatic initiatives (hosting conferences for stakeholders in Somalia's future, for example) and to speak out on controversial subjects (as UK Foreign Secretary William Hague has frequently done regarding Syria) means that on some issues the US can afford to take a step back, with its ally shouldering more of the burden.

Tier IV: Defence and security integration

Encompassing nuclear, intelligence, military and, increasingly, counter-terrorism and cyber capabilities, the bilateral defence relationship is the one element of wider US–UK relations that truly merits the term 'special'. This

---

41 Edelman, 'A special relationship in jeopardy'.

42 Obama and Cameron, 'United States and Great Britain'.

43 Ibid.

44 FAC, *Global Security*, pp. 54–5.

foundation stone represents more than 70 years of defence cooperation, crystallised through Cold War-era agreements, and the subsequent development of an exceptional level of trust and understanding that 'almost defies analysis'.[45]

To this day, the UK remains the only country with which the US shares nuclear technology, a unique cooperation established under the 1958 US–UK Mutual Defense Agreement and most recently reaffirmed in 2006. This is also one of few areas in which the UK adds real value in intellectual and practical terms, through its contribution of expertise in nuclear science, particularly in weapons and propulsion technology, and its position as a trusted ally with a different vantage point. Indeed, James de Waal argues that the 'alternative perspective the British bring [in these areas] in a safe context ... is not easily quantified but apparently beneficial'.[46]

In addition, the intelligence-sharing relationship between the US and the UK remains extremely strong. Formalised under the 1947 UKUSA ('Five Eyes') Agreement, collaboration since 2009 has become increasingly focused on counter-terrorism, in preparation for the London 2012 Olympic and Paralympic Games, for example, and most notably exposing planned attacks using air freight in 2010. It has also been formally extended into the cyber realm through a bilateral Memorandum of Understanding signed in 2011.

The controversial National Security Agency (NSA) and Government Communications Headquarters (GCHQ) internet surveillance schemes confirm this impression of a bilateral intelligence-sharing relationship that is fundamentally robust and useful to both parties. PRISM and Operation Tempora were launched by the two agencies in order to meet the challenge posed by counter-terrorism data-collection and the proliferation of communications technologies. Tempora in particular is a distinctive capability, benefiting from the UK's geographical position (as the point of landfall for fibre optic cables carrying global communications across the Atlantic), its reputedly more permissive legislation and, reportedly, US investment of more than £100 million.[47]

However, for the UK this raises considerable questions about the independence of its intelligence-gathering activities. Furthermore, despite vastly increased domestic capacity, the UK continues to rely on the NSA for 60 per cent of its refined intelligence.[48]

Nor has the intelligence relationship been entirely smooth during President Obama's first term. In October 2009, the UK High Court released 42 US intelligence documents relating to Binyam Mohamed, a British citizen suing

45 Interview with James de Waal.
46 Ibid.
47 Hopkins and Borger, 'Exclusive: NSA Pays £100m in Secret Funding for GCHQ'.
48 Ibid.

the UK for complicity in his alleged rendition and torture. Although parts of these documents had previously been made public by American courts, this prompted the Central Intelligence Agency (CIA) to suspend and review bilateral cooperation in this area,[49] a significant although not unprecedented step, with intelligence-sharing also halted temporarily in the late 1970s.[50] Foreign Secretary William Hague's announcement the following year of a judge-led inquiry into the UK's alleged role in such acts prompted equal concern. Although the 2013 Justice and Security Act addresses this issue more broadly – by extending closed material procedures into the main civil courts in England and Wales – this entire episode fuelled growing American fears over perceived judiciary activism in the UK.[51]

This collaboration between the two countries' intelligence services is mirrored in the deep coordination of their respective armed forces. The defence relationship is underpinned by the fact that 'Today it is impossible to imagine a mortal threat to each other's security that we would not face together'.[52] At its heart, meanwhile, is the interoperability and familiarity generated during decades of fighting side by side. Since 2001, the US and the UK armed forces have undertaken continuous operations in the Middle East – 'standing together' and 'bleeding together', to paraphrase President Obama.[53] The contributors of the two largest troop contingents in the International Security Assistance Force (ISAF), deployed without restrictive national caveats, the US and UK have also worked together in Operation Enduring Freedom, the simultaneous counter-terrorism mission in Afghanistan, as well as in Libya in 2011 and counter-piracy operations in the Gulf of Aden.

UK forces in Afghanistan were accorded both status and access to the operational planning process through the appointment of a British three-star general as ISAF's Deputy Commander, reflecting the long-standing, unrivalled integration of British officers throughout the US military structure, including in the Pentagon and US Central Command; the numbers of Ministry of Defence (MoD) personnel based in the US have varied greatly over the years, sometimes running into the thousands during major conflicts, but in recent times there have been a little over 700 military and civilian staff based all over the United States. A large proportion of these could be designated 'exchange posts', meaning that for every British member of staff in the US there is an

49 Interview with Mark Phillips, associate fellow, RUSI, London, Sep. 2013.
50 Dumbrell, 'The US–UK special relationship', p. 71.
51 Interview with Mark Phillips.
52 William Hague cited in Gardiner, 'Mind the gap: Is the relationship still special?'
53 'PM and President Obama remarks at White House arrival ceremony'.

American counterpart in the UK, indicating an extraordinary mutual trust.[54] While the UK gains all the benefits of 'being in the room' during discussion and planning, the US profits from the alternative viewpoint of an ally whose background is different but interests are similar.[55] Although the United States shares notably close defence relationships with other allies such as Japan and Australia, this integration of the US and UK armed forces at all levels remains unmatched by any of the United States' other allies.

The US also has over 9,000 personnel based in the UK[56] and makes frequent use of British bases elsewhere in the world, such as Diego Garcia, Cyprus and Ascension Island, which, according to James de Waal, represent 'politically reliable and important real estate in the US defence structure' that would be difficult to replace.[57] Beyond this, the forces sustain interoperability through the numerous joint training opportunities available to them. The year 2010, for example, saw the American and British navies come together with the French during Exercise Auriga,[58] while the statement of intent on aircraft carrier cooperation, signed in January 2012, is intended to help Royal Navy pilots maintain their skills while the UK regenerates a carrier-strike capability.

Collaboration between the armed forces is underpinned by the sharing of defence technology, joint procurement and bilateral defence sales. The UK is the only Tier 1 partner in the development of the F-35 Joint Strike Fighter, for instance; meanwhile, the UK imports US defence goods and services worth at least $2 billion each year, and approximately 17.5 per cent of all UK defence exports are destined for the US.[59] Moreover, in streamlining the sales process, the Defense Trade Cooperation Treaty, ratified in 2010 and in force from 2013, will likely increase bilateral defence trade.

Yet, the defence element did not survive the Obama administration's first term unscathed: the campaigns in Iraq and Afghanistan revealed weaknesses in the British defence capability, potentially causing lasting damage to the UK's martial reputation, especially in the eyes of its principal ally. The nadir of the British campaign in southern Iraq came in 2008, during the Iraqi-American Operation Charge of the Knights to wrest control of Basra back from the

54 Correspondence with Air Vice-Marshal Michael Harwood, Oct. 2013; The White House, 'Joint Fact Sheet: U.S. and UK Defense Cooperation'.

55 Interview with Air Vice-Marshal Harwood.

56 The White House, 'Joint Fact Sheet'.

57 Interview with James de Waal.

58 Ministry of Defence, 'Royal navy vessels exercise in the Atlantic', 20 May 2010, https://www.gov.uk/government/news/royal-navy-vessels-exercise-in-the-atlantic (accessed 13 Feb. 2014).

59 Ministry of Defence, 'UK–US defence equipment cooperation' (speech by the UK Minister for Defence Equipment, Support and Technology), Washington, DC, 23 April 2013, https://www.gov.uk/government/speeches/20130423-uk-us-defence-equipment-cooperation (accessed 13 Feb. 2014).

Mehdi Army. This was a deliberate attempt on the part of Iraqi President Nouri al-Maliki to compel the UK to re-engage – having withdrawn its forces to the airport outside of the city, under an agreement with local militias – or to force the US to assume the burden instead. From the US perspective, this episode exposed, first, decay in political will and, second, the British Army's failure to realise that its previous experience in Northern Ireland was not applicable to the situation in Basra and to adapt its approach accordingly.[60] Consequently, the impression held by the Bush administration by 2008 was of a less reliable ally, both politically and militarily.[61]

Helmand Province, on the other hand, was 'a different story but a better story', according to John Bassett. The contribution made by British special forces and intelligence was particularly valued, with the UK being one of a small number of ISAF contributors to stay the course until the end of 2014.[62] Nevertheless, there have also been many reports of US dissatisfaction with the performance of the British armed forces since they arrived in the province in 2006, undermined as they were by insufficient resources in terms of troops and equipment. A July 2013 study concluded that: 'By arriving with insufficient force, aligning themselves with local corrupt power-holders, relying on firepower to keep insurgents at bay and targeting the poppy crop, the British made matters worse', while, in a cable released by WikiLeaks, the US Embassy in Kabul reported back to Washington in late 2008 that 'we and Karzai agree the British are not up to the task of securing Helmand [without US support]' prior to the election of 2009.[63] This lends considerable weight to the suggestion that President Obama deployed US Marines into Helmand a year later because the British armed forces appeared incapable of securing the province alone.

These Middle East campaigns thus prompted substantive questions about British political will and military capabilities, but they also led to Britain scrutinising more closely the benefits of supporting the US in these endeavours. As Hew Strachan points out, the UK gained little in terms of political or operational influence, having barely been consulted during Obama's Afghanistan strategy review in 2009, for instance.[64] Once again, this indicates that access – in this case, at the operational and strategic levels – does not necessarily translate into policy influence.

The military element of what President Kennedy called the 'coral reef' of the US–UK relationship therefore suffered (perhaps irreversible) erosion

---

60 Interview with Mark Phillips.

61 FAC, *Global Security*, p. 64.

62 Interview with John Bassett.

63 Norton-Taylor, 'UK forces in Helmand "made matters worse", says report'; Boone et al., 'WikiLeaks cables expose Afghan contempt for British military'.

64 Strachan, 'British national strategy: who does it?', p. 51.

during the second half of the last decade. However, it would take a deliberate act to wrench apart the well-entrenched, structural elements of the defence relationship – from the stratified military integration to close intelligence and cyber collaboration, to the sharing of nuclear technology – which will therefore likely remain 'immunised'[65] from the political ebb and flow for some time to come.

Rebalancing towards Asia: a shift in the relationship?

Nevertheless, the headline foreign policy announcement of President Obama's first term – the 'rebalancing' towards the Asia-Pacific – raises significant strategic questions for the United Kingdom, whose latest National Security Strategy describes the US as continuing to be the central component of its foreign, defence and security policies.

What impact this proposed change in focus will have on Europe in the long term, and on the United States' involvement in it, is difficult to predict. The only observed effect on Europe so far has been the declared intention to shift some military resources away from the continent: in June 2012, then-Secretary of Defense Panetta announced that 60 per cent of US naval forces would be deployed in the Pacific by 2020, instead of the current 50/50 split with the Atlantic,[66] while the 2012 US defence strategy outlined plans to withdraw two heavy-armoured brigades from Europe, now that it is a producer rather than a consumer of security.[67] This may also reflect the increasing pressure on the US government to justify its permanent military presence in Europe now that it is no longer deemed essential to continental security, especially given growing domestic demand on limited funds.

Nevertheless, given that Europe remains the United States' leading trade partner by a large margin, it is difficult to imagine that the US would ignore a significant threat to stability in the region, and therefore to its own interests. Indeed, this was demonstrated by the recent deployment of 600 troops to Poland and the Baltic States for joint exercises designed to reassure and show solidarity with the United States' NATO allies, following Russia's annexation of Crimea in March 2014. Thus the United States' rebalancing would not leave Europe 'denuded or exposed'.[68] (Likewise, while some commentators predict that the so-called shale gas revolution in the US means it will soon have few vital interests in the Middle East,[69] it should be remembered that a major incident in that region would impact on the global price of oil and, in turn,

---

65 Interview with John Bassett.

66 BBC News, 'Leon Panetta: US to deploy 60% of navy fleet to Pacific'.

67 Department of Defense (DoD), 'Defense budget priorities and choices: January 2012', p. 6.

68 Interview with John Bassett.

69 Genté, 'Shale gas changes geopolitics'.

on the US economy.) This strategic emphasis on Asia might, however, mean that the US is much less willing to become involved in areas where its own national interests are not directly threatened, even if those of its European allies are, or where there are only moral imperatives at play, as in Libya in 2011 and Syria since then. Moreover, the impact of sequester-imposed budget cuts may also force this issue further than would otherwise be the case under the Asia 'rebalancing' policy.

It is in this context that the UK must consider its own strategic positioning, particularly in relation to where and how its national interests will converge with those of the US in the future. If the latter increasingly focuses on the Far East, the UK must review where the two countries can continue to collaborate effectively.

One option would be for the UK also to 'rebalance' eastwards in support of the US, deepening its engagement in the Asia-Pacific and 'backfilling' security commitments in the Middle East – a path formally set out in the UK's 2010 National Security Strategy in response to the development of 'new systems of influence'.[70] The coalition government has explored this in both word and deed: according to Hague, 'Today Britain is looking East as never before',[71] reflected in several visits by ministerial and trade delegations to China and India since 2010. Cameron's November 2012 trip to the Gulf also hinted at a return 'east of Suez' through the possible re-establishment of a permanent military presence, while uncertainty expressed by Japan over the United States' commitment to its security[72] may also constitute an opportunity for the UK, if a somewhat tricky one given the potential for friction with the US this entails.

An alternative would be for the UK to concentrate its efforts closer to home, focusing on maintaining stability – in political, economic and security terms – in Europe and its immediate neighbourhood. As an ally that tends to share the United States' values, interests and threat perceptions, 'there is scope for the UK to play a leading role in Europe which would in turn be of value to the US',[73] enabling the latter to divert more of its energies and resources to Asia.

These options are not, by nature, mutually exclusive; indeed, it is highly likely that the UK, and the US, would prefer to pursue them both wholeheartedly. However, ongoing fiscal restraints, limited resources and matters of national

---

70 HM Government, *A Strong Britain in an Age of Uncertainty: The National Security Strategy*, p. 15.

71 Second Fullerton Lecture, given by William Hague on 26 April 2012 at the International Institute for Strategic Studies, Singapore. See Think Defence in Blog, 'Britain in Asia – William Hague's speech', www.thinkdefence.co.uk/2012/04/britain-in-asia-william-hagues-speech/ (accessed 13 Feb. 2014).

72 Niblett, 'US foreign policy off-balance'.

73 FAC, *Global Security*, p. 76.

politics may mean this is not possible. These domestic drivers may also compel the UK to make policy decisions that will ultimately serve to weaken the US–UK relationship through a partial divergence of national interests or a diminishing ability on the UK's part to contribute in the areas traditionally valued by the US.

The shadow over UK defence

Despite the weaknesses exposed by the campaigns in the Middle East, the UK remains a first-rate military power. It is this primacy, along with its openness to trade, that enables it to sustain global influence. However, there is now real concern in both the UK and the US that the country's defence capability is being hollowed out as a result of the substantial cuts to the UK defence budget exacted under the coalition government.

The 2010 Strategic Defence and Security Review (SDSR) outlined a reduction in the defence budget by 7.5 per cent over four years, with the impact of this magnified by the large over-commitment in the forward defence budget – a 'black hole' estimated at £38 billion.

The fact that the scale of the cuts, and the speed with which they were implemented, caught some parts of the US government by surprise – with some policymakers in the White House and Pentagon seemingly more informed than, for instance, the embassy in London – signifies the deep institutional complexity of the bilateral relationship, with many constituencies on both sides.[74] As a sovereign matter for the UK, all elements of the US government had been greatly reluctant to intervene during the SDSR process.[75] Thus, although the broad preferences of the upper echelons of the Obama administration were known to UK policymakers – such as continuing to meet NATO's defence expenditure target of 2 per cent of GDP, and maintaining its presence in Afghanistan and its nuclear capability – it was less easy to be sure what mattered in terms of specific military capabilities. In some instances, this was because the fledgling government failed to ask the right questions of its principal ally;[76] more often, however, it was due to the conflicting answers it received from the different parts of the US government with which it engaged. This highlights how difficult it is even for an intimate ally to determine clearly the impact of domestic decisions on alliance relations.[77]

74 Correspondence with James de Waal, Oct. 2013.
75 Interview with Mark Phillips.
76 Ibid.
77 Correspondence with James de Waal.

Nevertheless, the United States' initial response to the SDSR was fairly positive:[78] indeed, there was relief, reportedly, in the Pentagon and the White House, not least because the UK remained committed in Afghanistan.[79] However, as the top-line figures were fleshed out in the ensuing months, it appeared, from the US perspective, that it might have been preferable for the UK to invest in niche areas (enabling it to perform discrete but useful tasks well) rather than trying to maintain a balanced but shallow force (with which it would take control of a section of the 'front line', as had traditionally been the case). The inability of the UK and France to conduct the operation in Libya without substantial US assistance – in crucial areas such as command and control, surveillance and air-to-air refuelling – only confirmed that it would be even more challenging for the US to focus on Asia if the military capabilities of its principal European allies declined further.

However, of greatest interest to some in the US, especially within the US Army,[80] were the changes to the size and structure of the British Army announced in July 2012. The additional reduction in numbers of Regulars to 82,000 (from 95,000 under the SDSR) prompted concern that the army would be unable to make a meaningful contribution to future land operations; while the plans regarding the Reserves element – to be increased in number and integrated fully into the army structure – were deemed unrealistic.[81] The US also concluded that the MoD had underestimated the costs and difficulties, and overestimated the effect, of implementing another key component of the Army 2020 concept: defence engagement abroad to tackle the causes of conflict before it materialises.[82]

Nor did defence cuts end with the 2010 SDSR: with the UK economy failing to recover as predicted, spending reviews in 2012 and 2013 outlined a further £1.4 billion in savings for 2014–16.[83] In addition, the more difficult strategic defence questions were not even asked during the last review process, an avowedly short-term exercise circumscribed by the ongoing campaign in Afghanistan. The successor to the Trident nuclear weapons programme is one such issue that will need to be addressed in the coming years but, at an anticipated cost of £25 billion,[84] this would severely reduce the funds available for other big-ticket items within the defence budget.

78   Interview with James de Waal.

79   Correspondence with James de Waal.

80   Ibid.

81   Interview with Mark Phillips.

82   Ibid.

83   Chalmers, 'Respite from the storm? Defence and the 2013 Spending Review outcome'.

84   Blitz, 'The price of deterrence'.

There was, however, some sympathy for the UK within US defence policymaking and military circles, as well as interest in the SDSR process itself, not least because in January 2012 the US announced defence cuts of $487 billion to be implemented over the following decade.[85] Furthermore, there had been fears in the UK that, despite the cutting-edge design and technology of the sea and air platforms due to be delivered after 2020, it would be priced out of US-led operations in the future by the newly-established American military concept Air-Sea Battle, with its emphasis on high-end technology and unprecedented interoperability between the armed services.[86] However, due to the imposition in January 2013 of sequestration – a 'blunt instrument' compared to the 2010 SDSR[87] – it remains to be seen whether the US will ultimately implement the concept as intended.

As the 2015 SDSR looms, the UK must therefore carefully consider the military capabilities it will need to continue playing a full part in the upkeep of global security, the cornerstone of its relationship with the US. Without certain capabilities – such as command and control, intelligence, surveillance and reconnaissance – and a critical mass of ground troops, the UK risks becoming a secondary military power, capable only of plugging into, rather than assuming a primary role within, US-led operations. It also risks being relegated as a European military ally below France which, having reintegrated into NATO structures, recently demonstrated its political will and independent military prowess in Mali.

The UK should also learn the lessons of the last SDSR and engage fully with its international allies as part of the review process; it should not, for example, complete the next review without asking what support US policymakers and military personnel might expect, should the country be drawn into military operations in the Pacific, and whether it would be in British interests to meet those expectations.

Heading for a 'Brexit'?[88]

Prime Minister Cameron's announcement in January 2013 that a re-elected Conservative government would hold a national referendum on EU membership by the end of 2017 prompted a rare public intervention by US diplomats. Assistant Secretary of State for European Affairs Philip Gordon made it clear that the United States' strategic interests lie in the UK being a 'strong voice' within the EU,[89] both because it commonly shares US values

---

85 DoD, 'Defense budget priorities and choices'.

86 Schwartz and Greenhert, 'Air-sea battle: promoting stability in an era of uncertainty'.

87 Interview with Air Vice-Marshal Harwood.

88 A blend of 'British' and 'exit'.

89 US Department of State, 'Media roundtable in London: remarks by Philip H. Gordon'.

and threat perceptions and because it is essential to the development of a more robust European defence and foreign affairs agenda. This strongly refutes the argument that the relationship with the US can substitute for membership of the EU. Indeed, as Gordon observed: 'I wouldn't underestimate the increasing weight of the EU in the world'[90] – a pointed hint that, despite long-standing defence collaboration and the shared outlook implicit to the US–UK relationship, the UK would not remain as important to the US 'outside' of Europe as it is 'inside'.

Nothing underscores the strategic significance of this question to the UK more than President Obama's announcement of the Trans-Atlantic Trade and Investment Partnership (TTIP), which could augment UK trade revenues by £10 billion a year.[91] Like the Trans-Pacific Partnership (TPP) and the Middle East and North Africa Trade and Investment Partnership Initiative (MENA-TIP), TTIP is an attempt to succeed where the World Trade Organization's negotiations in Doha have so far failed: in re-writing international trade rules so that they are more appropriate to today's globalised economy, the Obama administration is seeking to bind emerging economies and powers to an economic system rooted in the western principles of open and fair markets. Negotiations regarding the TTIP will be slow and incremental; it will also be difficult to overcome the 'many political forces [including Congress] that could de-rail' the process. Nevertheless, as Robert Singh observes, there remains 'cause for optimism'.[92]

Thus, regardless of the domestic debate, should the UK eventually withdraw from the EU, its global standing will be weakened and it may well lose the benefits of a free-trade agreement negotiated with the economic clout of the EU.

'Hand', not 'heart': looking ahead

The now-hackneyed and somewhat discredited phrase, the 'special relationship', no longer reflects the reality of US–UK relations, in which the 'hand' is rightfully emphasised over the 'heart' – that is, common interests are placed above historical and cultural ties. Its use, particularly by the British media and some political commentators, therefore undermines the credibility of a partnership which is important precisely because the two countries continue to 'join hands across so many endeavours'.[93]

90 Ibid.
91 Centre for Economic Policy Research, 'Estimating the economic impact on the UK of a Transatlantic Trade and Investment Partnership (TTIP) Agreement between the European Union and the United States', p. 6.
92 Interview with Robert Singh.
93 Obama and Cameron, 'United States and Great Britain'.

More importantly, it suggests an almost unthinking support on the part of the UK for US policy and, to a much lesser extent, vice versa, particularly in relation to matters of defence and security. However, this is a disservice to the relationship: as changes within the geopolitical order increasingly threaten the countries' respective international standing and influence, it is vitally important that both the US and the UK consider what they want from the relationship in practical terms. Of course, no alliance is purely transactional; but given President Obama's pragmatism and his emphasis on a more functional relationship,[94] the two countries should take this opportunity to assess where their national interests continue to converge and where their collaboration will be most valuable. For this process to be truly beneficial, they should also recognise, implicitly at least, that it is – in Cameron's words – 'a relationship not of sentiment but of choice'[95] and that states' interests do diverge. In other words, the US–UK relationship is not a 'shibboleth' to be conserved despite reality; instead, its strength derives from its utility.

Despite the geopolitical changes over the course of the last decade and the subsequent shift in the United States' attention to the Asia-Pacific, the US and the UK continue to share the aims of upholding the western-built international financial, legal and governance systems and of maintaining global stability. This is evident in their ongoing efforts to address major transnational threats such as non-proliferation and terrorism. Moreover, the preservation of global stability now extends beyond ensuring freedom of trade across the seas to the protection of information and trade in the cyber-sphere, with the globalisation of contemporary threats to security manifested in the growing prevalence of cyber-crime and cyber-attacks, transnational organised crime and cross-border tax evasion.

The UK has much to offer in these areas, potentially using its diplomatic expertise and networks to address such matters at the policy level (as seen at the UK-hosted G8 summit, in June 2013,[96] where corporate tax evasion was on the agenda) and broadening the focus of its intelligence capabilities beyond counter-terrorism in support of efforts to tackle these issues. Thus, while the bilateral relationship may change with evolving security threats and geopolitical conditions, it will still be significant – perhaps even essential – because there will remain substantial ground for collaboration where national interests converge and areas where the UK can really add value.

However, it will be important not to over-emphasise the military aspect of the relationship – despite its long-standing centrality – not least because there are real question marks over the UK's future defence capabilities, in terms

94 FAC, *Global Security*, p. 69.
95 Cameron, 'A staunch and self-confident ally'.
96 The Group of Eight forum for the governments of eight leading industrialised countries.

of both resources and political will. Indeed, while the Obama administration
seems to have quietly accepted the coalition government's House of Commons
defeat on proposed strikes against Syria in August 2013, the vote did serve to
illuminate the lingering shadow of Iraq. Should the UK body politic continue
to shy away from military action, and should the UK's armed forces prove less
capable of making a significant contribution to future operations, the US will
increasingly question what was once the 'central plank' of the relationship.[97]
In this respect, the UK must decide what sort of power it wants to be in the
coming years, measuring its ambition against its resources; sustaining niche
capabilities where it boasts both operational and intellectual excellence, such
as special forces and intelligence; and communicating its limitations honestly,
with itself and its principal ally, so that it proves reliable in the tasks it does
undertake.

Looking ahead, therefore, the resilience and agility of the US–UK
relationship will be tested – indeed, it should be tested – as both countries
determine, in a post-ISAF world of continuing challenges, opportunities,
contingencies and complexities, where they can continue to 'join hands' across
endeavours, even if the 'heart' of the relationship is no longer fundamental to
its health.

References

J. Blitz (2013) 'The price of deterrence', *Financial Times*, 9 Jan., www.
    ft.com/cms/s/0/c569db3a-4947-11e2-9225-00144feab49a.
    html#axzz2t7SRYmSo (accessed 12 Feb. 2014).

J. Boone, J. Steele and R. Norton-Taylor (2010) 'WikiLeaks cables expose
    Afghan contempt for British military', *The Guardian*, 2 Dec., www.
    theguardian.com/uk/2010/dec/02/wikileaks-cables-afghan-british-military
    (accessed 12 Feb. 2014).

BBC News (2012) 'Leon Panetta: US to deploy 60% of navy fleet to Pacific',
    2 June, www.bbc.co.uk/news/world-us-canada-18305750 (accessed 12
    Feb. 2014).

D. Cameron (2010) 'A staunch and self-confident ally', *The Wall Street
    Journal*, 20 July, http://online.wsj.com/news/articles/SB10001424052748
    70491330457537129218681599 2 (accessed 12 Feb. 2014).

Centre for Economic Policy Research (2013) 'Estimating the economic
    impact on the UK of a Transatlantic Trade and Investment Partnership
    (TTIP) Agreement between the European Union and the United States',
    March, https://www.gov.uk/government/uploads/system/uploads/
    attachment_data/file/198115/bis-13-869-economic-impact-on-uk-of-

---

97 FAC, *Global Security*, p. 23.

tranatlantic-trade-and-investment-partnership-between-eu-and-us.pdf (accessed 13 Feb. 2014).

M. Chalmers (2013) 'Respite from the storm? Defence and the 2013 Spending Review outcome', 28 June, www.rusi.org/analysis/commentary/ref:C51CD74A8B34FD/#.UvzxrqNFDL8 (accessed 13 Feb. 2014).

H. Clinton (2011) 'America's Pacific century', *Foreign Policy*, 11 Oct., www.foreignpolicy.com/articles/2011/10/11/americas_pacific_century (accessed 12 Feb. 2014).

J. Dumbrell (2009) 'The US–UK special relationship: taking the 21st-century temperature', *The British Journal of Politics and International Relations*, vol. 11, no. 1, http://dro.dur.ac.uk/5601/ (accessed 12 Feb. 2014).

Economist, The (2013) 'Time to engage', briefing, 19 Jan., www.economist.com/news/briefing/21569719-barack-obamas-first-term-caution-was-understandable-he-must-now-show-greater-resolve-time (accessed 12 Feb. 2014).

E. Edelman (2010) 'A special relationship in jeopardy', *The American Interest*, vol. 5, no. 6 (July/Aug.), www.the-american-interest.com/articles/2010/07/01/a-special-relationship-in-jeopardy/ (accessed 12 Feb. 2014).

Foreign Affairs Committee, House of Commons (2010) *Global Security: UK–US Relations*, HC 114 (London: The Stationery Office), March, www.publications.parliament.uk/pa/cm200910/cmselect/cmfaff/114/114.pdf (accessed 12 Feb. 2014).

N. Gardiner (2011) 'Mind the gap: is the relationship still special?', *World Affairs Journal* (March/April), www.worldaffairsjournal.org/article/mind-gap-relationship-still-special (accessed 12 Feb. 2014).

R. Genté (2013) 'Shale gas changes geopolitics', 6 Aug., www.middle-east-online.com/english/?id=60586 (accessed 12 Feb. 2014).

R.N. Haass (2013) 'The irony of American strategy: putting the Middle East in proper perspective', *Foreign Affairs*, vol. 92, no. 3 (May/June), www.foreignaffairs.com/articles/139106/richard-n-haass/the-irony-of-american-strategy (accessed 12 Feb. 2014).

HM Government (2010) *A Strong Britain in an Age of Uncertainty: The National Security Strategy*, Cm 7953 (London: The Stationery Office), Oct., https://www.gov.uk/government/uploads/system/uploads/attachment_data/file/61936/national-security-strategy.pdf (accessed 12 Feb. 2014).

N. Hopkins and J. Borger (2013) 'Exclusive: NSA pays £100m in secret funding for GCHQ', *The Guardian*, 1 Aug., www.theguardian.com/uk-news/2013/aug/01/nsa-paid-gchq-spying-edward-snowden (accessed 12 Feb. 2014).

W. Inboden (2010) 'Is there still time to save the special relationship?', *Foreign Policy*, 29 March, http://shadow.foreignpolicy.com/posts/2010/03/29/is_there_still_time_to_save_the_special_relationship (accessed 12 Feb. 2014).

C.A. Kupchan (2013) 'No dilemma between Europe and Asia for Washington strategists', *Global Times*, 28 March, www.globaltimes.cn/content/771437.shtml (accessed 12 Feb. 2014).

E. MacAskill and J. Borger (2004) 'Iraq war was illegal and breached UN charter', *The Guardian*, 16 Sep., www.theguardian.com/world/2004/sep/16/iraq.iraq (accessed 12 Feb. 2014).

D.E. Mix (2013) 'The United Kingdom and U.S.–UK relations', Congressional Research Service, 15 April, www.fas.org/sgp/crs/row/RL33105.pdf (accessed 12 Feb. 2014).

R. Niblett (2013) 'US foreign policy off-balance', Chatham House, 25 Sep., www.chathamhouse.org/media/comment/view/194306 (accessed 12 Feb. 2014).

R. Norton-Taylor (2013) 'UK forces in Helmand "made matters worse", says report', *The Guardian*, 10 July, www.theguardian.com/world/2013/jul/10/uk-forces-helmand-afghanistan (accessed 12 Feb. 2014).

B. Obama and D. Cameron (2012) 'United States and Great Britain: an essential relationship', *The Guardian*, 13 March, www.theguardian.com/commentisfree/2012/mar/13/barack-obama-david-cameron-essential-relationship (accessed 12 Feb. 2014).

W. Russell Mead (2008) *God and Gold: Britain, American and the Making of the Modern World* (London: Atlantic Books).

N.A. Schwartz and J.W. Greenhert (2012) 'Air-sea battle: promoting stability in an era of uncertainty', *The American Interest*, 20 Feb., www.the-american-interest.com/articles/2012/02/20/air-sea-battle/ (accessed 12 Feb. 2014).

H. Strachan (2013) 'British national strategy: who does it?', *Parameters*, vol. 43, no. 2 (Summer), www.strategicstudiesinstitute.army.mil/pubs/parameters/Issues/Summer_2013/5_Strachan_Article.pdf (accessed 13 Feb. 2014).

The White House (2010) 'U.S. National Security Strategy', 1 May, www.whitehouse.gov/sites/default/files/rss_viewer/national_security_strategy.pdf (accessed 12 Feb. 2014).

— (2013) 'Joint Fact Sheet: U.S. and UK defense cooperation', 14 March, www.whitehouse.gov/the-press-office/2012/03/14/joint-fact-sheet-us-and-uk-defense-cooperation (accessed 13 Feb. 2014).

G. Thompson (2010) 'Clinton urges talks on the Falkland Islands', *New York Times*, 1 March, www.nytimes.com/2010/03/02/world/americas/02clinton.html?_r=0 (accessed 12 Feb. 2014),

US Department of Defense (2012) 'Defense budget priorities and choices: January 2012', www.defense.gov/news/Defense_Budget_Priorities.pdf (accessed 13 Feb. 2014).

US Department of State (2012) United Kingdom 'Fact Sheet', 22 March, www.state.gov/outofdate/bgn/unitedkingdom/197883.htm (accessed 13 Feb. 2014; now archived).

— (2013) 'Media roundtable in London: remarks by Philip H. Gordon', 9 Jan., www.state.gov/p/eur/rls/rm/2013/jan/202650.htm (accessed 13 Feb. 2014).

US Embassy Cable (2009) 'Subject: the British ask, is our relationship still special in Washington?', 9 Feb., www.theguardian.com/world/us-embassy-cables-documents/191116 (accessed 12 Feb. 2014).

F. Zakaria (2008) 'The future of American power: how America can survive the rise of the rest', *Foreign Affairs*, vol. 87, no. 3 (May/June), www.foreignaffairs.com/articles/63394/fareed-zakaria/the-future-of-american-power (accessed 12 Feb. 2014).

9. Obama's foreign policy: process, personnel and policy direction

John Dumbrell

When he entered the White House in January 2009, Barack Obama had some clear foreign policy objectives. These included the negotiation and identification of exit routes from Afghanistan and Iraq, as well as a general retreat from exposed foreign policy positions inherited from President George W. Bush. Obama sought to improve America's global popularity; to repair some of the global ruptures associated with Bush's War on Terror; and generally to develop a foreign policy approach suited both to lean economic times and to shifting global conditions. Where earlier presidents had been forced to learn the (admittedly rather ambiguous) 'lessons of Vietnam', Obama had to fashion a foreign policy which recognised the 'lessons of Iraq'. There were dangers both in over-learning and in under-learning these lessons.

The Obama administration thus found itself torn between the attractions of severely limited international engagement on the one hand, and active human rights and democracy-promotion on the other. In general, Obama tended to favour cost-conscious realism – a fairly restricted definition of 'national interests'. He kept alive, however, a generalised commitment to foreign policy humanitarianism, along with other 'idealist' objectives such as the commitment to global 'nuclear zero'.[1]

Obama's success in developing a foreign policy suited to our new 'age of limits' is questionable and indeed will no doubt be further tested in the last phase of his two-term presidency. Like his Democratic presidential predecessor, Bill Clinton, Obama has been assaulted from both right and left: condemned as an appeaser and foreign policy 'Apologist in Chief'; but also attacked by liberal critics for not breaking sufficiently decisively with the George W. Bush administration approach. My intention here is to switch discussion away from foreign policy substance – away from debates about Obama's theory and practice of American global leadership – and towards foreign policy process, including an assessment of the performance of leading personnel. To what extent have

---

1   Important studies of Obama's foreign policy include: Indyk et al., *Bending History: Barack Obama's Foreign Policy*; Sanger, *Confront and Conceal: Obama's Secret Wars and Surprising Use of American Power*; Singh, *Barack Obama's Post-American Foreign Policy: The Limits of Engagement*.

the processes and foreign policy leaders within the administration enhanced, or alternatively held back, the achievement of consistent and coherent policy direction?

Foreign policy process

Presidential foreign policy is often vitiated by inappropriate and poorly functioning process. A catalogue of recent woes might stretch from President Lyndon B. Johnson's failure to develop an appropriate decisional structure for rational consideration of American options in Vietnam, to the intense élite faction-fighting within the George W. Bush administration. That various administrations have not functioned effectively is not in question. Only the administration of George H.W. Bush was, among recent presidencies, relatively immune from crippling procedural inadequacies.[2]

It clearly is not easy to create effective foreign policy processes. They are such that they cannot simply be translated from presidency to presidency. As with the 'lessons' of Vietnam and Iraq, presidents need to learn from the mistakes of their predecessors without over-compensating for such perceived errors. Decisional processes need to be consciously tailored to specific presidential priorities, to particular personalities and emotional needs, and to shifting international conditions. Presidents, many of whom (like Obama) have come into office with woefully inadequate foreign policy experience, are often tempted (like the first-term Bill Clinton) to treat foreign policy process as a matter of flexible trial and error. Such presidents, lacking a network of élite foreign policy contacts, tend to find it difficult to make suitable appointments and may make overly 'safe' ones, or be tempted to fall back on loyalists from the campaign trail. They may not appreciate the need to think long and hard about *process*. Is success in foreign policy leadership not simply a matter of talking to the right people, making clear decisions in the White House, and then communicating those decisions to the foreign policy bureaucracy? In fact, the academic literature actually has quite a lot to offer incoming presidents by way of advice about how to construct an effective foreign policy process.

Presidents, even those rare recent presidents who have had some significant foreign policy experience, should consciously select a process that is suited to their priorities, to their ways of working, their 'cognitive style'. Unless the terms of intra-administration foreign policy decision-making are set by the president, they are unlikely to be set by anyone else. Processes (and indeed dominant personnel) selected at the start of the administration may continue to affect policy for years to come. Incoming presidents need to choose between more or less hierarchical patterns of access to the centre of decision-making in

2   See Dumbrell, *The Making of US Foreign Policy*, pp. 89–91; Inderfurth and Johnson (eds.) *Fateful Decisions: Inside the National Security Council.*

the presidential Oval Office. 'Collegial' patterns of administration behaviour encourage a 'hub in the wheel' advisory style, with several advisers from across the administration having direct access to the president.

Such advisers may have little idea of who else the president is consulting. The president may or may not employ a 'gatekeeper' (often his National Security Advisor – NSA) to bring some kind of order to such patterns of access. An effective NSA will probably be some kind of 'honest broker' between different interests, feeding into the president, though he or she will almost certainly also tend to advocate policy. Some presidents prefer pyramidical advisory structures, with a widely recognised hierarchical route for advice and information to reach him. Many presidents have attempted hybrid versions of 'hub in the wheel' and pyramidical systems, and indeed most recent presidencies have oscillated between hierarchical and more collegial structures. No system is perfect, but a successful chief executive is likely to be one who has considered carefully which is best suited to his own needs and priorities. In terms of information flow to the centre, presidents must set in place a system which identifies emerging international crises, but which also prevents the president becoming overloaded with second-order priorities.[3]

The literature also reveals that a successful president will be one who recognises that bureaucratic tensions within his wider administration are inevitable. Top appointments (especially to bodies such as the State Department, the Pentagon and the CIA) will inevitably be made with political considerations in mind, not least the need to secure confirmation of these appointments in the US Senate. Top appointees must be people who are likely to combine loyalty with the willingness to offer frank advice. The president will appreciate that the State and Defence Departments are almost bound to interpret international problems and crises in different ways. For its part, the White House – in foreign policy terms, essentially National Security Council (NSC) staff, headed by the NSA, plus some of the political staff – will tend to frame problems in political and electoral terms.

White House relations with the State and Defence Departments are unlikely to be trouble-free. The emergence of strong foreign-policy vice presidents under Presidents Clinton and George W. Bush, and continued under Obama, has further complicated these relationships. A sensible president will accept the inevitability of bureaucratic conflict but will try to ameliorate and control it. He will aspire to decisional rationality but will appreciate that good foreign policy involves value trade-offs. To quote Richard Haass, presidents need the information and ability to 'assess a situation accurately and, where applicable, prescribe a course of feasible policy that does the most to advance recognized

3   See Burke, 'The neutral/honest broker role in foreign-policy decision making', pp. 229–58; Haney, *Organizing for Foreign Policy Crises*.

interests and bring about desirable outcomes at the lowest possible direct and indirect costs'.[4]

A good president will weigh options, but not become paralysed by the prospect of cost or by the complexity of the international environment. He will not simply assume that a 'middle way' between options presented by his advisory structure is the best way. He will run a tight ship, appreciating the need to learn, adapt and always to expose himself to competing lines of argument. Nevertheless, the pursuit of 'multiple advocacy' must not be allowed to degenerate into randomness. A successful foreign policy president will also possess 'contextual intelligence' – an understanding of the domestic and international contexts in which decisions are made, an understanding of *when* he can make key policy changes. He will draw on his own experience but will understand that history does not simply repeat itself. A good president will be able to communicate effectively with Congress, the American public and with foreign leaders. He will not forget that decisions need to be implemented and that implementation requires constant evaluation and re-evaluation[5]

Obama and Biden

Plausible accounts of Obama's personal foreign policy belief system may be constructed from his pre-presidential biography and publications, and from 2008 campaign statements. From such sources, Robert Singh identified 13 key themes, ranging from 'smarter' prosecution of the 'good war' in Afghanistan and the search for fairer trade terms with China, to direct negotiations with 'rogue states' such as Iran and Syria, and 'cap-and-trade' commitments on global climate change.[6] From the 13 themes, there emerges a tension between 'idealism' (broadly, the values-oriented agenda promoted by Obama in the 2008 primary race against Hillary Clinton) and 'realism' (broadly, the orientation which emerged more clearly after Obama secured the nomination).

The various pre-election statements are difficult to read, not least because of the dynamics which encourage 'insurgent' Democratic candidates to cleave leftwards during the pre-nomination phase of the contest, and rightwards as election day approaches. The idealism/realism tension, however, persisted beyond 2008 and indeed has become the conventional way of understanding not only Obama's beliefs but also the internal dynamics of the entire administration. The tension was evident in the contrasting promises of 2008,

---

4   Haass. 'Why foreign policy is not pornography', p. 252.

5   See George and George, *Presidential Personality and Performance*, p. 2; Kegley and Wittkopf, *American Foreign Policy: Pattern and Process*, pp. 466–99; Larson, 'Good judgement in foreign policy'; Neustadt and May, *Thinking in Time: The Uses of History for Decision Makers*; Nye, *The Powers to Lead*.

6   Singh, *Barack Obama's Foreign Policy*, pp. 31–2; Obama, *The Audacity of Hope: Thoughts on Reclaiming the American Dream*; Obama, 'Renewing America's leadership', pp. 2–16.

with moves away from the War on Terror being balanced by the assertion of the right to take unilateral US military action in Pakistan. Early speeches also revealed these tensions. Obama's Prague address of April 2009 offered US support for nuclear disarmament. His Cairo speech, delivered two months later, promised a new dialogue between the US and the Moslem world. Yet, poignantly and pointedly, Obama used the occasion of his Nobel Prize acceptance (December, 2009) to emphasise his commitment to the necessary and measured use of military force.

Obama tends to stress the importance of consensual multilateralism – though certainly not at any cost. He often discusses 'values' in the context of America's role as democratic exemplar. Such a view tends to prioritise the need for constant domestic renewal and re-adjustment. Democracy-promotion abroad should also be tempered by acute cultural sensitivity and an awareness of shifting international conditions. American global leadership should be preserved, but can only be maintained if the US adjusts to a world of emerging powers and appreciates the perils of overstretch. At a press conference in January 2009, the president proclaimed: 'when we are at our best, the United States represents a set of universal values and ideals'. However, 'I also believe … that other countries have different cultures, different perspectives, and are coming out of different histories, and that we do our best to promote our ideals and our values by example'.[7]

The 'exemplar' theme, which could be the basis for a new kind of isolationism, is usually balanced in Obama's speeches by a resounding commitment to America's role in leading other nations to 'a new era of cooperation', as he explained it in his Westminster Hall address in London (May 2011). Here is Obama addressing graduates of the Air Force Academy in Colorado in May 2012: 'I see an American century because no other nation seeks the role that we play in global affairs, and no other nation can play the role we play … As president, I've made it clear the United States does not fear the rise of peaceful, responsible emerging powers – we welcome them. Because when more nations step up and contribute to peace and security, that doesn't undermine American power, it enhances it'. The Colorado speech should be placed in the context of Obama's desire to rebuff Republican party election year charges that the president saw himself simply as a manager of American global decline. However, the speech embodied a striking rhetorical commitment to the union of ideals, US national interest, and sustained international American leadership.[8]

Obama's background and status as the first African American president may be presumed to have bequeathed him something of an 'outsider' self-image.

7   Cited by Murray, 'Military action but not as we know it: Libya, Syria and the making of an Obama doctrine', pp. 146–66, esp. p. 150.

8   Cited in Stepak and Whitlark, 'The battle over America's foreign policy doctrine', pp. 45–66, esp. p. 54.

204   OBAMA'S WASHINGTON

However, efforts to depict Obama as a bitter and obsessive anti-colonialist are risible.[9] As James Mann argues, his post-primary education – from private colleges in Los Angeles and New York City to Harvard Law School – was fairly similar to the education of Presidents Kennedy, Nixon, Ford, Clinton and the two Bushes.[10] Belief systems are frequently linked to adolescent or early adult formative experience. Obama is not a member of the Vietnam War generation, though he has plausibly shown sensitivity to its 'lessons' – notably the need to question assumptions and to avoid rash military commitments.[11] More than Vietnam, however, Obama's formative foreign policy experiences included George H.W. Bush's handling of the end of the Cold War, with Washington finding a precarious balance between strategic pragmatism and being on the wrong side of history. Obama is a conspicuous admirer of the Republican pragmatic tradition exemplified in the foreign policy of the elder Bush and his NSA, Brent Scowcroft.[12]

During the Clinton years, Obama observed fraught national debates about the dangers of humanitarian intervention, as well as the need to protect American global leadership in a world transformed by the collapse of Soviet communism. Obama seems to have drawn some important lessons from the 1990s. These included the realisation that America neither should nor can duck the demands of global leadership, though the way in which the US exercises such leadership must be constantly adjusted to shifting circumstance. Like Bill Clinton, Obama has a legal training and a tendency to judge problems on a case-by-case basis.[13] More obviously, from the years that passed since the terrorist attacks of 11 September 2001, Obama took a variety of lessons: the US must never again became so exposed and internationally isolated as it was following the Iraq invasion; terrorism remains a potent threat, but one which cannot be eradicated by military action alone; the 'Iraq syndrome' – the ironic legacy of the Bush years – must not be allowed to inhibit judicious and 'smart' use of American military power.

Many Obama commentators have been struck by his caution and constant asking of the 'can-we-afford-it' question.[14] His natural inclination, as evidenced in his 2006 book *The Audacity of Hope*, favours consensual leadership – the slow building of support for a particular line of action, with constant reference

9   As in D'Souza, *The Roots of Obama's Rage.*

10   Mann, *The Obamians*, p. 73.

11   See Sanger, *Confront and Conceal*, p. 26.

12   See Lizza, 'The consequentialist: how the Arab Spring remade Obama's foreign policy', pp. 44–55, esp. p. 47.

13   Sanger, *The Inheritance: The World Obama Confronts and the Challenges to American Power*, p. 450; Lizza, 'The consequentialist', p. 55.

14   See Sanger, *Confront and Conceal*, p. 430.

to potential risks and costs.[15] However, Obama seems sensitive to the danger of consensus-seeking becoming a substitute for personal leader responsibility. He is frequently criticised for favouring the 'middle way' between options presented to him, as in the case of the 'surge and exit' decision in Afghanistan. Obama's decision-making style – apparently consensual, 'accommodationist' and tending to 'split the difference' – is often linked to his favoured ways of proceeding as a community organiser on the South Side of Chicago, just as Lyndon B. Johnson's ostensibly somewhat similar style was conventionally traced to his days as Senate Majority Leader.[16] Obama can act decisively: witness the sacking of General Stanley McChrystal in June 2010, and the April 2011 decision (taken against the advice of Defence Secretary Robert Gates and Vice President Joe Biden) to insert Navy SEALs directly into the Abbottabad compound being occupied by Osama bin Laden.[17] Perceptions of Obama as an ultra-cautious leader should also be balanced by awareness of his commitments to American leadership – albeit a transformed leadership, suited to shifting global circumstances – and to judicious (and preferably only semi-visible) direct action.

The attraction of having Joe Biden as running mate in 2008 was obvious. The Senator from Delaware, and current head of the Foreign Relations Committee, was something of a living archaeological site of recent Democratic party foreign policy debates. A dove in the Vietnam years, Biden had supported President Bill Clinton's interventions in the Balkans and voted to authorise action in Iraq in 2002. Biden supplied Obama with foreign policy credibility and was soon being described as a figure who brought unity to competing 'idealist' and 'realist' factions within the new administration, who (according to *New York Times* writer James Traub in November 2009) 'has largely realized his wish to be the president's all-purpose adviser and sage' and attends most daily briefings and principals' meetings. According to White House chief of staff Rahm Emanuel, Biden brought contacts and a flair for the kind of political schmoozing that Obama tends to shun. Biden, in Emanuel's words, 'has everything – gravitas, political smarts, the confidence of the players and knowledge of the issues, at the end of the day, this is a political process, and you need a politician to work on the process. And he has the authority of the White House'.[18]

Biden seems to have pondered at some length whether he wished to leave the Senate to serve a president, whom he opposed for the nomination and whom he had portrayed as a foreign policy tyro in the primary campaign.

15 Obama, *The Audacity of Hope*, pp. 90–7.
16 See Dueck, 'The accommodator: Obama's foreign policy', pp. 161–84.
17 Sanger, *Confront and Conceal*, p. 87.
18 Traub, 'After Cheney'.

One of his dilemmas was how to secure a prominent place within the advisory structure of the new administration without too obviously recreating the kind of relationship which Vice President Cheney had enjoyed with George W. Bush. Michael Hirsh, writing in *The Atlantic* in December 2012, speculated that Biden had become the most influential vice president in history, quoting one of Biden's remarks made during the 2012 re-election campaign: 'I literally get to be the last guy in the room with the president'.[19] The 'Cheney problem' was to some extent ameliorated by the simple fact of personality. Where Bush's vice president was a silent and glowering presence – or indeed a glowering but conspicuous non-presence – at principals' meetings under Bush, Biden is incapable of verbal self-restraint. Obama might lack foreign policy experience but, despite his instinct for caution and deliberation, does not lack confidence. Unlike Cheney, Biden also took on domestic policy tasks: notably budgetary negotiation with congressional leaders and responsibility for gun control initiatives. Biden was given special responsibility for White House liaison with senior State and Defence Department personnel – a task that no-one could imagine being given to Cheney. It is also worth noting that several 'inner circle' foreign policy staffers under Obama had strong links with Biden.[20]

As vice president, Biden has been given greater leeway than most 'inner circle' Obama advisers in terms of how far he is permitted to drift from the agreed presidential line. In the parlance of the Obama administration, Biden conforms to 'team of rivals' rather than 'inner circle' rules.[21] Biden's reputation as a garrulous committer of verbal infelicities probably underestimates the vice president's political sophistication. Some of Biden's public wanderings from the stated White House line may be interpreted as a conscious policy of testing presidential caution (most obviously over gay marriage but also arguably over Russian policy, with Biden tending to lead criticisms of Vladimir Putin's rule). Some of Biden's most widely publicised policy preferences include his severe disillusionment with possibilities of successful counter-insurgency, either in Afghanistan or Iraq. He advocated what was in effect an abandonment of Afghanistan, balanced by a concerted switch to counter-terrorism in Pakistan. The 'surge' part of Obama's 'surge and disengage' decision in 2009 was widely interpreted as a defeat for the vice president, though subsequent Afghanistan decisions bore more of a Biden fingerprint. Although initially favouring Iraqi partition, Biden was given explicit responsibility for negotiating the US withdrawal in 2010. His conduct in relation to this seems to have been skilled,

---

19 Hirsh, 'Joe Biden: the most influential vice president in history?'

20 See Hudson, 'Jeff Prescott replaces Julie Smith as Biden's deputy national security advisor'.

21 Mann, *The Obamians*, p. 212.

though Biden failed to negotiate with Baghdad a lasting American residual military presence.[22]

White House direction of foreign policy

In January 2009 Obama set in motion a hybrid and unique version of the 'hub in the wheel' foreign policy process. Leading ultra-high-profile Cabinet appointments – notably Hillary Clinton at State and Robert Gates at the Pentagon – could scarcely be denied access to the president. However, it swiftly became apparent that the process would be controlled unambiguously from the White House and that its *political* staff (notably staff chief Rahm Emanuel) would enjoy significant foreign policy input. Rather extraordinarily, at least initially, this would be a process which combined strong White House direction with a weak NSA. It was as if President Nixon had retained his preference for central control of foreign policy but named William Rogers rather than Henry Kissinger as his NSA.

James Jones, Obama's first NSA, was a Marine general and former NATO chief. His appointment reflected Obama's desire to bring in an element of seasoned bipartisan expertise. He presumably saw Jones, who was much closer to Senator John McCain than to himself, as a conduit to a military establishment which was disappointed by the 2008 election result. Jones made a few policy interventions – for example, in relation to Pakistani nuclear weapons – but essentially presented himself as an 'honest broker' NSA. He veered increasingly outside of the charmed circle of foreign policy aides inside the White House.[23] A member of the NSC staff told David Sanger: 'there was one moment when we were all headed into the Situation Room to handle some crisis du jour and there was Jim, in his bicycle suit, headed out the West Wing door'.[24] Jones became a casualty of the intra-administration dynamics publicly revealed in Bob Woodward's *Obama's Wars*.[25] Tom Donilon, formerly deputy to Jones and chief of staff to Secretary of State Warren Christopher in the early Clinton presidency, took over as NSA in October 2010.

Obama's general desire for White House centralisation over policy was signalled in his early designation of White House 'czars'.[26] In foreign policy, there was no question that the White House, even with a weak NSA, would rule. Donilon commented that the system deliberately mirrored that put in place by Brent Scowcroft under the elder Bush, with the NSC (in effect,

---

22 See Indyk et al., *Bending History*, pp. 78–80; Nasr, *The Dispensable Nation: American Foreign Policy in Retreat*, pp. 24, 145.

23 See Pfiffner, 'Organizing the Obama White House', p. 79.

24 Sanger, *Confront and Conceal*, p. 201.

25 Woodward, *Obama's Wars: The Inside Story*.

26 Pfiffner, *The Modern Presidency*, pp. 88–9.

the inner White House foreign policy staff) 'the sole process through which policy would be developed'.[27] Key personnel included figures – such as Mark Lippert, Denis McDonough and Ben Rhodes – who had advised Obama on foreign policy in the 2008 campaign. Of these, only Lippert, a former Senate aide to Obama, failed to become a significant force within the new NSC system. According to James Mann, Lippert 'was forced out in White House infighting'.[28] McDonough became Donilon's deputy in 2010, later taking over as White House chief of staff, while Rhodes became the leading speechwriter on the NSC staff. Several prominent staffers had worked in the Clinton administration. Tony Blinken, who became deputy to Donilon, had worked on Bill Clinton's NSC, had been a leading staffer on the Senate Foreign Relations Committee, and worked in the Obama team initially as chief foreign policy aide to Joe Biden. Blinken and Donilon became identified with a highly regularised process of information flow, organised around weekly principals' meetings. Donilon emerged, however, as much more than a procedural chief. He operated as a cautious proponent of 'leading-from-behind': urging cuts in military requests for Afghanistan, supporting a low profile in Syria, backing the new focus on East Asia and constantly factoring in the domestic dimension to key international decisions. When Donilon left his post in 2013, Obama said that his outgoing NSA had 'shaped every single national security policy of my presidency'.[29]

Much has been made of the relative youth and generational identity – the post-Cold War formative experiences – of the inner circle. An anonymous 'high-ranking administration official', interviewed by James Mann, saw a key distinction between those (like Hillary Clinton) who 'believe that the world revolves around the United States' and those (notably the NSC inner circle) who 'don't think that'.[30] Despite this, the inner circle did not think with one mind. Distinctions have sometimes been made between those (like Donilon) who had worked in the Bill Clinton administration and those (like Rhodes) who had not. Intra-White House debate predictably became interpreted in terms of 'realists' – those, like Donilon, who tended to fight shy of anything resembling liberal, humanitarian or democracy-promoting intervention – and 'idealists', who saw a role for multilaterally based American-led, international promotion of democracy. Firmly placed in the latter camp were Samantha Power, author of a major academic indictment of global failure to deal with genocide in the Balkans in the 1990s, and Michael McFaul, an academic Russianist and

27 Lizza, 'The consequentialist', p. 47.

28 Mann, *The Obamians*, p. 338.

29 Pace, 'Tom Donilon resigning'; 'Action women', *The Economist*; Pfiffner, 'Organizing the Obama White House', p. 80.

30 Mann, *The Obamians*, p. 252.

proponent of educative and non-military pro-democracy initiatives.[31] Power and McFaul served on Obama's NSC staff until the former moved to become US Ambassador to the UN and the latter became US Ambassador to Russia in the second term.

A few general comments about the role of the NSC staff and the inner circle are in order. First, the inner circle was and is very powerful, but it has never operated in isolation from other parts of the administration. 'Realists' in the inner circle found allies outside the White House, such as James Steinberg, veteran of the Clinton years and Deputy Secretary of State. 'Idealist' ranks included Susan Rice, US Ambassador to the UN in the first term and Donilon's successor as NSA, as well as Anne-Marie Slaughter, prior to her 2010 resignation from the State Department.

Second, the 'realist-idealist' polarisation can be overstated. When Power and Rice shifted jobs in 2013, it was widely pointed out that, despite their reputation as strong human rights policy advocates, neither woman could reasonably be seen as an unequivocal champion of military action for humanitarian purposes. Neither Rice nor Power, prior to the summer of 2013, was especially identified with public advocacy of air strikes on Syria, though some reports indicated that Power had privately backed such strikes since December 2012.[32]

Third, the distinctive character of Obama's inner circle – especially its close identification with broadly-conceived presidential interests – is not that much out of line with other presidencies. White House employees (including NSC staff) are *bound* by the logic of bureaucratic politics to take a 'presidentialist' view of foreign policy. A relevant bureaucratic maxim is that if nothing succeeds like success, nothing propinks like propinquity. This is a major reason why many presidents choose to rely on such staff in preference to the regular diplomatic bureaucracy. Such dynamics were evident in the opposition of NSC staff (and of chief of staff Rahm Emanuel) to the 2009 'surge' in Afghanistan. Emanuel in particular was concerned about the possible negative electoral consequences of a surge.[33]

Mention of the 2009 Afghanistan decision brings us to the fourth point about the inner White House circle and its impact on foreign policy. The 2009 decision went against Donilon and Emanuel, although Obama did commit himself to a disengagement timetable even as he ordered 30,000 extra combat forces to Afghanistan. The Obama foreign policy process is as much president-centred as it is White House-centred, and his vantage point differs

31 Power, *'A problem from hell': America and the age of genocide*; Mann, *The Obamians*, p. 168; Broadwell, 'The doctrine of power', pp. 40–3.

32 See Hirsh, 'Susan Rice and Samantha Power: less change than meets the eye'; Stolberg. 'A new US player put on the world stage by Syria'.

33 See Marsh, 'Obama's surge: a bureaucratic politics analysis of the decision to order a troop surge in the Afghanistan war', pp. 1–24, esp. p. 10.

from that even of his most intimate staff. As Stephen Wayne puts it, Obama's style determined the decision. The style in 2009, and indeed subsequently, was 'initially expansive, increasingly structured, with the end being a consensus among his policy advisors' – across the administration, not just in the White House. It reflected the president's 'need to take charge' as well as his determination 'for deciding with his head, not his heart or gut'.[34] A senior aide quoted in the *Financial Times* declared in 2010: 'President Obama is his own Henry Kissinger'.[35] Obama himself is securely in charge. However, as will be seen below, being in charge is not necessarily the same as being decisive.

The team of rivals: beyond the White House

The appointment of Hillary Clinton as his first Secretary of State was a gamble for Obama in several senses. The legacy of the 2008 primary race and Clinton's own political stardom had the potential to undercut the integrity of the new administration. Once appointed, it would be politically difficult to sack Hillary Clinton, who after all had demonstrated her appeal to many traditional Democratic constituencies in 2008. Another factor for Obama to consider was the unpredictable behaviour of her husband, former President Bill Clinton. Hillary Clinton also dictated explicit conditions for acceptance of the job, notably respecting her control of top-level diplomatic appointments. A further dimension of the gamble related to Obama's commitment to White House control of foreign policy. How would Hillary, a disappointed presidential candidate, respond to being sidelined by the White House?

To state the obvious, Hillary Clinton was a major player in Obama's foreign policy during his first term. By 2011, she had attended over 600 White House meetings and emerged broadly on the winning side in the Afghanistan 'surge and disengage' decision of 2009. By supporting Susan Rice and Samantha Power over western powers' military intervention in Libya in 2011 to implement UN Security Council Resolution 1973,[36] Secretary Clinton arguably tipped the balance in favour of American action. She was part of the bureaucratic push towards announcing the 'pivot' to East Asia in 2011–12, and did much to publicise and publicly defend the policy shift. Hillary Clinton led a diplomatic opening to Myanmar (Burma); was a major player in the early 'Russia re-set' policy; crisis-managed the brief diplomatic spat with Beijing over Chinese dissident Chen Guangcheng; and stood near the centre of the

34 Wayne, 'Presidential character and judgement: Obama's Afghanistan and health care decisions', pp. 291–306, esp. p. 299.

35 Luce and Dombey, 'US foreign policy: waiting on the Sun King' (cited by Pfiffner, 'Organizing the Obama White House').

36 See http://en.wikipedia.org/wiki/United_Nations_Security_Council_Resolution_1973 (accessed 31 March 2014).

administration's policy of 'strategic patience' regarding North Korea. Yet, as many commentators pointed out on the occasion of her retirement from Foggy Bottom in early 2013, she never achieved the centrality to US foreign policy of a Dean Acheson or even a George Shultz or a James Baker.[37]

In 2012, Denis McDonough described Secretary Clinton as 'the principal implementer'.[38] And in 2013 Vali Nasr wrote: 'Had it not been for Clinton's tenacity and the respect she commanded, the State Department would have had no influence on policy making whatsoever'.[39] Such a view is rather extreme, and reflects Nasr's perspective as a former adviser on Afghanistan with particular grievances against White House control of policy there. However, there is little question that Hillary Clinton was tangential to Iraqi, Iranian and Arab-Israeli policy. Nevertheless, she actually did relatively little practical high-level diplomacy in the traditional sense. Secretary Clinton was also to some extent the victim of the appointment of Special Representatives George Mitchell (assigned the task of breathing life into the Israel-Palestine peace process) and Richard Holbrooke (pointman for Afghanistan and Pakistan – 'Afpak'). Mitchell and, particularly, Holbrooke were close allies of Clinton. They worked *for* the Secretary of State, but became embroiled in complex and counter-productive bureaucratic politics. Holbrooke set up the Special Representative's Office for Afghanistan and Pakistan in a deliberate attempt to fend off White House control. Mitchell's initiatives came adrift in the face of complex change in the Middle East, while Holbrooke found himself marginalised. He escaped dismissal only through the personal intervention of Secretary Clinton.[40]

From the day of her appointment, Hillary Clinton showed enormous determination to display loyalty to Obama and to deflect doubts about his 'team of rivals' strategy. Though fairly clearly a less apologetic globalist than her boss, Clinton was no rocker of the foreign policy boat. Kim Ghattas, a BBC correspondent who covered Hillary's State Department leadership, argues that this determination could become counter-productive, with Clinton sometimes over-enthusiastically reinforcing White House positions – for example, over Israeli settlements – in a way which subsequently tied Obama's hands.[41] In general terms, however, Obama was fortunate if his only problem with his high-profile Secretary was over-zealous loyalty. Despite all this, there were distinct differences of emphasis between the two senior figures in the administration.

37 See 'What Hillary did next'; Clinton, 'America's Pacific century'.

38 Packer, 'The long engagements', p. 22.

39 Nasr, *The Dispensable Nation*, p. 38.

40 Ibid., pp. 30–4; Indyk et al., *Bending History*, pp. 137–40.

41 Ghattas, *The Secretary: A Journey with Hillary Clinton from Beirut to the Heart of American Power*, pp. 118–19.

The Secretary's 2009 public advocacy of a 'defence umbrella' for Arab allies along Cold War lines was rapidly disowned by the White House. Clinton was widely reported during the first term as being well ahead of the White House in her enthusiasm for arming rebel forces in Syria.

Borrowing concepts from European diplomatic practice, Clinton lauded 'civilian power'. Her legacy, despite her distance from actual policy-development, was still extraordinary. To quote George Packer: 'Clinton's true legacy might be the countless public events that she held from Lahore to Kinshasa, where thousands of ordinary people got to question the US Secretary of State, and where the topic was often something like women's rights or access to clean water'.[42] Amid a phenomenal schedule of travel, Clinton aimed to re-make American diplomacy at the lower and mezzanine levels. Some of her initiatives represented direct developments from her husband's administration. Thus, her emphasis on 'economic statecraft' included the commitment that diplomats would unapologetically promote the US economic agenda.

Bureaucratic changes included a new Bureau of Energy Resources; a rebuilding of the US Agency for International Development, including a doubling of development-oriented staff; new secretarial guidance on promoting gender equality; and a new planning process, the inaugural 2010 State Department Quadrennial Diplomacy and Development review. Much of this activity – which Clinton's successor, John Kerry, undertook to continue – was designed to lift the morale of Foreign Service Officers as well as to counter the global anti-Americanism of the years before 2008.[43] What these initiatives could not achieve, however – nor indeed was this Clinton's intent – was to establish the US as a 'civilian power' on the European model. By the end of Obama's first term, US foreign policy remained extremely militarised, while many policy departures – including drones strikes and cyberwar initiatives – increased the authority of the intelligence community and the Pentagon, to some extent at the expense of the State Department.

Clinton's status as a team player was evident in the relative ease of her relationship with Joe Biden – arguably less acrimonious than her relationship as first lady with Vice President Al Gore in the 1990s – and especially with her 'natural' bureaucratic rival, Defence Secretary Robert Gates. Clinton-Gates joint appearances before Congress deliberately underpinned the contrast with the Colin Powell/Donald Rumsfeld relationship in the George W. Bush presidency. Gates did not always have easy relations with the White House inner circle – especially, according to Bob Woodward, with Donilon.[44] However, the holdover of Gates from the Bush years proved to be another Obama gamble

---

42 Packer, 'The long engagements', p. 2.

43 See 'Senator John Kerry's confirmation hearing statement, January 2013'.

44 Woodward, *Obama's Wars*, pp. 77–81.

which succeeded. The former deputy NSA to President Bush the elder, and former CIA chief, proved himself a team player and a protection for Obama against opposition from a military forced to contemplate major budget cuts and priority shifts. Gates largely won in the 2009 contest over the Afghanistan surge though argued forcefully against the 2011 Libyan intervention. He represented within the administration exactly that tradition of pragmatic, interests-oriented 'Brent Scowcroft Republicanism' which Obama frequently commended, but which represented just one strand within his administration. Some of Gates' more unbuttoned comments – about the failure of NATO allies to spend adequately on defence and about the need to avoid major future conflicts in the Middle East – no doubt echoed Obama's own private thoughts.

Senior defence personnel, both civilian and military, have intersected with leading intelligence appointments. Indeed, it can reasonably be argued that, under Obama, divisions between the Pentagon and the CIA amounted to little more than a 'blurred wall' (to use Micah Zenko's phrase). According to Zenko, a leading analyst of drone warfare, the Pentagon's Joint Special Operations Command is 'basically a mini-CIA within the Defense Department'.[45] On the intelligence side of the blurred wall, Obama's team has not been free of conspicuous bureaucratic and personal rivalries. Admiral Dennis Blair, appointed director of national intelligence in 2009 (the coordinating office created after 9/11) almost inevitably had tense relations with Leon Panetta (Obama's first CIA chief) and John Brennan (special NSC staffer for counterterrorism). Woodward has described major clashes between Blair and Rahm Emanuel and, following a critical report on national counterterrorism written by John Brennan, Blair was forced out in May 2010.

The report also criticised the CIA. Agency head Leon Panetta had been appointed in 2009 in preference to both the existing director, Michael Hayden, and to Brennan himself; both Hayden and Brennan, a CIA operative and adviser to CIA head George Tenet, were seen as too seriously implicated in some of the more controversial activities of the Bush era.[46] Efforts by the White House to root out from the defence intelligence communities some of the more controversial defenders of controversial interrogation techniques from the Bush years largely foundered in the face of institutional obstruction and Obama's own desire to minimise internal conflict. The leading White House proponent of such efforts, White House Counsel Greg Craig, left the inner circle in late 2009.[47]

45 See Council on Foreign Relations, 'Appointment of John Brennan as Director of Central Intelligence and US Drone Strike Policies'.

46 Mann, *The Obamians*, pp. 104–5.

47 Sanger, *Confront and Conceal*, p. 212.

tta moved to the Pentagon in 2011, to be replaced at the CIA by
l David Petraeus. The latter, though certainly not a career politician, was
:t a member of the 'team of rivals'. Like Gates, he represented continuity
with the Bush years; he enjoyed greater public recognition than Gates, and
was rumoured to be interested in running for the Republican presidential
nomination in 2012. Petraeus, a major proponent of the Afghan 'surge' in
2009, was given responsibility for the Afghanistan campaign following General
McChrystal's dismissal. Petraeus's move to the CIA arguably took some of
the impetus away from any possible 2012 election bid, even as it took away
from direct military leadership the strongest national proponent of counter-
insurgency just as Obama was showing signs of becoming disillusioned with
such strategy. Panetta's arrival at the Pentagon was interpreted as a victory
for counterterrorism, as against long-haul counter-insurgency, within the
administration.[48] At the CIA, Panetta had presided over not only the bin
Laden raid but also the major expansion in drone warfare. Following a brief
and personally difficult time at the CIA, Petraeus handed the Agency headship
over to Brennan, widely regarded as a strong proponent of drone-based
counterterrorism. In 2013, Panetta was replaced at the Pentagon by former
Republican Senator Chuck Hagel.

Interwoven among the intelligence and Pentagon politics of the Obama
era were some fairly severe problems within civilian-military relations. Obama
seems, for example, to have deeply resented leaks, designed to box the president
into accepting the military's troop number estimates, at the time of the 2009
Afghan 'surge' debate. Later military resentment at the tightness of White
House decision-making surfaced during the September 2013 Syrian crisis. At
that time, General Martin E. Dempsey, chairman of the Joint Chiefs, made
explicit his scepticism about military action in a way that did not necessarily
chime with the (admittedly rather confusing) messages emanating from White
House and Foggy Bottom. Yet, in general, White House military clashes under
Obama were broadly kept in check and certainly did not plumb the depths of
the Bill Clinton years. A sign of growing tension in the second term, however,
was the opposition of two ex-Defence Secretaries to Obama's decision to seek
congressional authorisation before ordering air strikes on Syria in September
2013. Robert Gates and Leon Panetta viewed the decision as undermining US
credibility following the Syrian regime's August 2013 chemical weapons attack
and the breaching of a 'red line' set rather casually by Obama a year earlier.[49]

The complex shifts of intelligence and defence personnel under Obama
should not necessarily be seen as evidence of procedural chaos. They do,

48 Ibid., p. 319.
49 See Baker and Gordon, 'Kerry becomes chief advocate for US attack'; Londono and
    Whitlock, 'Syria crisis reveals uneasy relationship between Obama and nation's military
    leaders'.

however, illustrate the impact of some damaging clashes between White House inner circle and 'outsider' personnel. They also point to the strongly politicised nature of Obama's appointments, reflecting the president's need to reconcile competing pressures: to be seen to be breaking with the Bush years, despite Obama's awareness of the need for continuity in the fight against terrorism; the genuine commitment to bipartisanship and the concept of the 'team of rivals'; the concern to disengage as soon as feasible from Middle Eastern conflict; and the increasing attraction of 'smart' counterterrorism.

Obama and Congress

The political context for the Obama presidency was set by the intensification of polarised partisanship across Washington and by the Republican gains in the 2010 elections. Given the intensity of what in 2010 retiring Senator Evan Bayh called 'brain-dead partisanship', it can be argued that Obama, in the foreign policy arena at least, has fared rather well.[50] Senate ratification of the New Start Treaty in December 2010 was the most obvious White House success on Capitol Hill. Free trade agreements with Panama, Colombia and South Korea were ratified in 2011. Some potentially tricky confirmation votes have gone the president's way. Samantha Power, for example, was confirmed as US Ambassador to the UN in August 2013 by a margin of 87–10. In 2012, Jeffrey Bader (ex-Obama NSC staffer for East Asia) wrote that 'the extreme polarization that marked domestic politics in the Obama years was absent from foreign policy'.[51] To some degree at least, Obama has been able to exploit cross-party cleavages. Such cleavages, notably at the time of the Libyan intervention in 2011, raised the prospect of neo-isolationist Republicans making common cause with anti-war Democrats. However, at least until the Syrian debates of 2013, these complications in brute Capitol Hill partisanship tended to work in Obama's favour. The president fed off a national mood, reflected in Congress, which supported his version of low-visibility, post-Bush, 'leading-from-behind' internationalism.

Some qualifications need to be made to a narrative of Obama navigating a way through partisanship in the way indicated in the preceding paragraph. For one thing, domestic and foreign policy are not discrete categories. Budget battles affect defence spending levels. Republican animosity towards Obama may be more obvious in the domestic policy context, but can easily spill over – despite GOP internal divisions over the proper scope for contemporary US internationalism – into foreign policy votes. The 'intermestic' agenda, including trade, immigration and climate change, looms large. As John Kerry told the

50 Bayh, 'Why I'm leaving the Senate'.

51 Bader, *Obama and China's Rise: An Insider's Account of America's Asia Strategy*, p. 141.

Senate during his 2013 confirmation, 'foreign policy is economic policy'.[52] Additionally, Obama has followed a pragmatic line in holding back measures likely to run into problems on Capitol Hill. Thus, despite undertakings in Obama's 2009 Prague speech, the Comprehensive Nuclear Test Ban Treaty was not presented for Senate ratification. It should also be noted that many of Obama's victories on Capitol Hill have been very hard won. The New Start Treaty was passed in the wake of complex concessions to Republican leaders on nuclear weapons funding. The confirmation of Chuck Hagel, the former Republican whose liberal voting record in the Senate upset many in his own party, squeezed through 58–41 in early 2013. This was the tightest margin for any Secretary of Defence since the post was created in 1947.

Congress has clearly affected the policy substance of Obama's foreign policy. Examples here include the destruction of administration plans to transfer Guantanamo inmates to facilities in the US; the withholding of US funds to Pakistan in the wake of the finding and killing of Osama bin Laden in Abbottabad; continuing restrictions on presidential trade negotiation authority under the (now expired) Trade Promotion Authority; and the adding of various exceptions to a December 2012 measure to promote normal trade relations with Russia. Worries about confirmation difficulties were also widely seen as being responsible for Obama's decision to name Susan Rice as his second-term NSA, rather than as Secretary of State.[53]

The putative switching of Rice to the White House position was in fact deeply ironic. As we have seen, throughout the Obama presidency, and certainly into the second term, policy has been directed from the White House. Rice was likely to wield more power as NSA than as Secretary of State. Obama has taken stances on White House-congressional relations which would not have shamed less coy proponents of an imperial presidency. The president has used signing statements, recess appointments and invocations of 'executive privilege' to circumvent legislative intent and oversight. Drone and cyberwarfare are essentially immune from effective congressional oversight. The CIA does report drone strike records to the Senate Select Committee on Intelligence (SSCI), though Joint Special Operations Command attacks come under broad biannual legislative rather than Armed Services Committee review.[54] The SSCI spent years seeking legal justification for the assassination of US citizens purportedly plotting attacks on the US from abroad. Attorney General Eric Holder simply asserted that the US government has the right to take such action without judicial process. The 2011 Libyan bombing campaign involved

---

52 See Peters, 'Hagel approved for Defense in sharply split Senate vote'.

53 See Johnson, 'Congress and US foreign policy'; Warren, *The Obama Administration's Nuclear Weapons Strategy*, pp. 78–80.

54 See *The Economist*, 'W's Apprentice'; Zenko, 'Reforming US drone strike policies', p. 15.

controversial, though not unprecedented, interpretations of legislative war power. Conspicuously 'imperial' was the issuing of opinion on war powers in 2011 from the White House Counsel (Robert F. Bayer) rather than the Justice Department.[55] There have been numerous expressions of legislative disquiet – by no means all motivated by narrow partisanship – at the high-handedness of Obama administration attitudes towards legislative oversight of foreign policy.

Obama's personalised decision in September 2013 to seek congressional authorisation for military action against Syria was, at least to some degree, a rather surprising recognition of legislative prerogative. Obama insisted that he had 'the authority to carry out this military action without specific congressional authorisation', though a vote in Congress would be appropriate since 'all of us should be accountable as we move forward'. He also referred directly to the rejection by the British House of Commons of UK action in Syria.[56] Whether the seeking of a vote in Congress before what was explicitly described by Obama as 'action limited in duration and scope' established a major precedent is debatable – not least in view of the fact that both Presidents Bush took broadly parallel action (while reserving the right to act without Congress) before military intervention in the Middle East. However, the 2013 vote, postponed indefinitely following Moscow's intervention in the Syrian chemical weapons dispute, was scheduled under very different circumstances from its predecessors in 1990 and 2002. Upon announcing his decision to seek a vote, Obama's administration embarked upon intense lobbying on Capitol Hill – 'flooding the zone', as insiders described it to reporters. It rapidly became evident, however, that such a vote, if it were to be taken, might well go against the president. At least in domestic political terms, the decision to seek the vote in Congress did not enhance Obama's reputation for possessing acute 'contextual intelligence'.

The debate over action in Syria illustrated the cross-cutting cleavages, especially among Republicans but also on the Democratic side, to which I have already referred. Such cleavages look certain to set the scene for any use of military power for the remainder of the Obama presidency. Significant numbers of Democrats take the view Senator Dianne Feinstein articulated on her website on 7 April 2011 in reaction to the wave of revolutionary protests that rose up in the early stages of the Arab Spring: 'These are essentially civil wars. If you get involved in Syria, you get involved in Bahrain, you get involved in Saudi Arabia, then it's big trouble'.[57] In his efforts to attract support for Syrian action in September 2013, the president even had difficulty in capturing

55 See Ackerman, 'Legal acrobatics, illegal war'; J. Gertler et al., 'No fly zones: strategic, operational and legal considerations for Congress'.

56 See 'Statement by the president on Syria', www.whitehouse.gov/the-press-office/2013/08/31/statement-president-syria (accessed 24 Feb. 2014).

57 http://feinstein.senate.gov.

the support of GOP hawks like Senator John McCain, who looked for much stronger action than that promised (initially, at least) by Obama and Secretary Kerry. Less predictably, Republican opinion, especially in the House, was clearly reflective of public unwillingness to take more military gambles in the Middle East. To some degree, anti-war Republicans echoed the conservative re-orientation – condemned by John Kerry as 'armchair isolationism' – which was symbolised in Senator Rand Paul's 13-hour filibuster against John Brennan's CIA nomination in March 2013. Objecting to drone assaults on US citizens, Paul reflected a revived conservative suspicion of executive power and antipathy to fighting remote wars for ends not immediately connected to US security.

Other strands of Republican opposition included a degree of hyper-partisan opposition to any recommendation emanating from the White House, plus doubts (shared by several Democrats) about the selection of allies. Senator Ted Cruz (the Tea Party-oriented Republican from Texas) asked if America really wanted to provide Al Qaeda with an air force.[58]

Conclusion

The test of an effective foreign policy process is the articulation and implementation of coherent strategy. The Obama administration has by no means been immune to bouts of policy incoherence. The Arab Spring in particular put the administration on the back foot. Its responses, for example, both to the 2011 revolutionary changes in Egypt, and to the overthrow of Egyptian leader Mohamed Morsi in 2013, were conspicuously confused.[59] The rapid policy departures which followed the August 2013 chemical weapons attacks in Syria revealed an administration in considerable disarray. Obama's decision to go for a vote in Congress embarrassed not only John Kerry, the chief public proponent of military action in Syria, but also his new NSA, Susan Rice, who had also vigorously asserted the case for swift military action against the Assad regime.[60] Even the East Asian 'pivot' – arguably the most fruitful example of Obama making priorities anew – was launched clumsily, with excessive emphasis on the military aspects of Asian rebalancing.[61] Despite such lapses, the Obama years have not witnessed the kind of debilitating personal rivalries which disfigured the Carter or indeed the early George W. Bush administrations. There have, as this chapter has shown, been personality

58 See Douthat, 'What hath Rand Paul wrought?' and 'Why Republicans miss the realists'; Landler and Weisman, 'Obama delays Syria strike to focus on a Russian plan'.
59 See Maddox, 'Obama must end aid to Egypt before more die'.
60 See Baker and Gordon, 'Kerry becomes chief advocate for US attack'; Milbank, 'Obama's Syria muddle'.
61 See Haass, *Foreign Policy Begins at Home*, pp. 107–8.

clashes and bureaucratic confusions, but these have been more or less contained by the tightness of White House direction.

The White House-centric system may be presumed to suit Obama's cognitive style and also what Stephen Wayne calls the president's 'need to take charge'.[62] The Obama system is a strange one, with the 'inner circle' rather than the NSA apparently dominant. Obama has appointed three very contrasting NSAs. The selection of James Jones as his first one seemed to indicate the president's failure to anticipate the needs of a White House-centred system. Following Jones' marginalisation, Tom Donilon operated as a mixture of 'honest broker' and policy advocate with a low public profile. The third, Susan Rice, is presumed to be an intense policy advocate, and has a high public profile, though she apparently enjoys only circumscribed influence. The dangers of a highly centralised system, with an uncertain role for the NSA, are clear. The 'inner circle' may become resented by 'outsiders' as arrogant and mutually reinforcing. The regular foreign policy bureaucracy may feel excluded.

The group dynamics within the White House may prematurely shut down the due consideration of a range of policy options. Under Obama, the emergence of such self-defeating 'groupthink' is lessened by the semi-institutionalised intra-White House debate between 'realist' and 'idealist' positions, with the president often (but not always) weighing in on the side of pragmatic, cost-conscious realism. Group dynamics in the Obama White House thus operate within the confines of a president-centred system, with Obama's own developing world view, his understanding of the 'lessons of Iraq', and his recognition of the nature of contemporary US public opinion (reflected in Congress) holding great sway. The centralised nature of the process conspires to magnify the impact of the president's own beliefs and decision-making routines.

Elite personality has profoundly affected the Obama foreign policy. The first-term system of tight White House direction was to some degree made to work only by Hillary Clinton's decision not to undermine her former rival for the Democratic nomination. Biden and Gates made immense contributions to the foreign and security policy operation in the first term. The 'last man in the room' – to use Biden's phrase – is, however, always Obama himself. The presidential world view would seem to have shifted towards a slightly jaded, 'realist' acceptance of limits. He told the UN General Assembly in September 2013: 'The United States has a hard-earned humility when it comes to our ability to determine events inside other countries'.[63]

The president's August–September 2013 Syrian decisions can be seen as illustrating once again his penchant for the 'middle way': supporting military

62 Wayne, 'Presidential character and judgement'.

63 Quoted in Patrick, 'The realist idealist'.

action but inviting, in the name of democratic consensualism, the emergence of obstacles to such action. Obama convinces as a leader who can generate feasible policy through a rational, if sometimes slow, consideration of options. He is less convincing as a president who is unparalysed by complexity. As already noted, extreme presidentialism in making foreign policy should not be confused with decisiveness. Maureen Dowd's verdict on the Syrian decisions – that a 'mindlessly certain' George W. Bush had been replaced by a 'mindfully uncertain' Obama – may haunt the remainder of this administration.[64]

References

B. Ackerman (2011) 'Legal acrobatics, illegal war', *New York Times*, 20 June, www.nytimes.com/2011/06/21/opinion/21Ackerman.html (accessed 24 Feb. 2014).

J.A. Bader (2012) *Obama and China's Rise: An Insider's Account of America's Asia Strategy* (Washington, DC: Brookings Institution).

P. Baker and M.R. Gordon (2013) 'Kerry becomes chief advocate for US attack', *New York Times*, 30 Aug., www.nytimes.com/2013/08/31/world/middleeast/john-kerry-syria.html (accessed 24 Feb. 2014).

E. Bayh (2010) 'Why I'm leaving the Senate', *New York Times*, 21 Feb., www.nytimes.com/2010/02/21/opinion/21bayh.html (accessed 24 Feb. 2014).

P. Broadwell (2013) 'The doctrine of power', *Prospect*, Aug., pp. 40–3, www.prospectmagazine.co.uk/magazine/the-doctrine-of-power-paula-broadwell-samantha-power (accessed 24 Feb. 2014).

J.P. Burke (2005) 'The neutral/honest broker role in foreign-policy decision making: a reassessment', *Presidential Studies Quarterly*, vol. 35, no. 2, pp. 229–58.

H. Clinton (2011) 'America's Pacific century', *Foreign Policy*, 11 Oct., www.foreignpolicy.com/articles/2011/10/11/americas_pacific_century (accessed 24 Feb. 2014).

Council on Foreign Relations (2013) 'Senator John Kerry's Confirmation Hearing Statement, January 2013', www.cfr.org/elections/senator-john-kerrys-confirmation-hearing-statement-january-2013/p29874 (accessed 24 Feb. 2014).

— (2013) 'Appointment of John Brennan as Director of Central Intelligence and US Drone Strike Policies: discussion: Gideon Rose, Sarah Holewinski, Micah Zenko: 4 February 2013', www.cfr.org/intelligence/appointment-john-brennan-director-central-intelligence-us-drone-strike-policies/p29922 (accessed 24 Feb. 2014).

64 Dowd, 'Who do you trust?'.

R. Douhat (2013) 'What hath Rand Paul wrought?', *New York Times,* 9 March, www.nytimes.com/2013/03/10/opinion/sunday/douthat-what-hath-rand-paul-wrought.html (accessed 24 Feb. 2014).

— (2013) 'Why Republicans miss the realists', *New York Times,* 31 July, http://douthat.blogs.nytimes.com/2013/07/31/why-republicans-miss-the-realists (accessed 24 Feb. 2014).

M. Dowd (2013) 'Who do you trust?', *New York Times,* 10 Sep., www.nytimes.com/2013/09/11/opinion/dowd-who-do-you-trust.html (accessed 24 Feb. 2014).

D. D'Souza (2010) *The Roots of Obama's Rage* (New York, NY: Regnery).

C. Dueck (2011) 'The accommodator: Obama's foreign policy', *Policy Review,* vol. 169, pp, 161–84, www.hoover.org/publications/policy-review/article/94006 (accessed 24 Feb. 2014).

J. Dumbrell (1997) *The Making of US Foreign Policy* (Manchester: Manchester University Press).

Economist, The (2012), 'What Hillary did next', 24 May, www.economist.com/node/21551105 (accessed 24 Feb. 2014).

— (2013) 'W's apprentice', 18 May, www.economist.com/news/united-states/21578047-presidents-use-executive-orders-many-them-praiseworthy-aims-will-end (accessed 24 Feb. 2013).

— (2013) 'Action women', 8 June, www.economist.com/news/united-states/21579027-president-defiantly-picks-two-liberal-interventionists-action-women (accessed 24 Feb. 2014).

A. George and J.L. George (1998) *Presidential Personality and Performance* (Boulder, CO: Westview).

J. Gertler, C.M. Blanchard, C. Dale and J.K. Elsea (2013) 'No fly zones: strategic, operational and legal considerations for Congress', Congressional Research Service Report, 3 May, www.fas.org/sgp/crs/natsec/R41701.pdf (accessed 24 Feb. 2014).

K. Ghattas (2013) *The Secretary: A Journey with Hillary Clinton from Beirut to the Heart of American Power* (New York, NY: Times Books).

R.N. Haass (2003) 'Why foreign policy is not pornography', in S.A. Renshon and D.W. Larson (eds.), *Good Judgement in Foreign Policy: Theory and Application* (Lanham, MD: Rowman and Littlefield).

— (2013) *Foreign Policy Begins at Home: The Case for Putting America's House in Order* (New York, NY: Basic Books).

P.J. Haney (1997) *Organizing for Foreign Policy Crises: Presidents, Advisers, and the Management of Decision-Making* (Ann Arbor, MI: University of Michigan Press).

M. Hirsh (2012) 'Joe Biden: the most influential vice president in history?', *The Atlantic*, Dec., www.theatlantic.com/politics/archive/2012/12/joe-biden-the-most-influential-vice-president-in-history/266729/ (accessed 24 Feb. 2014).

— (2013) 'Susan Rice and Samantha Power: less change than meets the eye', *The Atlantic*, June, www.theatlantic.com/international/archive/2013/06/susan-rice-and-samantha-power-less-change-than-meets-the-eye/276579/ (accessed 24 Feb. 2014).

J. Hudson (2013) 'Jeff Prescott replaces Julie Smith as Biden's Deputy National Security Advisor', *The Cable*, 18 June, http://thecable. foreignpolicy.com/posts/2013/06/18/jeff_prescott_replaces_julie_smith_as_biden_s_deputy_national_security_advisor (accessed 24 Feb. 2014).

K.F. Inderfurth and L. Johnson (eds.) (2004) *Fateful Decisions: Inside the National Security Council* (New York, NY: Oxford University Press).

M.S. Indyk, K.G. Lieberthal and M.E. O'Hanlon (2012) *Bending History: Barack Obama's Foreign Policy* (Washington, DC: Brookings Institution)

T. Johnson (2013) 'Congress and US foreign policy', 24 Jan. www.cfr.org/united-states/congress-us-foreign-policy/p29871 (accessed 24 Feb. 2014).

C.W. Kegley and E. R. Wittkopf (1996) *American Foreign Policy: Pattern and Process* (New York, NY: St Martin's Press).

M. Landler and J. Weisman (2013) 'Obama delays Syria strike to focus on a Russian plan', *New York Times*, 10 Sep., www.nytimes.com/2013/09/11/world/middleeast/syrian-chemical-arsenal.html (accessed 24 Feb. 2014).

D.W. Larson (2003) 'Good Judgement in foreign policy', in S.A. Renshon and D.W. Larson (eds.), *Good Judgement in Foreign Policy: Theory and Application* (Lanham, MD: Rowman and Littlefield).

R. Lizza (2011) 'The consequentialist: how the Arab Spring remade Obama's foreign policy', *The New Yorker*, 2 May, pp. 44–55, www.newyorker.com/reporting/2011/05/02/110502fa_fact_lizza (accessed 24 Feb. 2014).

E. Londono and C. Whitlock (2013) 'Syria crisis reveals uneasy relationship between Obama and nation's military leaders', *Washington Post*, 18 Sep., www.washingtonpost.com/world/national-security/syria-crisis-reveals-uneasy-relationship-between-obama-nations-military-leaders/2013/09/18/752bb828-1ca5-11e3-a628-7e6dde8f889d_story.html (accessed 24 Feb. 2014).

E. Luce and D. Dombey (2010) 'US foreign policy: waiting on the Sun King', *Financial Times*, 30 March, www.ft.com/cms/s/0/df53a396-3c2a-11df-b40c-00144feabdc0.html (accessed 24 Feb. 2014).

B. Maddox (2013) 'Obama must end aid to Egypt before more die', *The Times*, 29 July, www.thetimes.co.uk/tto/opinion/columnists/article3827944.ece (accessed 24 Feb. 2014).

J. Mann (2010) *The Obamians: The Struggle Inside the White House to Redefine American Power* (London: Viking Penguin).

K. Marsh (2013) 'Obama's surge: a bureaucratic politics analysis of the decision to order a troop surge in the Afghanistan war', *Foreign Policy Analysis*, vol. 7, pp. 1–24.

D. Milbank (2013) 'Obama's Syria muddle', *Washington Post*, 10 Sep, www.washingtonpost.com/opinions/dana-milbank-kerrys-not-so-clear-sailing-on-syria/2013/09/10/142fe5da-1a52-11e3-a628-7e6dde8f889d_story.html (accessed 24 Feb. 2014.

D. Murray (2013) 'Military action but not as we know it: Libya, Syria and the making of an Obama doctrine', *Contemporary Politics*, vol. 19, no. 2, pp. 146–66.

V. Nasr (2013) *The Dispensable Nation: American Foreign Policy in Retreat* (New York, NY: Doubleday).

R.E. Neustadt and E.R. May (1986) *Thinking in Time: The Uses of History for Decision Makers* (New York, NY: Free Press).

J.S. Nye (2008) *The Powers to Lead* (New York, NY: Oxford University Press).

B. Obama (2007) *The Audacity of Hope: Thoughts on Reclaiming the American Dream* (New York, NY: Crown).

— (2007) 'Renewing America's leadership', *Foreign Affairs*, 86 (4), pp. 2–16.

J. Pace (2013) 'Tom Donilon resigning', *HuffPost Politics*, 5 June, www.huffingtonpost.com/2013/06/05/tom-donilon-resigning_n_3388885.html (accessed 24 Feb. 2014).

S.M. Patrick (2013) 'The realist idealist', 24 Sep., http://blogs.cfr.org/patrick/2013/09/24/the-realist-idealist-obamas-un-speech/.

J.W. Peters (2013) 'Hagel approved for Defense in sharply split Senate vote', *New York Times*, 26 Feb., www.nytimes.com/2013/02/27/us/politics/hagel-filibuster-defense-senate-confirmation.html (accessed 24 Feb. 2014).

J.P. Pfiffner (2010) 'Organizing the Obama White House', in J. Thurber (ed.), *Obama in Office: The First Two Years* (Boulder, CO: Paradigm Publishers).

— (2011) *The Modern Presidency*, 6th edn. (Boston, MA: Wadsworth).

S. Power (2003) *'A Problem From Hell': America and the Age of Genocide* (London: Flamingo).

D.E. Sanger (2009) *The Inheritance: The World Obama Confronts and the Challenges to American Power* (New York, NY: Bantam).

— (2013) *Confront and Conceal: Obama's Secret Wars and Surprising Use of American Power* (New York, NY: Crown).

R. Singh (2012) *Barack Obama's Post-American Foreign Policy: The Limits of Engagement* (London: Bloomsbury Academic).

A. Stepak and R. Whitlark (2012) 'The battle over America's foreign policy doctrine', *Survival*, vol. 54, no. 5, pp. 45–66.

S.G. Stolberg (2013) 'A new US player put on the world stage by Syria', *New York Times*, 22 Sep., www.nytimes.com/2013/09/23/world/a-new-us-player-put-on-world-stage-by-syria.html (accessed 24 Feb. 2014).

J. Traub (2009) 'After Cheney', *New York Times*, 29 Nov., www.nytimes.com/2009/11/29/magazine/29Biden-t.html (accessed 24 Feb. 2014).

A. Warren (2014) *The Obama Administration's Nuclear Weapons Strategy* (London and New York, NY: Routledge).

S.J. Wayne (2011) 'Presidential character and judgement: Obama's Afghanistan and health care decisions', *Presidential Studies Quarterly*, vol. 41, no. 2, pp. 291–306.

B. Woodward (2010) *Obama's Wars: The Inside Story* (London: Simon & Schuster).

M. Zenko (2013) 'Reforming US drone strike policies', Council on Foreign Relations Special Report 65 (Council on Foreign Relations Press), www.cfr.org/wars-and-warfare/reforming-us-drone-strike-policies/p29736 (accessed 24 Feb. 2014).

Index

ABC News, 42 n.8, 62 n.74, 48, 94 n.18, 114, n.5

absenteeism, 92, 149

abortion law, 35, 49

Academy of Nutrition and Dietetics, 150

Adelson, Sheldon, 35

Affordable Care Act (usually known as ACA or Obamacare), 15, 46, 79, 113–5, 116, 120 n.31, 124–30

Afghanistan, 18, 176, 177, 182, 184, 185, 186, 189, 190, 199, 202, 205, 206, 208–11, 213, 214

Agency for International Development, 212

agribusiness, 145, 152

Alberta tar sands, 164, 165

American Association of Paediatrics, 147

American Recovery and Reinvestment Act (usually known as ARRA), 113

Annan, Kofi, 176

Arab Spring, 204 n.12, 217, 218

Armed Services and Appropriations Committees, 81

arsenic (in drinking water), 165, 166

Asia-Pacific, 175, 177, 178, 187, 188, 193

Asia pivot, 17

baby bonuses, 105, 107

Bachmann, Michelle, 160

Bader, Jeffrey, 215

Bahrain, 217

Bank of England, 181

Biden, Joe, 113, 121, 202, 205–7, 208, 212, 219

Bin Laden, Osama, 205, 214, 216

Blair, Tony, 18, 180

Bloomberg, Michael, 145

Blue Dog Democrats, 61

Boehner, John, 54–5, 74, 101

Breyer, Stephen, 32

BRIC countries, 177

Brookings Institute, 145, 149

Brown, Gordon, 180

Brown, Scott, 55, 79, 124

budget, 14, 42, 59, 62–3, 71–87, 92, 94 n.18, 97, 98, 99, 114 n.4, 115, 116, 125–6, 138, 188, 189, 190, 206, 213, 215

budget committee, House, 81, 38; Senate, 81, 114 n.4

Budget and Impoundment Act 1974, 98

Budget Control Act, 74–5, 82

budget, cuts, 62–3, 188, 213; deal, 59; surpluses, 71, 85

Bureau of Energy Resources, 212

Burma, 210

Bush, George H.W., 29, 57, 200, 204, 207, 217

Bush, George W., 18, 27–9, 48, 51, 53, 54, 57, 71, 73, 75, 76, 77, 78, 85, 86, 90, 119, 121, 161, 165, 166, 180, 181, 186, 200, 201, 204, 206, 213, 214, 215, 217, 220

Cadillac tax, 126, 127 n.55

California Citizens Redistricting Commission, 26

California Fresh Works Fund, 147

Cameron, David, 18, 175, 176, 179, 181, 188, 191, 193

cap and trade, 159, 160 n.67 and n.68, 168, 202

Carter, Jimmy, 33, 47, 57, 167, 218

Carville, James, 26, 27, 31, 37

CATO Institute, 144

Census 2010, 25–6

Center on Budget and Policy Priorities, 144

Center for Consumer Freedom, 148

Centers for Disease Control, 136, 143, 148

Central Intelligence Agency (CIA), 184, 201, 213, 214, 216, 218

Chamber of Commerce, 123

Cheney, Dick, 206

child allowances, 102–6

childcare, 16, 107

child health, 106

Child Nutrition Act, 147

child poverty, 102–4, 106–7

China, 158, 177, 180, 182, 188, 202, 215 n.51

Churchill, Winston, 17, 175

Clean Air Act, 161, 163, 168

clean coal technology, 159, 168

Climate Action Plan (CAP), 161

Clinton, Bill, 26, 48, 51, 57, 71, 115, 119, 121, 122, 123, 124, 138, 166, 200, 201, 204, 205, 207, 208, 210, 214

Clinton, Hillary, 120, 177 n.11, 179, 202, 207, 208, 210–12, 219

Cold War, 178, 183, 204, 212

Commerce Clause, 127

Comprehensive Nuclear Test Ban Treaty, 216

Conference of the Parties, 158

Congress, 17, 18, 25, 26, 31, 33, 41, 42, 47, 53–64, 71–7, 79, 82, 84, 89, 94, 95, 97, 98, 118–22, 124, 157, 159, 181, 192, 202, 212, 215–18; ideological division, 55; presidential support, 57, 60

Congressional Budget Office, 72, 99, 100, 116, 125, 126

congressional supercommittee, 75

constituencies, Democrat, 25–7, 36, 52, 58, 59, 61–2, 210; Republican, 25–7, 36, 52, 57, 58, 60, 63

constitution, 29, 30, 35, 47, 73, 79, 127

constitutional boundary design, 14

Consumer Price Index (CPI), 97–8

Cook, Rhodes, 24, 25, 122

Cooperative Congressional Election Study, 51, 52, 56

Cruz, Ted, 55, 76, 80, 83, 218

culture wars, 14, 19

death panels, 47; penalty, 36

debt, 15, 63, 73–5, 84, 85, 89, 165, 169; ceiling, 15, 73, 74, 75, 77, 78, 79–81, 83, 86, 87, 89; ratio, 72, 84–5; reduction, 74, 85; repayment, 74, 84, 85

Defense Trade Cooperation Treaty, 185

deficit, 15, 43, 44, 61, 63, 71, 73–4, 75, 76, 77, 78, 81–2, 84–6

Democratic Leadership Council, 122

Democratic party, 24, 26, 33, 34, 36–7, 120, 121, 122, 205

diabetes, 149

disability insurance, 102, 149–50

disease, 135, 149

Donilon, Thomas, 207–8, 209, 212, 219

Dowd, Maureen, 220

Drewnowski and Specter, 139, 142

drone use, 18, 86, 212, 213, 214, 216, 218

Earth Policy Institute, 162

economy, 14, 19, 26, 31, 37, 71–3, 76, 77, 78, 80, 83, 84, 85, 86, 89, 93–4, 113, 126, 137, 143, 144, 167, 188, 190, 192

economic, business cycle, 94; collapse 2008, 13, 15, 72; growth, 19, 91, 121, 161

Economic Recovery and Reinvestment Act (ERRA), 15

Edwards, John, 120

Egypt, 218

Eisenhower, Dwight, 26, 57

election, campaigning, 23, 27, 31, 36, 136, 137, 161, 206; campaign funding, 35

Election 2000, 27, 28, 58, 61

Election 2008, 13, 14, 16, 17, 18, 22–3, 24, 26, 33, 34, 35, 43, 49–50, 64, 72, 120, 136, 165, 176, 202, 205, 207, 208, 210

Election 2010, 14, 15, 22, 23, 24, 59, 71, 73, 76, 160, 215

Election 2012, 15, 23, 24, 25, 26, 33–7, 41, 42–3, 44, 46, 51, 52–4, 56–8, 60, 61, 63, 75, 76, 79, 93, 120 n.31, 136, 137, 142, 175, 206, 214

Election 2014, 36, 37, 58, 61, 63, 82, 83, 87, 114

Election 2016, 37, 63, 82, 87, 93

Electoral College, 76

Emmanuel, Rahm, 121

energy, 17, 164, 168–9

environment, 17, 49, 152, 157–69

Environmental Protection Agency, 157, 160–3

equal opportunity, 49

exit polls, 23, 49, 50, 52, 56

European Union (EU), 101, 102, 107, 166, 178 n.14, 182, 187–8, 190, 191–2, 212

Falkland Islands, 179

family allowance, 103–4

Fannie Mae and Freddie Mac, 84

Farm Bill, 136, 137, 142, 144

federal campaign funding, 35

federal Defense of Marriage Act, 29

Federal, Nutrition Service, 140; Reserve, 181; Board, 73

Feeding America, 142

Feed the Future, 177

Feinstein, Dianne, 217

filibuster, 55, 79, 80, 82, 99, 121, 124, 160, 218

fiscal, cliff, 15, 62, 89, 101; year, 72, 74, 84, 86, 98

Food and Beverage Consumption Survey, 140

food and beverage industry, 141, 145, 149–50

Food and Drug Administration, 147

food, assistance, 136, 138; crisis, 17, 135–8, 152; deserts, 147; insecurity, 16, 138–9; movement, 138, 152; stamps. See SNAP

Food Stamps Act, 137

foreign, policy, 18–19, 176, 181, 187, 199–220; personnel, 184–5, 200, 205–15; process, 199–220

Fox News, 23–4, 53, 114 n.5

France, 101, 116, 151, 152, 182, 190, 191

G20, 178, 181

Gallup polls, 44 n.14, n.15 and n.16, 45, 47, 52, 53 n.47

Gang of Eight, 60

Gang of Six, 61

Gates, Robert, 205, 207, 212–14, 219

gay, marriage, 29–30, 35, 206; rights, 30, 35

gerrymandering, 25–6

Gingrich, Newt, 74, 136

Gini coefficient, 91

Gioia, Eric, 142

globalisation, 90–1, 193

Global Health, 177

global warming, 17, 165

Gordon, Philip, 191 192

Gore, Al, 27, 28, 115, 212

Government Communications Headquarters (GCHQ), 183

Government, divided, 26, 27, 31 52, 54–6, 59; shutdown, 63, 79, 80, 87, 114, 115, 144; spending, 17, 46, 85–6, 92, 101–2, 109

Gramm-Rudman-Hollings Act, 75, 78

Grand Old Party (GOP), 14, 22, 24–5, 36, 37, 50, 53, 76, 119, 120 n.31, 123, 215, 218

grassroots organisations, 93, 152

greenhouse gases, 159, 160–5, 168

Greenstock, Jeremy, 179, 182

green, jobs, 17, 165, 167–9; technology, 17, 159

Greenstein, Fred, 19

gridlock, 14, 64, 144

Grocery Manufacturers Association, 149

Gross Domestic Product (GDP), 16, 72, 73, 77, 84, 98, 101, 102, 115, 116, 117, 189

Guantanamo, 18, 216

gun control, 36, 41, 63, 206

Hagel, Chuck, 214, 216

Hague, William, 182, 184, 188

Hansen, James, 164

Head Start, 96–7

healthcare, 16, 19, 22, 23, 49, 50, 71, 79–80, 113–30, 147

Health Savings Accounts, 120

Health Security Act, 120

Healthy Hunger-Free Kids Act, 147

Hillary-care, 120

Hispanic, population, 32–3, 34, 63, 118–19, 139; vote, 23, 32–3

Holder, Eric, 30, 32, 216

House Agricultural Committee, 144

House of Representatives, 24, 25, 36, 43, 57, 71, 72, 73, 76, 78, 79, 82, 83, 87, 124, 144, 160, 169

House Budget Committee, 81, 138

Huelskamp, Tim, 43

Hurricane Sandy, 54

ideology, political, 44–6, 55, 56, 61, 63; public, 45, 50, 59

Independent Payment Advisory Board, 126, 127

Independent voters, 23, 43, 44, 46, 49, 59

Institute of Medicine, 118

immigrants, illegal, 33, 47

immigration, 33, 60–1, 63, 215

income, distribution, 90, 91, 95, 100; inequality, 89, 92, 96

International Security Assistance Force, 184

Iran, 178, 182, 202, 211

Iraq, 18, 71, 73, 86, 176, 177, 180, 185–6, 194, 199, 200, 205, 206, 211, 219

Israel-Palestine peace process, 211

Johnson, Lyndon B., 30, 57, 96, 137, 147, 200, 205

Joint Committee on Taxation, 98

Jones, James, 207, 219

Jones, Van, 167–8

Kagan, Elena, 29, 32

Kennedy, Anthony, 32

Kennedy, Edward, 79, 121, 124

Kennedy, John Fitzgerald, 57, 186, 204

Kerry, John, 33, 115, 212, 215, 218

Keynes, John Maynard, 89, 91, 95, 109

Keystone XL pipeline, 157, 163–5

Kristol, William, 119

Krugman, Paul, 85, 120

Kyoto Protocol, 157, 162

labour force, 105

Latino. See Hispanic

League of Conservation Voters, 163

Lehman Brothers collapse, 73

Let's Move campaign, 136, 146–9, 150

Lewis, John, 31

Libya, 179, 180, 182, 184, 188, 190, 210, 213, 215, 216

Lieberman, Joe, 121 n.36, 123, 160

Limbaugh, Rush, 13

Lincoln, Abraham, 13

Low Cost Food Plan, 141

Luxembourg Income Study, 103, 104, 107, 108

McCain, John, 49, 72, 160, 207, 218

McConnell, Mitch, 23, 61, 83, 114, 124, 160

McKinsey Global Institute, 117

Machiavelli, Niccolo, 19

macroeconomics, 89, 91, 92, 93, 94

mandate, political, 42–4, 53, 54, 122, 127

maternity pay, 16, 108

media, 13, 15, 49 n.36, 77, 93, 143, 146, 151, 180, 181, 192

Medicaid, 36, 62, 74, 116, 125, 127, 128, 129, 149

Medicare, 47, 62, 74, 82, 84, 116, 119–20, 126, 129, 149

microeconomics, 89

middle classes, 42, 62, 100, 104, 137

Middle East, 176, 177, 181, 184, 186, 187, 188, 189, 192, 211, 213, 214, 217, 218

Middle East and North Africa Trade and Investment Partnership Initiative, 192

minimum wage, 16, 95–7

Murray, Patricia, 81, 82

National Ambient Air Quality Standard, 167

National Association for the Repeal of Abortion Laws (usually known as NARAL Pro-Choice), 27, 28

National Conference of State Legislatures, 25, 29

National Dairy Council, 150

National Federation of Independent Business, 79, 123, 127–8

National Security, Advisor, 201, 204, 207, 208, 213, 216, 218, 219; Agency, 18, 183; Council, 201, 207, 208, 209, 213, 215

Natural Resources Defense Council, 166

NBC News, 114

Needlecraft magazine, 31

New Deal, 13

New Jersey minimum wage, 95–6

New York Coalition Against Hunger, 152

New York Times, 23 n.2, 85, 91, 114 n.5, 120, 142, 148, 205

New Start Treaty, 215, 216

Nixon, Richard, 27, 47, 57, 119, 124, 141, 204, 207

North Atlantic Treaty Organization (NATO), 182, 187, 189, 191, 207, 213

North Korea, 211

nutrition, 16–17, 135–6, 137, 138–41, 142, 143, 146, 147–8, 150, 151, 152

Obama, Barack, burden, 41–64; electoral coalition, 26, 34, 36–7, 49, 56, 59; hope and change, 13, 18; leadership, 22, 37, 41, 42, 61, 158, 199, 200, 203, 204, 205; pragmatist, 18, 193, 204, 213, 216, 219; radical agenda, 14, 16–17, 19, 49, 55, 121, 176, 202, 215

Obamacare. *See* Affordable Care Act

Obama, Michelle, 17, 136, 146–7, 152

obesity, 16–17, 94, 135, 136, 138, 140, 142, 143–4, 145–7, 148, 149–51, 152–3; childhood, 136, 146, 147, 151

Office of Information and Regulatory Affairs, 167

Office of Management and Budget, 161, 167

O'Neill, Tip, 25

Operation, Enduring Freedom, 184; Redmap, 36; Tempora, 183

Organisation for Economic Cooperation and Development (OECD), 101, 102, 104, 116, 117, 135

paid parental leave, 102, 105, 106–8

Pakistan, 203, 206, 207, 211, 216

Panetta, Leon, 187, 213–14

Patient Protection and Affordable Care Act. *See* Affordable Care Act

Paul, Rand, 218

Pell grants, 98

Pelosi, Nancy, 43, 62

Pentagon, 86, 184, 189, 190, 201, 207, 212, 213, 214

Perry, Rick, 128

Personal Responsibility and Work Opportunity Act 1996, 138

Petraeus, David, 214

Pew Research Center, 34 n. 27, 46, 49 n.34, 50 n.38, 53 n.45, n. 48 and n.49, 59 n.56, 62 n.74, 114 n.5

Piketty (Thomas) and Saez (Emmanuel), 89, 97

polarization, political, 19, 50, 55–6, 64, 215; public, 48–53, 56

Political Action Committees (PACs), 93, 141; Super PACs, 93

political election cycle, 94

Pollan, Michael, 138, 139, 150, 152

poverty, 15, 16, 96, 102–4, 106, 107, 125, 126, 129, 135, 137–8, 139, 142–4, 152

Power, Samantha, 180, 208–9, 210, 215

pre-school education, 16, 95, 96–7, 102

presidential-congressional relations, 54, 202, 214, 215–18

PRISM, 183

productivity, 92–3, 149

Project for a Republican Future, 119

Public Interest Research Group, 139

public opinion, 22, 29, 31, 36, 41–53, 77, 87, 94, 114, 219

purchasing power parity (PPP), 116

Putin, Vladimir, 206

Reagan, Ronald, 33, 42, 48, 51, 57, 75, 122, 148, 167

Republican party, 14, 21, 25, 32, 33, 34 35, 37, 59, 71, 73, 86, 119, 120, 160, 203

reverse political business cycle, 94

Rice, Susan, 180, 209, 210, 216, 218, 219

Roberts, John (Chief Justice), 29, 30, 32, 79, 127

Roe v. Wade, 27

Romney, Mitt, 23, 25, 34, 35, 37, 43, 51, 52, 58, 61, 63, 76, 79, 81, 120 n. 31, 137, 159

Roosevelt, Franklin Delano, 13, 26, 137

Rove, Karl, 24, 35

Royal United Services Institute for Defence and Security Studies, 179 n.20, 184 n.49

Rubio, Marco, 59, 60–1, 82

Russia, 158, 177, 182, 187, 206, 209, 210, 216

Ryan, Paul, 43, 81–2, 138

same-sex marriage. *See* gay marriage

Saudi Arabia, 164, 217

Scalia, Antonin, 32

Scowcroft, Brent, 204, 207, 213

Sebelius, Kathleen, 79, 114 n.4, 127–8

Senate, 22–6, 28, 52, 55–9, 60–3, 72, 76, 77–83, 85, 87, 121–4, 144, 159, 160, 201, 215, 216; Finance Committee, 113; Select Committee on Intelligence, 216

sequestration, 41, 62, 63, 75, 77, 78–9, 81–3, 84, 85, 86, 87, 89, 162, 191

Sierra Club, 163

Simon, Michele, 141, 149, 151

smart power, 177

Social Security, 16, 62, 97–8, 106, 107, 121, 129

Sodexo, 147

Sotomayor, Sonia, 29

Souter, David, 29

Standard and Poor, 74, 86

Starbucks, 117

Stevens, John Paul, 29

stimulus package. *See* Economic Recovery and Reinvestment Act

Strategic Defence and Security Review, 189–91

Supreme Court, 14, 16, 27–32, 35, 36, 47, 79, 121 n.36, 127–8, 129, 160

sustainability, 135, 136

State of the Union 2011, 168

State of the Union 2013, 95

Stone, Deborah, 135, 136

Strategic Defence and Security Review, 189–91

Supplemental Nutrition Assistance Program (known as SNAP), 136–45, 151, 152; eligibility, 139–41; educational programmes (known as SNAP-Ed), 140

Syria, 86, 178, 182, 188, 194, 202, 208, 209, 212, 214, 215, 217–18, 219, 220

tax, brackets, 99, 102; breaks, 98–100; cuts (George W. Bush), 71; increase, 16, 59, 62, 63, 76, 77, 78, 79, 81, 82, 84, 85, 97, 100, 107; progressive, 89, 100; reform, 81, 98–101; on wealthy, 16, 43, 76, 77, 94, 97, 98, 99–100

Tea Party, 14, 15, 24, 50, 55, 60, 73–4, 76, 78, 80, 83, 122, 218

technological change, 90–1, 163, 165, 183, 191

terrorist attacks (11 September 2001), 71, 204
Thomas, Clarence, 32
Thrifty Food Plan, 141
Time magazine, 13
Trans-Atlantic Trade and Investment Partnership, 192
Trans-Pacific Partnership, 192
Treasury, 74
Troubled Asset Relief Programme (usually known as TARP), 50
Truman, Harry, 124
Trump, Donald, 24

United Kingdom (UK), 17, 91, 78, 101, 102, 103, 104, 105, 107, 108, 116, 175–94, 217
UKUSA Agreement, 183
UK House of Commons Foreign Affairs Committee (FAC), 178
UK Ministry of Defence, 184, 185, 190
unemployment, 15, 23, 73, 77, 86, 91, 92, 94, 95, 102, 143
United Nations, 157, 158, 176, 179, 182, 209, 210, 215, 219; UN Framework Convention on Climate Change, 157, 158
United States Department of Agriculture, 137, 138–9, 140–1, 142, 147, 149
US–UK, essential relationship, 175–6; Mutual Defense Agreement, 175, 178–80, 183; special relationship, 184, 192; relations, 17–18, 175–94

Vietnam, 199, 200, 204, 205
Violence Against Women Act, 54
voter turnout, 22, 23, 33–4, 37
voting behaviour, African American, 23, 33, 34; conservative, 23, 44–6, 49, 50, 52, 56; Hispanic/Latino, 23, 32–3, 34; liberal, 44–6, 49, 52, 56; moderate, 44–6, 49; white, 23, 33, 34, 43, 56 n.57, 59, 63.
voter identification law, 36
Voting Rights Act, 30, 31, 36

Walmart, 142, 143, 147–8
Wall Street Journal, 85, 114 n.5
War on Poverty, 96
War on Terror, 18, 86, 176, 199, 203
Washington Post, 42, 48, 62 n.74, 94 n.18, 114 n.5
Waxman-Markey Act, 159–60
welfare, benefits, 62, 92, 97, 98, 102–8, 137, 143; reform, 16, 101–8
White House, 114, 144, 165, 189, 190, 201, 206, 207–15, 216–18, 219
WikiLeaks, 186
Woodward, Bob, 207, 212, 213
Woonsocket, Rhode Island, 143
World Trade Organization, 192
World War Two, 91, 177, 178

x-efficiency, 92

INSTITUTE OF
LATIN AMERICAN
STUDIES
SCHOOL OF ADVANCED STUDY
UNIVERSITY OF LONDON

Founded in 1965, the Institute of Latin American Studies (ILAS) forms part of the University of London's School of Advanced Study, based in Senate House, London. Between 2004 and 2013, ILAS formed part of the Institute for the Study of the Americas.

ILAS occupies a unique position at the core of academic study of the region in the UK. Internationally recognised as a centre of excellence for research facilitation, it serves the wider community through organising academic events, providing online research resources, publishing scholarly writings and hosting visiting fellows. It possesses a world-class library dedicated to the study of Latin America and is the administrative home of the highly respected *Journal of Latin American Studies*. The Institute supports scholarship across a wide range of subject fields in the humanities and cognate social sciences and actively maintains and builds ties with cultural, diplomatic and business organisations with interests in Latin America, including the Caribbean.

As an integral part of the School of Advanced Study, ILAS has a mission to foster scholarly initiatives and develop networks of Latin Americanists and Caribbeanists at a national level, as well as to promote the participation of UK scholars in the international study of Latin America.

The Institute currently publishes in the disciplines of history, politics, economics, sociology, anthropology, geography and environment, development, culture and literature, and on the countries and regions of Latin America and the Caribbean.

Full details about the Institute's publications, events, postgraduate courses and other activities are available on the web at http://ilas.sas.ac.uk.

Institute of Latin American Studies
School of Advanced Study, University of London
Senate House, Malet Street, London WC1E 7HU

Tel 020 7862 8844, Fax 020 7862 8886, Email ilas@sas.ac.uk
Web http://ilas.sas.ac.uk

Recent and forthcoming titles published by the Institute for the Study of the Americas/Institute of Latin American Studies:

Joaquim Nabuco, British Abolitionists and the End of Slavery in Brazil: Correspondence 1880–1905 (2009)
edited with an introduction by Leslie Bethell & José Murilo de Carvalho

Contesting Clio's Craft: New Directions and Debates in Canadian History (2009)
edited by Christopher Dummitt & Michael Dawson

World Crisis Effects on Social Security in Latin America and the Caribbean: Lessons and Policies (2010)
Carmelo Meso-Lago

Caamaño in London: The Exile of a Latin American Revolutionary (2010)
edited by Fred Halliday

Evo Morales and the Moviemento Al Socialismo in Bolivia. The First Term in Context, 2006–2010 (2011)
edited by Adrian J. Pearce

Fractured Politics. Peruvian Democracy Past and Present (2011)
edited by John Crabtree

Organized Labour and Politics in Mexico: Changes, Continuities and Contradictions (2012)
Graciela Bensusán & Kevin J. Middlebrook

Traslados/Translations: Essays on Latin America in Honour of Jason Wilson (2012)
edited by Claire Lindsay

Broken Government? American Politics in the Obama Era (2012)
edited by Iwan Morgan and Philip John Davies

Democracy in Mexico: Attitudes and Perceptions of Citizens at National and Local Level (2014)
edited by Salvador Martí i Puig, Reynaldo Yunuen Ortega Ortiz & Mª Fernanda Somuano Ventura

Recasting Commodity and Spectacle in the Indigenous Americas (forthcoming 2014)
edited by Helen Gilbert and Charlotte Gleghorn

Lightning Source UK Ltd.
Milton Keynes UK
UKOW05f1616171214

243291UK00001B/44/P